GUY GRIFFITHS
The Life & Times of an
Australian Admiral

D1614473

This book is the story not just of a man but of a nation and a navy facing the challenges of a complex and dangerous world.

> Rear Admiral James Goldrick AO CSC RAN (Retired),
> prize-winning author of *After Jutland*

From country boy to gold-braided admiral, Guy Griffiths has led a richly-textured life of service to the navy and the nation. As a teenage midshipman he survived the disastrous sinking of the battlecruiser HMS *Repulse* off Malaya in 1941 and went on to fight at sea with distinction in another two wars: Korea and Vietnam. It is an unmatched record of courage, dedication and achievement.

With characteristic modesty, Guy was reluctant for his story to be told but Peter Jones—another retired admiral—has done him proud. This is the enthralling biography of a remarkable sailor and a genuinely great Australian.

> Mike Carlton AM, bestselling author of *Flagship* & *First Victory*

Peter Jones is one of the most distinguished and operationally experienced RAN officers of the post-Cold War era. His biography of Rear Admiral Guy Griffiths reflects this deep understanding, providing an insightful perspective not only on the man and his chosen profession of arms, but also on the challenges facing a previous generation of Australians through three of the most important wars of the 20th Century.

> Dr David Stevens AM, prize-winning author of *In All Respects Ready*

GUY GRIFFITHS
The Life & Times of an Australian Admiral

PETER JONES

ARCADIA

© Peter Jones 2021

First published 2021 by ARCADIA
the general books imprint of
Australian Scholarly Publishing Ltd
7 Lt Lothian St Nth, North Melbourne, Vic 3051

Tel: 03 9329 6963 / enquiry@scholarly.info / www.scholarly.info

ISBN 978-1-922454-67-6 Hardback
ISBN 978-1-922454-68-3 Paperback

ALL RIGHTS RESERVED

Cover design: Wayne Saunders
Front cover: photograph by heidesmith

Dedicated to the memories of two remarkable naval officers

Vice Admiral Ian MacDougall AC AFSM RAN (1938–2020)

&

Commodore Sam Bateman AM RAN (1938–2020)

both served under Guy Griffths and held him
in the highest regard.

Contents

Foreword

This book, which is thoroughly researched and elegantly written, is a superb account of the life experiences of a remarkable man, Rear Admiral Guy Griffiths AO, DSO, DSC, RAN Retired. It explores the aspects of his personality, his individual characteristics, and the concepts and methods he used to achieve success through his remarkable naval career. He applied his experiences in war and peace to excellent and extraordinary effect, particularly as an inspirational leader, who gave respect and earned great loyalty amongst all he served with, whatever the circumstances.

From World War II, where he won the DSC at the Battle of Leyte Gulf [one of the most significant naval battles in world history], he progressively combined his active service in the Korean War and then the Vietnam conflict, where he was awarded the DSO, to become an imaginative and decisive combat commander.

The book engagingly explains how Admiral Griffiths was able to apply his exceptional abilities. It explores his motivating leadership; for example, in HMAS *Hobart* (II) in Vietnam (where I served under his command). The superior training and morale of his crew was a fine match for his calm demeanour and masterful ability to create trust and commitment amongst his men. Outstanding performance and happiness invariably followed in whatever task the ship was given.

As a professional naval officer, he was technically knowledgeable and tactically excellent; his awareness and application matched changes in the technology of sea power throughout his 43-year career. He was a fit, focused and galvanising officer, often ahead of his time in the way he sometimes provocatively exercised his strategic leadership.

The book also shows his capacity to gain remarkable insights into developments that the RAN needed to adapt to or implement. He was a driving force for change in the Navy; this was particularly evident in the latter half of his service. Guy Griffiths was a fine role model and mentor to follow. He set the standards by which others in the RAN achieved results and their successes. I am proud to say I was privileged to serve with him.

I commend this exceptional book—and Admiral Griffiths—to you: I venture that you won't be disappointed in either.

Vice Admiral Rob Walls, AO, RAN Retired

Preface

This is the biography of Guy Griffiths, one of the Royal Australian Navy's most decorated Admirals. Besides capturing a quite remarkable life in a biography, my additional object was, through Guy's service, to shine a light on the RAN through those four decades.

Guy twice politely, but firmly, rebuffed the idea of a biography before he acceded to my request to write one. He felt he had not had a 'remarkable' career and others were more deserving of a book. The main reason why he agreed was that he wanted the service of his shipmates to be better remembered and appreciated in our collective history.

Guy was in his 96th and 97th years when this book was written. I was writing about a life that was long and fully lived, and I benefitted from his insightful comments on the drafts. I am sure it is many a biographer's dream to be able to ask the subject about a point of detail or their feelings on a particular issue. I have been most fortunate that Guy has an exceptionally well-ordered set of papers and he retains a remarkably accurate memory for detail.

In my first book, *Australia's Argonauts: The remarkable story of the first class to enter the Royal Australian Naval College*, the boys who were its subjects were all born in 1899 and some served in the RAN until the late 1950s. A surprising number of the parents of Guy's naval class were also born in 1899, and so this biography relates the times of the next generation of naval officers, some of whom served until the late 1970s. As such this biography covers a period of great peril as well as triumph. The events in which Guy was a participant still continue to shape our lives today.

Peter Jones
Canberra, 2021

Acknowledgements

Through writing this biography I have become keenly aware that dealing with a biographer can be an intrusive and unsettling experience for the subject. I sincerely thank Guy for his openness, perseverance and fortitude. To his credit Guy did not try and censor the manuscript. Through the drafting process his daughter Erica has been a great support to Guy and me, and I thank her for her considerable encouragement and assistance.

I have enjoyed the support and goodwill of a great many people who have either served with Guy or greatly admired him. Some helped initially to convince Guy to submit himself to a biography. In this regard I would like especially to thank Rear Admiral David Campbell, Mr Angus Hordern, Vice Admiral David Shackleton, Vice Admiral Rob Walls and Commodore John Stavridis.

Two of my Naval College classmates were of tremendous assistance with this project. They are Rear Admiral James Goldrick and Dr David Stevens, from whose seemingly inexhaustible knowledge of the Navy I drew; I benefitted from their many comments on the manuscript. Another classmate, Graeme Lunn was a great help when I was researching the UK archives.

I also benefitted from information from Commodore Malcolm Baird, Captain Rick Bailey, Rear Admiral Mark Bonser, Mike Carlton, Lieutenant Commander Ken Cartwright, Chaplain Gareth Clayton, Rear Admiral Simon Cullen, Commodore 'Toz' Dadswell, Rear Admiral Allan Du Toit, Vic Dzodz, Lieutenant Commander Brian Farthing, Commodore Tony Flint, Lieutenant Mike Fogarty, Rear Admiral Murray Forrest, Professor Tom Frame, Commander Richard Hannan, Rear Admiral Jeff Harley USN, Bill Hartnell, Rear Admiral

Jaimie Hatcher, Father Michael Head, Tony 'Doc' Holliday, Ian Holmes, Able Seaman Danni Humphries, Frank Jeanes, John Jeremy, Commander Dennis Jones, Paul Konings, Bill Krause, Robyn Lawrence, Ronald 'Dixie' Lee, Brian Love, Peter Manoel, the late Vice Admiral Ian MacDougall, David Mattiske, Jim McGeachie, Roland Millbank, Allan 'Shorty' Moffatt, John Mortimer, Captain Peter Murray, Angelika Nawroth of the Bundesarchive, Professor Gregory Nelson, Vice Admiral Michael Noonan, Captain John Peterson USN, Lieutenant Commander Lauren Rago, Commodore Lou Rago, Rear Admiral Neil Ralph, Major Martin Reese of the Bundeswehr, Dr John Reeve, Commander Bill Ritchie, the late Rear Admiral Andrew Robertson, Harold Sharp, Lieutenant Will Singer, John Smith, Professor Peter Stanley, Rear Admiral Rothesay Swan, Tony Terntori, Rear Admiral Tan Sri Dato Seri K Thanabalasingham RMN, John Thompson, Professor Geoffrey Till, Warrant Officer Alan Ward, Ralph Wollmer, Lieutenant Commander Desmond Woods and Commander Steve Youll.

I would like to acknowledge the unstinting support of the Seapower Centre Australia from the earliest days of this project. Captain Sean Andrews and his knowledgeable team provided ready access to their archival material and connected me to literary agent Joe Boschetti. I would particularly like to acknowledge the support of John Perryman, Commander Richard Adams, Rob Garratt and Petar Djokovic at the Centre. I am also appreciative of their intention to acquire copies of the book for the benefit of those serving in the contemporary RAN. Also of tremendous assistance has been the helpful staff at the Australian Defence Force Academy Library, the Australian and UK National Archives, the Caird Library and Archive at Greenwich and the National Library of Australia.

Among the quoted works in copyright I am grateful for permission to reprint excerpts. For those literary heirs and original publishers I have been unable to trace, may I here record my acknowledgements. I would like to particularly thank Lionel and Myrtle Logue's grandson

Mark Logue for his successful efforts in unearthing the family correspondence that related to Guy's stay with his famous grandparents. I have tried where possible to trace the copyright of photographs, but some appear in multiple collections and so their original copyright owner remained unclear. I would particularly like to acknowledge the fine cover photograph of Guy Griffiths by Heidi Smith which so well captures the essence of the man.

At various stages of the project, the late Commodore Sam Bateman, Rear Admiral David Campbell, Commodore Peter Leschen, Commodore Jack McCaffrie, Vice Admiral David Shackleton, my wife Rhonda as well as my sons Dion and Evan were kind enough to comment on draft chapters which greatly improved the manuscript.

In turning the manuscript into a book I would like to acknowledge the efforts of my literary agent Joe Boschetti for his unstinting efforts in finding a willing publisher and for his professional advice and encouragement. I thank Pablo Mandel and his team at Circular Studio for the creation of the maps and the family tree. I am indebted also to Nick Walker and the Australian Scholarly Publishing team for their willingness to take on this biography and apply their many talents to make it a reality. Finally, notwithstanding my debt to so many people, I take responsibility for any errors in this book.

Author's Note

Writing about nautical history inevitably poses problems for both the author and the reader when it comes to distances and lengths. This is particularly the case for Australian readers, many of whom have only grown up in the metric world. If for no other reason that latitude and longitude have a direct relationship with the nautical mile, and a knot of speed is a nautical mile in an hour, it is likely that mariners are destined to use both the imperial and metric systems. As such, this book uses imperial measurements when discussing nautical matters, but uses metric measurements in geographical distances. A table of equivalents is provided below. Similarly, the sizes of guns are expressed in the unit of measurement that was used at the time. Once again, a conversion table is provided. Times in this biography are expressed in the naval 24-hour clock, so 9am is 0900 and 1pm is 1300.

On the issue of place names, the local name at the time is used, with the modern or other common name also provided if needed. In regard to Vietnamese place names, which can incorporate up to nine diacritics or accents, such as in Đà Nẵng, I decided not to use them in the text. This is because most readers will be unfamiliar with their sound or tonal indication.

In conformance with the 2020 Japanese Government change to convention for expressing Japanese people's names in English, they are now written in order of family name followed by given name.

Abbreviations

AA	Anti-Aircraft
ADO	Air Defence Officer
ARG	Amphibious Ready Group
ARVN	Army of the Republic of Vietnam
CIC	Combat Information Centre
CNP	Chief of Naval Personnel
CNS	Chief of Naval Staff
DASH	Drone Anti-Submarine Helicopter
DESRON	Destroyer Squadron
DDG	Guided Missile Destroyer
DSC	Distinguished Service Cross
DSO	Distinguished Service Order
DMZ	Demilitarised Zone
FOCAF	Flag Officer Commanding HM Australian Fleet
HACP	High Angle Control Position
H&I	Harassment and Interdiction
HDML	Harbour Defence Motor Launch
HMAS	His/Her Majesty's Australian Ship
HMCS	His/Her Majesty's Canadian Ship
HMNZS	His/Her Majesty's New Zealand Ship
HMS	His/Her Majesty's Ship
HNMS	His/Her Majesty's Netherlands Ship
IFF	Identification, Friend or Foe
LCM	Landing Craft Mechanized
MID	Mention in Despatches
NTDS	Naval Tactical Data System
OOW	Officer of the Watch
PAVN	People's Army of Vietnam
PIRAZ	Positive Identification Radar Advisory Zone
PT	Patrol Torpedo boat
RAAF	Royal Australian Air Force
RAF	Royal Air Force
RAN	Royal Australian Navy
RANC	Royal Australian Naval College
RANVR	Royal Australian Navy Volunteer Reserve

RMN	Royal Malaysian Navy
RN	Royal Navy
SAGW	Surface to Air Guided Weapon
SS	Steam Ship
TF	Task Force
TG	Task Group
TU	Task Unit
USAF	United States Air Force
USN	United States Navy
USS	United States Ship
VC	Victoria Cross
Viet Cong	National Liberation Front of South Vietnam & Cambodia
VERTREP	Vertical Replenishment
WBLC	Water Borne Logistics Craft
WRNS	Women's Royal Naval Service

Table of Equivalents

1 yard = 0.9144 metres

1 nautical mile = 1,853.2 metres = 6,080 feet

1 ton = 0.907185 tonne

Guns

Metric	Imperial
20-mm	0.8-inch
40-mm	1.6-inch
76-mm	3-inch
102-mm	4-inch
114-mm	4.5-inch
127-mm	5-inch
133-mm	5.25-inch
152-mm	6-inch
203-mm	8-inch
38-cm	15-inch
40.6-cm	16-inch

Prologue

So suddenly you were there. You were in the war.

Guy Griffiths

The *Karamea* was finally nearing safety from the threat of German U-boat attack. Hopefully, it was just two more nights at sea and then landfall and a berth somewhere up the Clyde. *Karamea* was a refrigerated cargo ship with a maximum speed of just 15 knots. Up to this point in the voyage she had sailed uneventfully from New Zealand across the Pacific, with just a glimpse of the Galapagos Islands to break the monotony of a clear horizon. This was contrasted by the busy and highly organised passage through the Panama Canal.

Karamea was carrying butter, frozen lamb and other produce for Britain. By the time of her planned arrival in February 1941, food shortages were already a fact of everyday life. Her only passengers were six Royal Australian Navy (RAN) officers who had joined *Karamea* in Port Lyttleton on 6 January, after their cross-Tasman passage in *Mauriganui*. They were Commander Alvord 'Rosie' Rosenthal, who was to command a RAN destroyer, then building in Britain, and in his charge, five midshipmen. They were Guy Griffiths, John Austin, Bruce Dowling, Robert Davies and Peter Gyllies, all newly graduated from the Royal Australian Naval College. The midshipmen were destined to join the cruiser *Australia*, then in British waters, and so commence their sea training. Onboard *Karamea*, Rosenthal had kept them busy with keeping watches on the bridge and unravelling the mysteries of celestial navigation.

After entering the Atlantic, *Karamea* had steamed up the east coast of the United States with the crew being struck by the well-lit coastline in contrast to their home waters where the war had led to black-out measures. On reaching the New England coast, the weather turned and the midshipmen experienced their first blizzard. Successive gales struck the ship as she then made her solitary passage across the North Atlantic. To the young seafarers it was an incredible experience. The dangers of the elements were intertwined with the violence of the enemy. This was brought home when a less fortunate merchantman was torpedoed only about fifty miles way.

On that penultimate evening out, the familiar sounds of the ship and the sea were broken by a distant thud and then a starshell burst overhead and drifted down near *Karamea.** It brilliantly illuminated her. This was followed by the appearance of a warship out of the gloom with someone on her bridge asking by loud hailer 'What ship? To where are you bound?' Bruce Dowling later wrote, 'Our tormentors, were one or two destroyers of the Royal Navy. With the same courtesy they apologised for upsetting us and then vanished.'[1]

The following morning the midshipmen were either on watch or down below packing. Ahead, two aircraft appeared and altered their course towards *Karamea*. Air protection at last. The aircraft continued towards the ship and then descended as they approached. The now uneasy Master pressed the Action Stations alarm. The aircraft were two German Heinkel bombers and proceeded to bomb and strafe *Karamea*. Guy ran down the starboard side of the ship towards the bridge. He saw a bomb drop. It hit one of the booms of the forward derrick and deflected over the side and then exploded in the sea. Guy ducked inside at the first open door to shelter from the machine gun bullets. Another three or four more bombs were dropped, but all missed. The aircraft returned to strafe the ship. The faces of some of the aircrew could be clearly seen. As suddenly

---

*   A starshell is a projectile fired from a gun which has a fuse that activates at a
      given height igniting a magnesium flare which illuminates an area. The flare's
      descent is slowed by a parachute.

as the attack began it was over.

Miraculously besides the upper decks being riddled with bullets *Karamea* was otherwise intact. The only casualty was the cook who received cuts when he fell when carrying plates. For Guy and his fellow midshipmen, the attack, so close to the Clyde, was their initiation to the war at sea. Years later Guy reflected of the moment, 'So suddenly you were there. You were in the war.'[2]

The next day, 16 February, *Karamea* proceeded up the River Clyde where some of the midshipmen saw snow-capped hills for the first time. *Karamea* passed the busy shipyards where battleships, cruisers and destroyers were being fitted out and finally a berth among many merchantmen near the city of Glasgow. To complete a memorable day, the midshipmen went into Glasgow and took in a show at the Alhambra Theatre.

The swift and unexpected attack on the *Karamea*, with fortunately benign results, was emblematic of Guy Griffiths' naval career. In three wars, by chance or fortune, Guy took part in or was witness to some of the most significant naval battles of his time. Through it all he would be physically unscathed, but many of his friends and shipmates would be lost or badly injured. As a result of these wars Guy was to be informed and altered in such a way that he would try to use those experiences to benefit the Royal Australian Navy.

A naval officer's career demands skills in practical seamanship, navigation, and leadership, as well as technical competence in various forms of naval warfare. At a relatively young age naval officers must develop an awareness of strategy and international relations. Overlaying these demands is a need to be resilient against the dangers of the sea, not to mention the ill intent of the enemy. It was a vocation that Guy Griffiths revelled in.

1

A Country Boy

We may look forward with confidence to the day when the ingratiating juice of the grape shall appear as an item in the annual exports of Australia.

On the efforts of Mr James Busby,
The Sydney Herald, 1834[1]

I

Guy Richmond Griffiths was born in Sydney on 1 March 1923 to Guy Griffiths (Snr) and the former Edith Lewis Chalmers Kelman. Although born in the city, Guy's parents were country folk who hailed from the winegrowing area of Pokolbin in the Hunter Valley, north of Sydney. Guy's childhood was that of a country boy and he never lost either his rural roots or an appreciation for the land.

Guy descended from four British pioneering families. Three were English: the north country Busby family, the west country Griffiths and the Holmes from Exeter. The other family, the Kelmans, were from Fraserburgh in Scotland. Guy's ancestors came to the colony of New South Wales in the mid- and late-nineteenth century. Each of these families was to make important contributions to the founding and growth of the Hunter Valley wine industry. Their experiences in the growing colony were to prove formative to Guy and his immediate family.

The first two families to sail to Australia were Guy's maternal great-great-grandparents John and Sarah Busby accompanied by their daughter and four of their sons.* Also onboard was Guy's great-grandfather, William Dalrymple Kelman. They departed Leith on 17 September 1823 onboard the Australian Company's *Triton* bound for Hobart. The vessel was just eight years old and although only 35 metres long and displacing just 400 tonnes, was typical for this trade route. The Master was the experienced and well-regarded Captain Creer and he had 23-man crew. Remarkably for such a small ship there were 23 cabin and 33 steerage passengers. In addition to their effects for their new life in the colony, there was also cargo and livestock. The Busbys and Kelman were among the cabin passengers.

The 134-day voyage was not uneventful. The initial gales gave way to calmer weather *en route* to Teneriffe. On leaving that port the *Triton's* two cannon were prepared and the men onboard were given musket drill in case they encountered pirates. This threat became more real one night when a sail was sighted. The mystery ship continued to close and fired a couple of cannon shots which fell astern of *Triton*. The ship then disappeared into the night. As they passed into the Southern Hemisphere a 'Crossing the Line' ceremony was duly held. About twenty passengers demurred from receiving the tender mercies of King Neptune and his court. They appeared to have good reason, for each initiate was blindfolded, had his face covered with cow dung, his mouth filled with tar, an iron hoop drawn over the mouth to retain the tar. He was then thrown into the jolly boat, which had been filled with sea water and cow dung. According to one of the passengers 'the rest of the day was spent in conviviality'.[2] This, however, involved much grog, which led some of the sailors to invade the steerage class to tar the still uninitiated; general brawling then broke out which led one of the ladies among the cabin class to have a fit in consequence. The rest of the voyage was less tumultuous but there were still occasional fights in the cramped steerage class.

---

* The sons were James, John, Alexander and William.

William Kelman's ambition was to take up a land grant in Van Diemen's Land.* The older John Busby, an experienced mining engineer, was to go on to take up a post in Sydney to develop the town's water supplies as well as to scope the Hunter Valley coal deposits.† While onboard *Triton,* the 23-year-old William was befriended by the two oldest Busby children, 19-year-old Catherine and 22-year-old James. The latter was a budding viticulturist who had already spent time in the Bordeaux region. On the voyage James wrote *A Treatise on the Culture of the Vine and the Art of Making Wine.*[3] William was both attracted to Catherine and greatly enthused by James's ideas on winegrowing in New South Wales. Whilst at Cape Town William, the three toured the Constantia vineyard where the owner 'treated us with a glass of the different kinds of wine, white and red Constantia and Frontignan, the finest wines in the world'.[4] After this tour William resolved that once he had developed his land grant to a workable farm, he would sell it and move to New South Wales to pursue viticulture.

Triton arrived safely in Hobart Town on 20 January 1824. The following month William Kelman was granted 650 acres on Macquarie River near Ross Bridge. He named the property 'Glen Kelman'. The Busbys spent a couple of weeks in Hobart before re-embarking in *Triton* for the voyage to Sydney. In May 1824 John Busby was granted 2,000 acres on the Hunter River near Lower Belford which he named 'Kirkton'. William and Catherine maintained correspondence and on 16 February 1827 they were married at St James Church in Sydney. They returned to Glen Kelman where their first daughter Sarah was born later that year.

For his part, James Busby had secured a position as a teacher at the Male Orphan School near Liverpool where he was to take charge of the school farm and teach viticulture. In addition to his £100 salary, Busby would receive one third of the farm's produce. In 1827 the school came

---

* In 1856 the name 'Van Diemen's Land' was changed to 'Tasmania' after grant of self-government.

† John Busby designed and built Sydney's second water supply, named Busby's Bore, 1827–37. It is located in present-day Centennial Park.

under the Church Corporation and his 'generous' remuneration came under scrutiny. After considerable wrangling James lost his position. For the next two years he temporarily had the position of Collector of Internal Revenue until the permanent appointee arrived from England. Fortunately for John Busby, in 1828 William Kelman had secured a land grant in the Hunter Valley near Kirkton, and so in the following year Glen Kelman was sold and the young family moved to the Hunter Valley. In the absence of James, William took on the management of Kirkton.

In 1830 James Busby wrote his highly influential *A Manual of Plain Directions for Planting and Cultivating Vineyards, and for Making Wine in New South Wales*.[5] An immediate by-product of Busby's *Manual* was the distribution of vine cuttings from the Botanical Gardens in Sydney to prospective winegrowers for the purpose of developing an industry. William Kelman was one of the recipients and planted vines at Kirkton in the early 1830s. So began wine production which continued in the family for some eighty years.

But James Busby's life was to take an unexpected direction. He had become dissatisfied with his treatment by the government and in 1831 sailed for England to take his complaint to the Colonial Office. He took with him ten gallons of local wine to encourage interest in New South Wales' wines. While waiting for an outcome on his complaint James spent four months touring the vineyards of Spain and France and took nearly six hundred vine cuttings, which were shipped back to the Botanical Gardens in Sydney*.

The outcome of James Busby's complaint was that in 1832 he was appointed as the British Resident in New Zealand. He had a prefabricated house shipped from Australia and he erected it at Waitangi in the Bay of Islands. Of his new residence Busby said, 'It is my wish when I have erected my house, that all the (Maori) Chiefs shall visit me and be my friends. We shall then consult together by what means they can make

---

*   Once established, cuttings from some of these vines were sent from Sydney to Adelaide for further propagation.

their country flourishing, and their people rich and wise, like the people of Great Britain.'[6] Busby's achievements include helping design the first New Zealand flag in 1834, drafting the Declaration of the Independence of New Zealand in 1835, which was signed by thirty-five chiefs, and most importantly co-drafting the 1840 Treaty of Waitangi.

James Busby did not return to the Hunter Valley and his vision for Australian farmers to have small vineyards as part of their holding for their own wine consumption, after the French fashion, was not realised. His biographer Eric Ramsden described him as 'the Prophet of Australian viticulture'[7] whose achievements were to the benefit of both his family's economic prospects and that of New South Wales. The Victorian Government Viticulturist, François de Castella, wrote in 1935 that 'the crowning achievement of having introduced most of the valuable wine sorts of France and Spain, certainly place James Busby in the front rank of those who contributed to the development of John Bull's vineyard in the Antipodes'.[8]

In 1841 John Busby and his sons bequeathed Kirkton to William Kelman.[*] After the Kelman family's arrival in the Hunter, Catherine had a further ten children over the next twenty years. One of them was Guy's maternal grandfather, Lewis Chalmers Kelman, who was born in 1842.

II

The next strand of Guy's forebears to arrive in Australia was Joseph Broadbent Holmes and his wife Harriet. Joseph had previously been to sea on the China–England run and rounded Cape Horn on a number of occasions. The couple arrived in Sydney on 6 May 1842 from England onboard the *Kelso*, after a remarkably quick passage of 103 days. Harriet had been so seasick that she never went to sea again.

Also onboard *Kelso* was Monsieur Faramond, the inaugural French

---

[*]   *Kirkton* remained in the Kelman family until 1914 when it was sold to another notable wine growing family, the Lindemans, who were related through the marriage of one of William Kelman's sisters.

5

Consul to the colony, and seventeen French immigrants, including a vine dresser.[9] Joseph Holmes bought 1,300 acres of land at Allandale, not far from Kirkton. Joseph soon sourced some local vines and established an orchard and vineyard he called 'The Wilderness'. The fledgling Hunter Valley wine industry prospered with the growth of Sydney; this was assisted by the duty placed on imported wine, including that from other colonies. The Holmes family, led by Joseph, also developed two more vineyards at Caerphilly and Palmers Lane. The combined business became J. B. Holmes and Sons Ltd, with his son Charles as chairman.

In 1872 William Kelman's fourth son Lewis married Joseph Holmes's eldest daughter Edith. It was one of the many marriages that intertwined the Hunter Valley winegrowing community. Lewis and Edith soon established a small farm, Rota, near Sawyers Gully and they had four children. March 1884 brought triumph and tragedy to the Kelman and Holmes families. On 11 March Edith gave birth to her fourth child, destined to be Guy's mother. She was named Edith Lewis Chalmers Kelman. Two days later a cablegram was received from India advising that a Kelman wine had won a Gold Medal at the 1884 Calcutta International Exhibition.[10] This news was overshadowed by the death on the same day of Lewis Kelman of the painful Bright's disease.* Poignantly, baby Edith's birth notice appeared just above her father's death notice in the *Maitland Mercury and Hunter River General Advertiser*.[11] With the sudden loss of her husband and the need to support a young family Edith moved from Rota into town to run a boarding house. Her clientele were mainly 'young bank boys'.

---

* Bright's Disease was identified by Dr Richard Bright in 1827. It is now considered a historical term for several inflammatory kidney related maladies. Therefore the details of Lewis's condition are not precisely known. Some notable people fell victim to Bright's Disease including the first wives of Theodore Roosevelt (Alice Hathaway Lee Roosevelt, also in 1884) and Woodrow Wilson (Ellen Axson Wilson, 1914) and cricket legend Victor Trumper (also in 1914).

GUY GRIFFITHS FAMILY TREE

Guy's direct ancestors who migrated to Australia

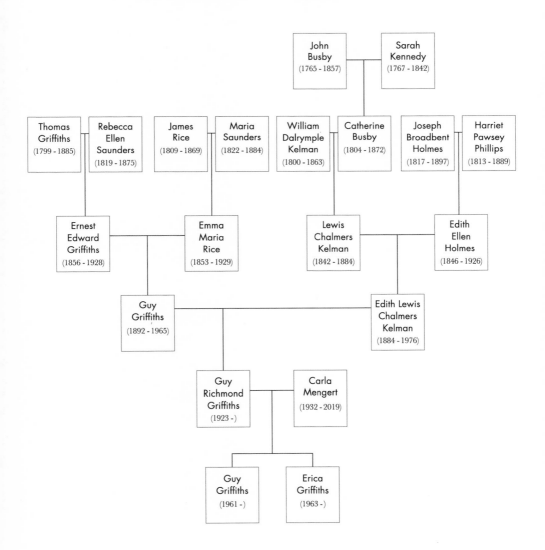

III

The final strand to Guy's pioneering roots was the arrival in Australia of the Griffiths family. On 26 November 1881 the clipper *La Hogue* entered Sydney Harbour after a 14-week voyage from London. *La Hogue* had a cargo of building supplies that were eagerly sought after in the growing colony.[12] The ship's surgeon for the voyage was Guy's paternal grandfather, the 25-year-old Dr Ernest Griffiths. Born in Bideford, Devon, Ernest like many before him had worked his passage and now looked for a new life in New South Wales. The following year Ernest became the Government Medical Officer and Vaccinator in the settlement of Blayney, 240 kilometres west of Sydney. In 1885, having sufficiently established himself, Ernest returned to England where he married his cousin Emma Rice. The newlyweds soon sailed to Australia via the Suez Canal, travelling First Class on the modern steamship *Orient*, and then on landing to the growing Blayney township. They remained in Blayney for the next twenty years and in that time produced four children, Frank, Harvey, Guy and Mary.

Ernest Griffiths became a pillar of the local community and, in 1890, he was initiated into the Freemasons at the local Lodge, 'Carringtonia'. For reasons now unclear he sold his medical practice and moved to Sydney. In 1906 Ernest became a general practitioner, first in Bellingen and then in Coopernook, both in northern New South Wales. The family remained on the north coast for a decade until 1918 when Ernest and Emma finally returned to the Western Slopes and settled in Oberon. Ernest helped found Oberon's local Freemason Lodge.

Of Ernest and Emma's sons, their second oldest Harvey, after being educated in Bathurst, was the first to leave the Blayney district. In 1908 he joined the Colonial Sugar Refining Company as a clerk and progressed steadily through the firm, firstly in mills in northern New South Wales. By 1920 Harvey had become the overseer of a mill in Fiji. Except for a short stint in the Anglo-French condominium of the New

Hebrides (now Vanuatu), Harvey held key positions in Fiji until his retirement as Chief Manager in 1951. Harvey was a colourful figure in the family. In Fiji, he and his wife Molly became highly respected for their character and hospitality. They both enjoyed the culture and the company of Fijians leading them to involve themselves in works of social benefit. Professionally, Harvey was esteemed for his ability to get on with local Fijian chiefs, Indian businessmen, politicians and workers. Harvey was a role model for Guy and he later wrote of his uncle, 'Harvey had a good brain and a very balanced mind, both characteristics we know to be of inestimable value, and so well placed with him as he worked tirelessly for the well-being and help of others.'[13]

Ernest and Emma's oldest son Frank obtained a position in the Bank of Australasia. While working at a branch in Newcastle he lived in Edith Kelman's boarding house. It was no doubt through Frank that his younger brother Guy (Snr), after having completed training at the Hawkesbury Agricultural College in 1912, came to the Hunter Valley. He gained a position working at The Wilderness, now run by Edith's brother Charles Holmes. Guy (Snr) found that the Hunter Valley vineyards were emerging from some difficult years. At the turn of the century they, like most rural areas, had to survive the severe 'Federation Drought'. Commercially, Federation had removed the trade barriers between colonies. At about the same time the Hunter's dry wines were losing favour among a public becoming more attracted to sweeter interstate wines. This led to some adjustment in the wines being produced.

At the outbreak of war in 1914 there was great patriotic fervour in the district for men to enlist in the Army. The numbers of local young men that joined were regularly reported in the local newspapers.[14] Guy (Snr) was not among them because as a boy he had had an accident which resulted in most of his left bicep being removed.

IV

In 1916 the 23-year-old Guy (Snr) married Edith's youngest daughter Edith Lewis Chalmers Kelman. Because she had the same name as her mother and perhaps in memory of her father, she was known within her family as 'Lewie'. Although eight years older than Guy, Lewie did not have their first child, Guy, until she was 39 years old. A daughter, Dorothy, was born three years later.

There exists a curiosity in the Griffiths' family history. The marriage certificate for Guy (Snr) and Lewie has several unexplained entries. Guy (Snr) wrote that his middle name was 'Fawkes', a name which does not appear on his birth certificate. But 'Fawkes' does appear in some Electoral Rolls. The marriage certificate also erroneously listed the groom's place of birth as 'at sea', which his son Guy has always found mysterious. There was also a mistake in which Guy's mother's maiden name was 'Richmond' instead of her correct name of Rice. Because of this error the new-born Guy received the middle name of Richmond.

Initially, the young Griffiths family lived in a small cottage on The Wilderness, but moved to the two-storied Caerphilly, formerly occupied by Lewie's uncle, Arthur Holmes. It was the main homestead for the Caerphilly Vineyard and next to the house was the large cellar and cooling water tower. By this time Guy (Snr) was Assistant Manager to Charles Holmes for the whole Holmes winery enterprise. Caerphilly was to prove a wonderful family home. For young Guy there was much to explore in the vineyard, the buildings where the wine was produced and the adjacent fields and bush. Much of Guy's youth was spent outdoors playing sport, rabbit shooting or just 'mucking about' with friends.

Among the pupils at Rothbury Public School[*] were surnames that became synonymous with the Australian wine industry. Guy would maintain some of these friendships for over eighty years. One of his teachers was Mr Jim Shaw. He winced at the country accents of

---

[*] Rothbury Public School was established in 1883 but was closed in 1964.

9

his students. His daughter, who was attending elocution lessons, was regularly brought to the front of the class to properly pronounce words to the benefit of the class. At school the children thought Guy's middle name was Richard, hence he was known to many, including his family, as Dick.

In the late 1920s drought once again hit the area. This, combined with the Depression and an outbreak of downy mildew, made life very difficult for those in the wine industry. In 1931 *The Report on the Wine Industry of Australia* was produced. The survey said that the Hunter Valley was well suited to its dry wines, but the commercial demand for them was bleakly assessed as scant, and doubts were raised as to whether the area could continue production.[15] At the time, the young Guy was conscious that the family 'didn't have many pennies to rub together'.[16] Although Guy was 'mad keen' on the machinery of wine producing, the associated hardships killed any interest he had in following in his father's footsteps.

Owing to his mechanical bent Guy commenced attending West Maitland Junior Technical School in 1934.* To get there, his father bought him a Malvern Star bicycle which he rode ten kilometres to the Allandale Station. The stationmaster let him keep his bicycle at his house and Guy took the 18 kilometre journey by train.

Periodically, Uncle Harvey would visit Caerphilly during leave from Fiji. Harvey always left an impression on Guy who later wrote, 'I was enthralled with his tales of the sugar mill, the Indians and Fiji in general; he was a great talker and storyteller.'[17] It was a glimpse of a wider world beyond the Hunter Valley. On one such visit Harvey took the 8-year-old Guy and his father on a memorable road trip to visit Uncle Frank, then a bank manager at Crow's Nest on Queensland's Darling Downs. The inland route was rugged, and on one back road that crossed the border they had to open a farm-style gate to enter Queensland.

In early 1936 during a family gathering at Caerphilly, Guy's future came up. A relative suggested that as Guy had an interest in machinery,

---

* Most Technical Schools became Comprehensive Schools.

the Navy might be career for him. This seemed attractive to Guy, as was the prospect of seeing the world. So, the seed was sown. Guy decided 'to have a crack' at entering the Royal Australian Naval College as a 13-year-old cadet midshipman. As a Depression-era economy measure, the Naval College had in 1930 been moved from its impressive purpose-built facilities at Jervis Bay and relocated to the Flinders Naval Depot on the shores of Westernport Bay in Victoria. Flinders Naval Depot now conducted all initial and some specialist training for officers and sailors. If Guy was selected he would undertake four years of academic and naval training at the Naval College before proceeding to sea.

Entry into the Naval College was very competitive, and it was clear that Guy would need some help academically if he was to be sufficiently ranked to get through to the final interview stage. Typically, only about the top 4% were selected. Mr Fuller, a science teacher at West Maitland Tech, coached him in the sciences. In September 1936 Guy sat the examinations which comprised ten different papers and then a medical examination. He passed all sufficiently to progress to assessment by a final selection board, to be held in Sydney.

Guy's first sea voyage was in the coastal steamer *Gwydir* that took him from Newcastle to Sydney to attend his final interview for the Naval College. The selection board was chaired by Captain Cuthbert Pope, who was Commanding Officer of the Flinders Naval Depot and, as such, also of the Naval College. The other key member of the board was the Director of Studies, Mr R. F. 'Bill' Cowan, easily identifiable in his academic gown. The demeanour of board members was severe, and the interview was a daunting experience for the 12-year-old Guy. He was asked a series of questions about the Navy, general affairs and other areas to test his mental agility. He was then ushered out and left to ponder his chances.

On 22 December 1936 the Minister for Defence, Sir Archdale Parkhill, announced to the Press the successful candidates for the Royal Australian Naval College.[18] There were two special cadetships for sons of men who had served in the Great War and fifteen ordinary cadetships. Guy was among the list of successful candidates.* His selection was from nearly five hundred applicants and his success was proudly reported in the *Maitland Daily Mercury*.[19] In Guy's words, 'I had won the Lotto.'[20]

---

* The Special Cadetships were awarded to Guido James Willis and Bruce Dowling.

2

Life at the Naval College

This world of ours is small enough,
But circumstances state
The queerest of all freaks at large
Are first year, small and great.
Now when the breakfast pipes do blow
Quite queer it is to see
The first year's lean and hungry look
Transformed to one of glee.
If through this world at large you roam
You never there will see
A stranger, yet more hungry crowd,
Than the 'germs' at F.N.D.

Cadet Midshipman Robert Davies[1]

I

On 28 February 1937 Guy Griffiths and sixteen other 13-year-old boys assembled at Victoria Barracks in Melbourne prior to being taken to the Royal Australian Naval College. They were met by two cadet captains from the senior year at the college who would help them settle in until the remainder of the cadets from the senior classes returned from summer leave two days later.

The 1937 'Phillip' Year,* as Guy's class was called, was a diverse group of boys. There were seven Victorians, six New South Welshmen, three Queenslanders and a sole South Australian. Their families were either from the middle or working classes. Among their fathers' occupations were three clerks, two engineers, a doctor, a lawyer, a farmer and a vigneron. Of service connections, few had any naval links. The most prominent was John Goble's father James, who had served in the Royal Naval Air Service in World War I. Now an Air Vice Marshal and former Chief of the Air Staff of the Royal Australian Air Force, he was presently serving in the UK.† The young John Goble travelled unaccompanied from London in the *Tuscan Star*.[2] Three other fathers had served in the Australian Imperial Force on the Western Front. This was of an era when their mothers' occupation was invariably listed as home duties on the electoral roll.

The 80-kilometre trip to Westernport in the Naval College charabanc‡ that had faithfully transported cadet-midshipmen for over twenty years. James Willis, who as a former boarder in a private school, seemed more relaxed about proceedings and decided to pass the time by throwing peanuts at the two cadet captains sitting up front. His hits were ignored but, in the words of one of the class, they were 'storing up trouble'. On arrival at the Naval College precinct within Flinders Naval Depot, the boys piled out of the charabanc and many crossed a white line on the asphalt. The cadet captains then fell the boys into a line and told them that the line represented the 'Quarterdeck' boundary where they should have saluted. As they hadn't they were all beaten on their backside with a gym shoe. They were then told to go to their dormitory where their uniforms were laid out on their bunks to get dressed and return. It was a stark welcome to the Naval College.[3]

---

* Each of the four classes were named after Cook, Phillip, Jervis & Flinders. After 1938 the classes were referred to by their year of intake.

† Air Vice Marshal Stanley James 'Jimmy' Goble, CBE, DSO, DSC (1891–1948). During World War I, Goble became a fighter ace with ten victories.

‡ A charabanc was an open motor car typically with four to five rows of seats. Popular until the in the 1920s they were replaced by motor coaches.

The Naval College's training regime involved high school studies intermixed with naval training such as parade drill, seamanship and engineering. The weekdays began with an early morning bugle call, a quick shower and then a run before breakfast. The junior cadets had to wash and dress in three minutes, but some senior supervising cadets reduced this to two and a half minutes. This was followed by parade training or Divisions after which academic and naval study occupied the day until 1600. There was then sport until dinner.

In the early days at the Naval College the Phillip Year had to learn the nautical terms for their surroundings. Floors became 'decks', walls 'bulkheads' and beds 'bunks'. There was method to this nautical immersion as it would help them once they got to sea. More demanding was the imperative to know how to properly wear and maintain their various naval uniforms. Phillip Year were the subject of much scrutiny in this area and punishments were meted out for poorly worn or maintained 'rigs'. The boys soon learnt how to shine their boots to a parade-ground standard as well as to darn and sew. Fortunately, they were given an adequate uniform allowance which proved essential as the 13-year-olds quickly grew in this physically active environment.

Since its move to Flinders, the Naval College occupied repurposed buildings, but in 1937, as funds became available, a new E-shaped Studies Block with classrooms, laboratories and assembly hall was under construction. There was a sentiment that there needed to be a delineation between the Naval College and the rest of Flinders Naval Depot. Physically, the Naval College precinct was surrounded by a cypress hedge and the grounds were out of bounds to other personnel.

Due to the Depression, the size of the Fleet was cut and therefore the required cadet intake much reduced. In its Jervis Bay heyday the Naval College trained 120 cadet-midshipmen, but by 1937 the total was only 50. In 1938 the Naval College was divided into two 'Houses'— Flinders and Cook. This structure contributed to the cohesion of the college, helped with sporting competitions and provided a means for the younger boys to less formally engage with the senior cadet midshipmen.

Captain Pope had served at the original Naval College before World War I and had then been the Navigating Officer in the cruiser *Sydney* during her famous 1914 battle against the German cruiser *Emden*. Because Pope was also in command of the entire Flinders Naval Depot, the day-to-day running of the college was the domain of the Commander. That was Commander Henry Palmer who had been a member of the 1914 Entry to the College. He was a physical training specialist and a keen rugby player. At the end of 1937 Palmer left the College to join the new cruiser *Sydney*. After a six-month gap he was replaced by Commander James Armstrong, a natural leader and destined to have distinguished war service.

There were just two other officers who each had responsibility for two of the 'Years'. Initially they were Lieutenant Commander Arthur Skipwith, RN and Lieutenant Commander Harley Wright. While they taught some naval subjects, such as seamanship, they had less contact with the cadet midshipmen than the masters and cadet captains. There were also several senior sailors who gave instruction and the most notable was Chief Petty Officer John Mackay, who taught the young boys seamanship. Mackay had been part of the Naval Brigade in the 1900 Boxer Rebellion and the boys were much more interested in his tales of China than knots and splices.

The academic staff just numbered a Director of Studies and four masters. They included the well-regarded Frederick Eldridge, who first joined the college in 1913, and later wrote its first history.* The influential Director of Studies, Bill Cowan, was another long-time member of the academic staff who joined the college in 1919 as a mathematics instructor. Cowan had played first class cricket for South Australia and for many years had coached the college's cricket teams.

---

* Eldridge, F.B. *A History of the Royal Australian Naval College: From its inception in 1913 to the end of World War II in 1945*, Melbourne, Georgian House, 1949.

Guy was a member of Flinders Division and in 1940 he became the junior of its two cadet captains. Classmate David Hamer thought that Guy was the 'natural selection'.[4] Cadet captains were like boarding school prefects but with a naval twist. To distinguish cadet captains, their uniforms were embellished with a gold-braided insignia on the left sleeve.[5] One cadet opined that 'Cadet-Captains lived lordly but somewhat lonely lives'.[6] They largely ran the daily routine, each presided over a table at meals and they 'cast a disciplinary eye over the herd'.[7] For minor infractions the chief cadet captain and the cadet captains administered punishments which included a gym shoe on the backside 'in interests of public order'.[8] It was not uncommon for a junior cadet to receive such punishment at least once a week. This delegated approach to discipline could be fraught as it gave great power to immature boys in an environment often unseen by the officers.

In practice the discipline at the Naval College at that time was strict. One cadet midshipman, Andrew Robertson,* who was two years junior to Guy, described the College as 'hell on earth'.[9] Rothesay Swan,† of the 1940 Entry, thought that on reflection the purpose of this regimen was to turn boys into men in short order.[10] Perhaps to the good fortune of Guy's class one of its members contracted mumps and the entire class was placed in isolation for a period. Guy's assessment was that this discipline sometimes crushed rather than developed the boys.[11]

This strict regime was most heavily felt by the most junior class. This inadvertently served to bond the boys and so it was with the Phillip Year. Their diversity of background, particularly whether from 'city' or 'country' created a strength of collective skills. Guy felt that while the boys who came from boarding schools seemed to adjust quickest to the college routine, and the 'city' boys were generally ahead academically, the 'country' boys were more resilient and confident. Collectively the boys formed, in Guy's view, a great team and 'a happy bunch of characters'.[12]

---

* Later Rear Admiral A.J. Robertson, AO, DSC, RAN (1925–2020).

† Later Rear Admiral R.C. Swan, AO, CBE, RAN (1926–).

Bruce Dowling and John Austin became Guy's close friends and Guy spent a leave with Austin's family on the coast.

In the first week the cadet captains told the Phillip Year everyone had to have a nickname. A few names were relatively easy to assign. Colin Russell was the smallest in the class and so became 'Squirt'. John Austin became 'Boots' after the Austin Boot Company. Lyster Tatham was given the less prepossessing moniker of 'Snoz' because of his big nose, while another boy became 'Trunky' for another physical feature. As inspiration diminished Guy was relieved to be just 'Guy', using this new phase of his life to leave 'Dick' behind. Another rite of entry was an initiation ceremony. In the history of the Naval College, the staging of an 'initiation ceremony' waxed and waned.* In Guy's time at the college it consisted of a fight with the Second Years and then a dunking in a putrid duck pond.

Field and water sports figured large in the life of the cadet-midshipmen. For Guy and other boys who were good at sport, this was a welcome release from the classroom. The cadets played sport among themselves, as well as against Victorian schools such as Geelong Grammar and Melbourne Technical College. The latter included the very competitive girls' hockey team from Merton Hall. Before the match was afternoon tea and Guy wrote, as a budding sports reporter in the *Royal Australian Naval College Magazine*, 'It was good to see how our team turned out in spotless togs and with hair plastered down. Treloar's shorts were a sight for sore eyes, Merson's boots were just about good enough for Sunday Divisions, and Reed must have used fully half a bottle of oil on his hair.'[13]

The boys won 6–2; the day concluding with a dance at the College. Guy was a natural athlete and the editions of the *RANC Magazine* record his achievements over his four years at Flinders. With a small body of cadets, the boys became adept at many sports. Guy was 'a very good all-rounder' in the cricket team and as he grew became a breakaway in the

---

* In Naval College folklore, it was said that an initiation ceremony had taken place on the evening of the HMAS *Melbourne–Voyager* collision on 10 February 1964. As a result future ceremonies were banned.

rugby team. He also played hockey, soccer, tennis and, in particular, he excelled at athletics. Probably most notable was his performance as a cross-country runner. In 1937 he won the age handicap in the Cross Country Championship for which he was awarded a cake. In 1938 and 1939 he was beaten by the older Jack Lester but he finally won in 1940. Also that year Guy won the One Mile Shield and the Best Athlete Award. Guy would eventually be awarded 'Colours' in athletics, boats, hockey and rugby.*

Towards the end of 1938 Guy made the decision that would shape his naval career. He had joined the Navy with the intention of being an engineer, but after two years the Navy gave the boys, after some exposure to the Service, the opportunity to alter their proposed specialisation. It was a tour of the old destroyer *Vampire,* then a training ship attached to Flinders, that led to a change of heart. Guy recalled,

> We went down one sort of cold wet and windy Bass Strait
> day and walked around the dear old ship and went through
> the engine room and boiler room which I didn't find
> particularly attractive … I can remember quite distinctly
> coming back and standing on the quarterdeck in the light
> drizzle and thinking to myself, as I looked at the bridge,
> I don't want to be down below. I think I'd like to be up
> there driving the ship. And so I changed my initial bid for
> engineering, and when it came to the decision at the end
> of the second year I said 'No thanks, I'll be an Executive
> Officer'. Never regretted the change.[14]

In 1939, as the international situation continued to deteriorate, there were considerable changes at Flinders Naval Depot. More and larger intakes of officers and sailors were taken in for training. The 1939 Naval

---

* At the Naval College Sporting Colours, more often known as Colours, were awarded to cadet midshipmen who excelled in a sport. Colours were worn on the college blazer.

College intake was twenty-one boys, the largest since 1920. In August it was also decided that the senior class would forego their Passing Out Parade and instead expeditiously join the ships of the Australian Squadron.* On 3 September, two days after the Parade was due to take place, war was declared against Germany.

On the departure of the 1936 Entry, the 1937 Entry became senior and Guy was made the Chief Cadet Captain of the Naval College. That came with both leadership and disciplinary responsibilities. Guy thought this was quite an achievement for one of the 'country' boys. Andrew Robertson said their new Chief Cadet Captain was the fittest boy at the Naval College and the best turned out in uniform. 'He was a great role model, a stern disciplinarian, but at that time his fine sense of humour was not too evident.'[15]

Within the Australian Squadron, ships in reserve were progressively brought back into service. This necessitated officers, such as Commander Armstrong and then his very brief relief Commander William Moran,† leave their shore appointments to be replaced by retired World War I veterans.

The new Commander was 58-year-old Commander Alexander Loudoun-Shand. He was a Scot who first went to sea in sailing ships and had rounded Cape Horn seven times. During World War I he was First Lieutenant of the small cruiser *Psyche* and at war's end he was made a Year Lieutenant at the Naval College. Loudoun-Shand was keen on sports and soon his stentorian voice from the side-lines became familiar to the boys. He was also invariably seen with his pipe and on one occasion on the parade ground he had placed his still smouldering pipe in his pocket. To the intense interest of the cadets, but unnoticed by Loudoun-Shand, the smoke continued to emanate from the pocket until the pipe

---

* From 1926 to 1949 the Australian Fleet was officially called the Australian Squadron.

† Commander W.T.A. Moran died when his destroyer *Vampire* was sunk by Japanese aircraft in 1942.

clattered to the ground having burned through the Commander's pocket. Of the three Commanders, Guy considered that Loudoun-Shand best understood the young. He endeared himself to Guy and other country boys by getting them to bring their rifles and shotguns from home at term break so they could go shooting for rabbits in the nearby countryside.

The Term Officers, Skipwith and Wright, also went to sea. They were replaced by Lieutenant Commander 'Arch' Harrington* and Lieutenant Rupert Robinson. Harrington had a strong presence and placed a particular emphasis on boat work. On one occasion he took some of Guy's class in the cutter for rowing practice. The repeated drill of tossing and shipping oars – that is, raising the blades vertically in the air and then bring them down horizontally into the rollocks – required some strength. One of Guy's weary classmates dropped his oar on Harrington's head.

Academically Guy was in the middle of the class and his strengths were in engineering and the sciences. During the four years, the stand-out student was David Hamer and Guy would later rate him as probably the smartest naval officer he ever met. Others who shone academically were Bob Davis, James 'Jim' Willis, Bruce Dowling and Lyster Tatham. At the end of the first year David Manning was withdrawn by his parents from the Naval College. While in the third year John Goble, who had struggled academically, was back-classed one year, but would eventually graduate.

At the end of the academic year there was a period of more advanced naval training for Guy's class to better prepare them for their first ship. The fifteen soon-to-be-graduates were hosted to a dinner in the Wardroom where they were given a beer for the first time. It was traditional for the Governor General to be the Reviewing Officer at the Passing Out Parade. However, on 12 December 1940 Lord Gowrie was detained in Canberra for war-related matters. The First Naval Member, Admiral Sir Ragnar Colvin, took the salute at the march past and presented the prizes

---

*   Later Vice Admiral Sir Hastings Harrington KBE, CB, DSO, RAN (1906–65). He was Chief of Naval Staff 1962–65.

to the Phillip Year. Although the weather at Flinders could go from bleak to balmy within the same day, the sun shone upon the Graduating Class and those parents that could make the journey. In his address Colvin said, 'On your efficiency, the efficiency and even the lives of the men you command will depend. You dare not, therefore, miss any opportunity to gain knowledge.'[16]

Of the prize-winners, unsurprisingly David Hamer was the Dux, winning four out of the seven academic prizes. He was followed by Jim Willis with three, plus the Otto Albert Prize for Seamanship. John Austin won the Governor-General's Cup while John Kennedy was awarded the coveted King's Medal for 'gentlemanly bearing, character, good influence among his fellows and officer-like qualities'. For his part, Guy received a prize for engineering.

On graduation the 1937 Entry were promoted to Midshipmen, designated with a white patch on each lapel. For the boys the promotion was significant within the enclosed world of the Naval College, but now the Squadron beckoned. They were to be posted to the Navy's two heavy cruisers. The first five alphabetically were to join *Australia* while the remainder went to *Canberra*. Onboard they would start to learn the intricacies of their naval profession from both officers and sailors. Whilst as Midshipmen they were officers, there was a time-honoured convention that sailors would take midshipmen under their wing to impart their seasoned wisdom from years at sea. For the sailors this was an investment in the future well-being of the Service. For many naval officers their midshipman's time was one of the most crucial periods of their careers. For Guy Griffiths it was to be significantly so.

3
Midshipman at Sea:
HMS *Repulse*

Among the qualities of those battlecruisers which perhaps most impressed was their dignified grace. Fast, unarmoured and powerful as they were, They evoked more the feminine presence than that of the cruising battleship.

Vice Admiral Sir John Hayes[1]

I

The day after *Karamea*'s safe arrival in Glasgow, Guy Griffiths and his comrades took the night train to London. On arrival they reported to Australia House only to learn that *Australia* had already sailed from UK waters and was probably near the Cape of Good Hope bound for Australia. The revised plan was to initially billet the five boys out with Australian expatriate families in the London area until an alternate RN warship could be found for them. Commander Rosenthal also learnt at Australia House that his impending destroyer command was changed and instead he would take command of the already commissioned *Nestor*. Her captain had been removed pending court martial for that career pitfall of drunkenness.[2]

Guy and two other midshipmen were assigned to a Mr Lionel and Mrs Myrtle Logue who lived at Beechgrove, an imposing house with grounds in Sydenham, an outer suburb of London. The boys, guided by Mrs Logue, took a tram with just a small bag each. They found the Logues to be 'wonderful people' and were quickly made at home. Lionel Logue was a speech therapist who specialized in helping people with a stutter. His most notable client was King George VI.* It was on one of their first nights with the Logues that the boys first heard the air raid sirens sound and saw the flak rising into the sky. They were hustled down into the basement of the house to wait till the 'All Clear'. It was a happy and welcoming household, but after a couple of days the boys were moved away from London; first to a delightful Mrs Marchant, who had a little cottage in the village of Chalfont St Giles north-west of London. Their stay was punctuated by enormous meals, walks around the village and pints at the local pub. Their final billet was with another charming hostess, Lady Pelham Byrne, and her family at nearby Beaconsfield.

II

By early March 1941 the Admiralty had nominated a ship to take the Australian midshipmen to progress their training. She was *Repulse*, a 32,000 tonne battlecruiser and World War I veteran. With a main armament of six 15-inch guns, a speed of 32 knots and complement of over 1,300 officers and men, *Repulse* would be unlike anything the midshipmen had hitherto experienced. *Repulse* was at Greenock waiting to escort a convoy. On 7 March the midshipmen caught a crowded overnight train back to Glasgow. The next day they made their way to *Repulse* anchored off Greenock. Thus 8 March 1941 began their operational life in the Navy. Guy had just turned 18 but he was not the youngest onboard with over twenty 17-year-old boy seamen in the ship. Guy and his classmates had 'some apprehension as to just how one would measure up to the challenge'.[3]

---

* This relationship was made famous in the 2010 Academy award-winning film *The King's Speech*.

Like the other two remaining battlecruisers in the Fleet,* *Repulse* still maintained the elan imbued into the battlecruisers by their charismatic Great War commander Admiral Sir David Beatty. The Australian midshipmen soon caught on, and Guy recalled:

> Beatty was a nonconformist in his fashion and instead of buttoning up his jacket with four rows of buttons Beatty decided to have a jacket with three. So as nobody else was allowed to have a jacket with three, all the battle cruiser officers undid their top right button. That was their privilege. And so we used to proudly undo the top right button as midshipmen to positively show, we were in the Battle Cruiser Squadron. It was great fun.[4]

As glamour ships during the inter-war years, the three battlecruisers had at different times undertaken world or Royal tours. *Repulse* had done so three times† and had been slated to take the King and Queen to Canada in 1939. With storm clouds brewing they instead went by the Canadian Pacific liner, the *Empress of Australia*. The legacy for *Repulse,* however, was a handpicked crew and the senior captain in the Fleet. He was Captain William Tennant,‡ a navigator by specialisation. During World War I he had survived the sinking of the cruiser *Nottingham* and between the wars had navigated both *Repulse* and sister-ship *Renown* on Royal tours. Most recently, Tennant had been the Senior Naval Officer ashore at Dunkirk during the epic evacuation.§ His fame spread throughout the Fleet. While the King made him a Companion of the Order of the Bath, sailors gave him the sobriquet *Dunkirk Joe.*

Repulse made an immediate impression on the Australian

---

* The other two battlecruisers were *Repulse*'s sister-ship, HMS *Renown* and the world's largest warship, HMS *Hood.*
† Royal and World Tours in 1923, 1925 and 1927.
‡ Later Admiral Sir William Tennant KCB, CBE, MVO, DL (1890–1963).
§ In the 2017 film *Dunkirk*, Captain Tennant was played by Kenneth Branagh.

midshipmen. Bruce Dowling wrote she was 'a world away from the *Karamea* … She was fantastic. The pride and morale of the crew made her a happy and therefore an efficient ship.'[5] Guy would say in later years that *Repulse* was the most efficient ship in which he had served. Memoirs and oral histories of former *Repulse* officers and sailors underscore this assessment.

The Australians lived in the gunroom which was located near the aft twin 15-inch gun turret. What armour there was in the ship ended in this area. As a result the quarterdeck could flex disconcertingly in heavy seas. Guy described the effect as '… the back end would waggle like a duck's tail'.[6] The gunroom bathroom had a propensity to overflow if the ejector system did not shut off for speeds over 16 or 18 knots. On a few occasions the midshipmen would look down from their hammocks to find their boots floating in a couple of inches of cold seawater.

In a more serious vein, gunrooms in the fleet could be hierarchical places that made life miserable for new joiners with petty cruelties and hazing. Not so in *Repulse*. There were 25 midshipmen and 3 sub-lieutenants onboard; one of latter, Sub-Lieutenant Richard Pool,[*] was in charge. Fortunately, for the Australian midshipmen, Pool had recently reformed the gunroom from its Victorian era idiosyncrasies to operate more like an officers' wardroom. Pool reasoned that, with the influx of older midshipmen from different backgrounds because of the war, a more mature approach was required. One popular improvement was the hanging of framed artwork of swimsuit clad beauties from an American magazine. While popular with the midshipmen it caused Captain Tennant some angst when he saw them when doing rounds. He called for Pool. Tennant was both a devout Christian and a lover of country shooting weekends. He gave Pool some money to buy some framed country scenes the next time *Repulse* pulled into Rosyth. The opportunity did not present itself and the beauties continued to adorn the Gunroom.

Repulse was a 'West Country Ship' with most of her sailors coming

---

[*] Later Commander R.A.W. Pool DSC, RN (1919–95).

from that part of England and Wales. At this time Guy was unaware of his familial ties with the West Country. He had, however, been told that by reputation West Country ships were friendly and good humoured, and so it proved. Guy's early impressions of *Repulse* and her gunroom were positive,

> The ship sailed at about 5 o'clock and there we were at sea with our hammocks slung on our first night at sea as a midshipman in a warship. And we had a great time. Wonderful captain. A great, great crew, a friendly team in the gunroom. … we were quite warmly greeted … there was no sort of 'who on earth are these colonials?' Although I think probably people might have thought it, they didn't say it.[7]

Other newly joining officers and sailors have also commented in their reminiscences of the welcoming attitude onboard *Repulse*. They were assisted and encouraged to get their sea legs, learn the layout of the ship, its routines, their duties and integrate into the ship's company.[8] It was another sign of a happy and efficient ship.

Guy was to find that socially the gunroom was friendly but stratified with the junior midshipmen, senior midshipmen and sub-lieutenants going ashore in separate groups. The other important figure for Guy and his compatriots was their training officer or 'snotties' nurse'.* This was Lieutenant 'Jock' Hayes.† Highly intelligent, Hayes had been a skilled navigator whose career was put off course because of failing eyesight. He was now the Signals Officer onboard. Hayes proved to be an encouraging and empathetic training officer.

On the day of their joining, *Repulse* sailed to escort a southbound

---

* Midshipmen were known as 'snotties' because they had three buttons on the sleeves of their dress jackets. It was said that the buttons were put there to stop midshipmen wiping their noses on their sleeves. The officer in charge of the midshipmen's training was therefore known as the snotties' nurse.

† Later Vice Admiral Sir John Hayes, KCB, OBE, DL (1913–98).

Atlantic convoy. This duty had largely been *Repulse*'s lot, interspersed with fruitless hunts for German warships trying to break out into the Atlantic. Guy found Captain Tennant initially forbidding and to a midshipman a god-like figure onboard. Tennant observed the tradition of the Captain inviting a couple of midshipmen to breakfast in his cabin in order to learn something of them. When Guy had his turn he was initially too petrified to speak to the great man, but Tennant soon put him at ease and on reflection Guy thought it was 'really a very nice' experience.[9] Over time Guy formed the view that his captain was quiet, conservative, efficient, understanding and, importantly, a skilled ship-handler of a battlecruiser. In terms of Tennant's relationship with the ship's company Guy thought his Captain 'knew his people and so he knew more about you than you thought he did'.[10] For his part Tennant would later report that Guy was 'a most determined, able and exceptional young officer. He should do very well in the Service'.[11]

On 22 May 1941 *Repulse* was once again in the Clyde to escort a convoy, this time a fast troop convoy to the Indian Ocean – WS.8B. The WS code letters signified the port of origin. The sailors took the initials to be shorthand for *Winston Specials*. The tasking was, however, short-lived and instead *Repulse* sailed north to join the battleship *King George V,* wearing the flag of Admiral Sir John Tovey,[*] the aircraft carrier *Victorious*, 4 cruisers[†] and 7 destroyers off Cape Wrath early the following day. The modern and powerful German battleship *Bismarck* and her consort the heavy cruiser *Prinz Eugen[‡]* had been sighted off the Danish coast and were probably going to sortie into the North Atlantic. There was huge excitement within *Repulse* as she joined the formation. On a clear and blustery day they steamed at 27 knots on a course hopefully to close the Germans. That evening it was reported that the Germans had been

---

* Later Admiral of the Fleet Sir John Tovey, 1st Baron Tovey, GCB, KBE, DSO (1885–1971).

† The cruisers were the 6-inch-gunned light cruisers *Aurora, Galatea, Hermione* & *Kenya*.

‡ A heavy cruiser is armed with 8-inch guns.

sighted and were being shadowed, amid snow flurries and mist, by the heavy cruisers *Suffolk* and *Norfolk*.

Bismarck's reported location put another British formation, the battlecruiser *Hood*, wearing the flag of Vice Admiral Lancelot Holland, and the new battleship *Prince of Wales*, closer to the Germans and they were likely to intercept them at first light the next morning. The next day during breakfast in *Repulse* it was announced that *Bismarck* had sunk *Hood* and damaged *Prince of Wales*. To Guy and many onboard it was surprising and sobering news. If *Hood*, the pride of the Navy and the largest warship in the world, had been sunk, with just three survivors, how would *Repulse* fare?

Suffolk and *Norfolk* still shadowed *Bismarck* and Tovey altered course to the south west to close *Bismarck* with the expectation that battle would be joined on the morning of 25 May. Down below in *Repulse* the sustained high speed in the sea conditions had taken its toll. Bruce Dowling later wrote,

> The chase was immensely exhilarating. We were steaming at some 27 to 28 knots into a very heavy Atlantic sea. The old *Repulse* would dig her mighty bow into a huge wave and then shudder as the bow lifted and hundreds of tons of water were flung over the Bridge and the decks. The force was so great that some anchors, though they were heavily secured, were swept overboard.[12]

Half an hour before sunrise the ships went to action stations and lookouts scanned the faint horizon. *Bismarck* was not to be seen. She had slipped her trackers during the evening. For *Repulse* the news got worse. The high-speed steaming meant she was low on fuel and had to detach to top up. Tennant was able to get a few more hours with the force after suggesting *Repulse* could refuel Conception Bay in Newfoundland instead of Scotland.

Once again, the opportunity to engage the enemy eluded *Repulse*. Jock Hayes captured the mood in the wardroom when he wrote that, 'the anticlimax was debilitating. Keyed up for action, hopefully to have been an actor on the stage we must now vanish into the wings.'[13] Guy later recalled 'the whole ship fell absolutely flat, absolutely flat and frustrated'.[14] On the lower deck Seaman Robert Fraser reflected that 'we always seemed to be out of it'.[15]

While *Repulse* refuelled at anchor, local fishermen readily sold large quantities of fish to the ship. Meanwhile, Guy and some of the other midshipmen took the chance to have a walk ashore. Whilst at anchor news came of *Bismarck's* demise at the hands of the battleships *King George V* and *Rodney*, and their consorts. After *Repulse* fuelled from an oiler sent up from Halifax she returned to sea, initially looking for *Prinz Eugen*. *Repulse* then visited Halifax for some much-needed repairs to her anchors and hull. The Nova Scotian port seemed a throwback to pre-war years with its lively nightlife along the waterfront and the absence of rationing or blackout restrictions. To Guy and his Gunroom messmates Halifax was heaven compared to war-time Britain. On sailing, *Repulse* escorted a large convoy, which contained the Canadian 3rd Division, across the North Atlantic.

III

In July 1941 *Repulse* went into dock in Rosyth. Among other things she received additional close-range anti-aircraft weapons. The period under repair provided a welcome break from the sea-time. Guy and his fellow midshipmen savoured innocent pleasures such as afternoon tea with some WRNS* at nearby Dunfermline. Rumours abounded about *Repulse's* next employment, ranging from a full modernisation in America to more convoy work.

Following the refit, *Repulse* sailed to the protected waters of Scapa

---

* The acronym WRNS stood for the Women's Royal Naval Service.

Flow in the Orkney Islands for a shakedown. During one of the 15-inch gunnery firings Guy marvelled at being able to see the large shells leave the guns. As part of their training the midshipmen had to sail the ship's whalers and then bring them alongside *Repulse* without damaging either the whaler or the ship's gangways or ladders. The whalers had a main and a smaller mizzen mast and required some expertise to handle well. Under watchful eyes the five Australian midshipmen were assigned the one whaler. Each took a turn at the helm to bring the cutter alongside the starboard-side accommodation ladder. Fortunately, at the Naval College they had considerable practice in whalers and each competently completed the evolution. Guy later remarked,

> Suddenly people realised 'oh these Australians can sail'. We knew we had acquitted ourselves that day. Quite fun. I suppose in a way back in those days we felt just a little bit smug about it, but we were only doing what we had been trained to do and we had obviously been taught well at home.[16]

There was, however, much to learn, even in boat-work. For example, some of *Repulse*'s motorboats were fitted with the notoriously difficult 'Kitchen Rudder'.* This consisted of two steerable curved plates that partly encased a single propeller to give more manoeuvrability. It had the added complexity of both a tiller and a tiller wheel. This required much practice and until mastered coming alongside could be quite spectacular. Guy was much helped early on by two who had learnt the Kitchener rudder art. They were one of the RN midshipmen, James Bremridge and the very experienced Leading Seaman Lew Higgins.

After a spell in Scapa Flow, convoy work became *Repulse*'s assignment once more. It was to be another 'Winston Special' – WS.11

---

* Kitchen rudder or more correctly, 'Kitchen's Patent Reversing Rudders' was invented in 1916 by Mr John Kitchen. It is variously referred to as 'Kitchener gear' or 'Kitchener rudder'.

that comprised 22 troopships departing the Clyde and Liverpool at the end of August 1941 bound for the Indian Ocean. Once there the ships would split into smaller convoys taking the troops to various ports from Suez to Singapore. *Repulse*, the major escorting warship, was joined by the aircraft carrier *Furious*, armed merchant cruiser *Derbyshire*, the destroyers *Encounter*, *Highlander* and *Legion*, the cutters *Sennen* and *Totland*, as well as the Indian sloop *Sutlej*.

Once into the Atlantic, *Repulse* and the destroyers escorted the faster units, leaving *Derbyshire* and the other escorts to look after the slower ships. All were initially bound for the West African port of Freetown, which was a major convoy hub. During the day *Repulse* took station between the two centre columns of the convoy, while at night she placed herself ahead. On 4 September, as the convoy came abreast Gibraltar, the escort was strengthened by *Nestor*, commanded by Guy's former 'sea-daddy' Commander Rosenthal. The reconstituted convoy reformed and sailed from Freetown on 18 September. Four days later, despite the war, honours were paid to King Neptune and his court in a 'crossing the line' ceremony as *Repulse* passed over the Equator. A canvas swimming pool was also rigged which proved very popular in the un-airconditioned ship.

Repulse briefly left the troop convoy to anchor off St Helena to take fuel from an oiler. During this interlude each watch was given two hours ashore to stretch their legs. This remote volcanic island had not only been a place of internment for Napoleon but also for a troublesome Zulu king and Boer rebels. On reaching the Cape, *Repulse* detached once more, this time for fuel in Durban. During the visit the locals extended their hospitality to the ship's company with the city becoming a favourite for the sailors. On re-joining, the convoy passed through the Mozambique Channel. At this point, on 13 October, *Repulse* handed over her convoy to the cruiser *Ceres* to join the small aircraft carrier *Hermes* and the light cruiser *Emerald* to form Force T. Their role was to search for and destroy German surface raiders[*] that were then plaguing shipping routes. The

---

[*] German surface raiders or auxiliary cruisers were merchant ships typically

British East Africa port of Kilindini (Mombasa) became Force T's base, between what were to prove fruitless sweeps of the Indian Ocean. As at all the ports visited, the hospitality of the locals was generous. The District Commissioner, Mr Geoffrey Hodges and his wife, were friends of Captain Tennant. As a result Guy and the other officers enjoyed afternoon teas and the swimming pool at their residence.

During a refuelling stop in Durban, South Africa's Prime Minister Field Marshal Jan Smuts addressed *Repulse's* ship's company. To many of the men it was going to be just another long speech. Standing on a dais on the catapult deck it was soon apparent he was speaking as a battle-hardened soldier and soon had their rapt attention. He welcomed their presence in the Indian Ocean, but then he warned them of the growing menace of Japan. He said, 'let it be known that the Japanese weren't some myopic servile race who'd be scared of confrontation with the British'. To the contrary, he stated emphatically that 'they'd openly encourage it'.[17] It was clear to Guy that Smuts had a deep appreciation of the Far East situation and *Repulse* needed 'to be bloody careful'.[18] Smuts had made an 'indelible impression'[19] on *Repulse*. To Guy, Smuts came across as 'a great bloke and one hell of a statesman'.[20] Smut's words were prescient for the strategic situation was changing rapidly.

One of the cornerstones of the British Imperial defence strategy in the Pacific was Singapore. During the interwar period, a series of conferences in which Australia had taken part had discussed both the fortification and the deployment of naval, land and air forces to Singapore. Funding never met these aspirations. While it was realised that a battle fleet could not be permanently stationed at Singapore, it was hoped that Singapore, and to a lesser extent Hong Kong, would hold off any aggressor until the main battle fleet could arrive from British waters. By 1941 it was clear this strategy was flawed. Firstly, neither the planned strengthening of Singapore's defences had occurred, nor had the

covertly armed with six 5.9-inch guns, close-range guns, torpedoes, mines and a seaplane. They preyed on unescorted merchant ships as well as mining coastal shipping routes.

deployment of forces, particularly aircraft and submarines. This was partly the result of the changed global situation. Secondly, it was not foreseen that all of Western Europe would be occupied and Britain would have to shoulder the global struggle alone.

As such there were insufficient battleships and aircraft carriers to send as a viable force to counter the substantial Imperial Japanese Navy. The question was therefore whether to send any heavy ships at all or send a deterrent force. Churchill chose the latter course of action. The force would comprise *Prince of Wales*, still in British waters; the new aircraft carrier *Indomitable*, then undergoing work-up in the Caribbean and *Repulse*, then in the Indian Ocean. Only 4 destroyers were available to round out this force.* Inauspiciously, *Indomitable* ran aground off Jamaica and had to proceed to Norfolk, Virginia for repairs. A replacement carrier was unavailable.

The commander of the now depleted force was to be current Vice Chief of Naval Staff in the Admiralty, Rear Admiral Tom Phillips. His was an unusual selection, as there were more senior and seasoned admirals; indeed, his designated Chief of Staff, Rear Admiral Arthur Palliser,† had more recent seagoing experience. Phillips' personal relationships with both the First Sea Lord and Churchill were factors in his selection. On appointment Phillips was promoted to substantive Vice Admiral and then made an Acting Admiral to ensure he was senior to the other admirals in theatre. Phillips had seen little action at sea in World War I and none in this present conflict. In addition, he had never commanded formations of major warships at sea. Perhaps more troubling was his attitude to the threat of aircraft attack on warships. Whilst at the Admiralty, when reviewing British warship losses due to air attack during the 1940 Norwegian campaign, Phillips found it difficult to accept the lethality of modern aircraft and thought 'greater courage and resolution' was needed to counter them.[21]

---

* The destroyers were *Electra*, *Express*, *Encounter* and *Jupiter*. They were later joined by HMAS *Vampire*.

† Later Admiral Sir Arthur Palliser KCB, DSC (1890–1956).

Onboard *Repulse* nothing was known of these developments. The ship arrived in Colombo on 22 November to find there was a dock strike. Sailors were used to help restore order and man the wharves. The strike ended two days later. *Repulse* then undertook a successful sea efficiency test for the Commander-in-Chief East Indies, Vice Admiral Sir Geoffrey Arbuthnot. After landing the Admiral, *Repulse* sailed to Trincomalee for fuel and then on 29 November proceeded into the Bay of Bengal. On clearing harbour Captain Tennant announced on the ship's broadcast that *Repulse* would meet *Prince of Wales* the next morning and proceed to Singapore. They would form the nucleus of the new Far Eastern Fleet.

On 30 November *Repulse* rendezvoused with *Prince of Wales* and her destroyers. Admiral Phillips had flown ahead to Singapore, so as Tennant was senior to Captain John Leach in *Prince of Wales* he ordered the battleship to form up astern of *Repulse*. This may not have sat well with those on the bridge in the *'Prince'*, as *Repulse* sailors called her, but so be it. During the afternoon of 2 December the ships approached Singapore and Tennant ordered *Prince of Wales* to take station ahead of *Repulse*. For many on *Repulse*'s upper deck it was the first opportunity to view this modern battleship. At about 1700 *Prince of Wales* went alongside, whilst *Repulse* went to a buoy off the naval dockyard. Their arrival was a morale boost for the garrison city.

For the next two days the ships were busy refuelling, storing and availing themselves of dockyard assistance for minor repairs. Soon a rumour spread through *Repulse* that she would sail to Darwin and other ports to advertise the presence of the two capital ships to the region. The 'scuttlebutt' proved correct and *Repulse* sailed on 5 December for Darwin. On the same day Admiral Phillips flew to Manila to meet the Commander-in-Chief of the US Asiatic Fleet, Admiral Thomas Hart. The American admiral, through his interest in the code-breaking and signal traffic analysis efforts of his cryptanalysis team, felt he had a good sense of Japanese intentions. On the strength of this work, Hart deployed Catalina reconnaissance aircraft to track Japanese warships and transports, as well as deploying his forces in case of attack.* Hart impressed upon Phillips that the Japanese plans probably involved multiple points of attack and they would be launched within days not weeks.[22] Both men were keen to work together when the inevitable attacks occurred. Hart wrote in his diary of Phillips, 'Well I acquired considerable respect for Phillips – looks like as good an Englishman to work with as I have seen for some time.'[23]

The prospect for the Australian midshipmen of returning home to Australia in *Repulse* was short lived. On Phillips' return to Singapore he recalled *Repulse*. She was back at the Singapore Naval Base late on 7 December. Soon more rumours swept the ship, this time about possible Japanese troop convoys off the Malay coast. At about 0400 the bugle call 'Repel aircraft' was heard over the ship's broadcast. Those on the upper deck could see searchlights from the city playing over aircraft in the sky. There was a formation of 9 aircraft and *Repulse*'s port-side 4-inch high-angle guns opened fire. They were soon followed by the *Prince of Wales'* 5.25-inch guns as well as Bofors guns in the dockyard. The aircraft were at a height of about 10,000 feet and largely untroubled by the barrage. Soon after the raid, the ship's Commander announced on the broadcast that the aircraft were likely Japanese bombers from Saigon. Of more import, he announced the US Fleet had been attacked at Pearl Harbor and that the Japanese had landed troops on the Malay coast. Britain and the USA were now at war with Japan.† The reaction by many onboard *Repulse* was that at last the ship would see action.

IV

At 1230 on 8 December Captain Tennant attended an urgent meeting with Phillips, Palliser, Leach and Phillips' Chief Staff Officer Captain Leonard

---

*   The Asiatic Fleet cryptanalysis team based at Corregidor was code named Station C or CAST). Later elements would help form the RAN-USN Fleet Radio Unit Melbourne or FRUMEL.

†   The Commander in a major warship is the second in command or executive officer and is of the rank of Commander. In *Repulse* he was Commander Ronald Dendy. Later Captain R.J.R. Dendy (1900–80).

Bell. It was briefed that the Japanese had made landings at Singora and Khota Bahru and these had been supported by the battlecruiser *Kongo* and heavy cruisers. Phillips outlined his intent to 'make a raid on the Japanese communications to Khota Bahru, Singora and Pattani'.[24] He thought his ships had the opportunity of 'smashing the Japanese forces'.[25] This operation would proceed on the basis of having fighter protection and maintaining surprise. There was unanimous support for the plan. Indeed, in the face of the Japanese invasion in Malaya and the reported reverses by Commonwealth land and air forces, it was felt that the Navy could not remain in port. Bell later wrote, 'the plan for a sudden raid, though hazardous, was acceptable. There was also the psychological effect of the fleet putting to sea in the grave emergency.'[26] The ships were now designated Force Z.

Leaving the Naval Base just prior to Force Z was the armed merchant cruiser HMAS *Manoora*. As she passed close by *Repulse* the Australian sailors could hear her band playing on the quarterdeck as her anchor was being weighed. Force Z sailed at 1700 and as the flagship steamed down Johore Strait and passed Changi Naval Signal Station, Admiral Phillips received a signal that fighter cover would not be available. He decided to proceed in any case. As the ships steamed into the South China Sea Tennant addressed his ship's company over the broadcast. Guy vividly remembers his Captain telling them they were going north to 'We are off to look for trouble. I expect we shall find it.'[27]

The following morning the portents were promising, with low cloud and rain showers making Force Z's detection by aircraft difficult. Palliser, who had remained in the Singapore Headquarters, signalled to Phillips that the air force had lost the Kota Bharu airfield, reducing the prospect of fighter protection. Equally worrying was an assessment that the Japanese air attacks on Malaya had come from a strong bomber force located in Indo-China. The implication was that this was a long-range threat to Force Z.

The Japanese naval forces were commanded by the Commander of the 2nd Fleet, Vice Admiral Kondō Nobutake.* In order to detect any sweeps north by the British he had deployed submarines in a line north east of Singapore to act as a trip wire. At 1400 his submarine *I-56* reported the Force Z's presence. This report resulted in 'Babs' reconnaissance aircraft being launched from Indo-China and 'Jake' seaplanes from the cruisers *Kinu* and *Kumano*. It was the latter Jakes that located Force Z at about 1645 but they could not maintain contact into the night. Rear Admiral Matsunaga Sadaichi,† Commander of the 22nd Air Flotilla, based at Saigon, had hoped to launch 90 aircraft to attack Force Z that day. The attack was delayed because the aircraft were armed with bombs for Singapore and it took time to rearm with torpedoes. Once launched, the aircraft could not locate Force Z in the dark.

Of these Japanese actions, Phillips was only aware of the Japanese seaplanes shadowing his ships. At 1900, in accordance with the navigational plan, the ships altered course to the north west and increased speed to 26 knots to close Singora. At the same time short-legged *Tenedos* was detached to return to Singapore. At this point, Phillips, following discussions with Leach and Bell, changed the plan. The element of surprise had been lost and what shipping was in the Singora area might not be there in the morning. Phillips was also concerned about the prospect of air attack although he believed the Japanese shore-based bombers did not possess anti-ship bombs or torpedoes. He thought his destroyers particularly vulnerable but was less concerned about his big ships.[28] At 2030 Force Z altered course to the south east to return to Singapore; speed was later reduced to 20 knots to conserve the destroyers' fuel.

Just after midnight Phillips received a fateful signal from Palliser to say there were reports of another Japanese landing at Kuantan. The landing site was not far off Force Z's planned track and being 400 miles from the Japanese airfields may be clear of that threat. Bell later wrote 'the Admiral therefore decided that surprise at Kuantan was probable

---

* Later Admiral Kondō Nobutake (1886–1953).
† Later Vice Admiral Matsunaga Sadaichi (1892–1965).

and the risk justifiable. Just before 0100 Force Z altered course towards Kuantan and increased speed to 24 knots. At 0220, unknown to Phillips, Force Z was not only detected and reported by *I-58* but subjected to an unsuccessful torpedo attack. At 0630 Force Z came under aerial surveillance once more with the aircraft sighted in *Repulse*. Undeterred, at 0800 the ships reached the approaches to Kuantan only to find an empty sea. *Express* was sent further inshore and reported 'All quiet as a wet Sunday afternoon.'[29]

Repulse, on Tennant's suggestion, launched a 'Walrus' seaplane to conduct an anti-submarine sweep ahead of Force Z's planned track toward Singapore. The city was only 140 miles distant and the Walrus would go on to Singapore. On receipt of *Express'* report, Force Z resumed passage to Singapore, but with a slight diversion to investigate some barges seen on approaching Kuantan. Critically though, Phillips, who had been concerned about maintaining radio silence, had not told Palliser of his Kuantan diversion nor sought air cover for the coming day.

At dawn Matsunaga launched 51 'Nell' bombers and 34 'Betty' torpedo bombers. Owing to Phillips' diversion to Kuantan, only one formation of Nells, armed with bombs, located a British ship. This was the lone *Tenedos* at 0950. The old destroyer successfully evaded the bombs. The large Japanese strike force had turned back to their bases in Indo-China to refuel. Then the Babs reconnaissance aircraft relocated Force Z.

At 1030 Phillips received the report from *Tenedos* of the attack. He altered course to the south east to clear the coast and increased speed to 25 knots. The ships went to the First Degree of Readiness (Action Stations) in preparation for an air attack. Onboard *Repulse* Guy went to his Action Station which was in charge of the forward High Angle Control Position (HACP). Within the compartment was a mechanical computer operated by a small crew which took bearing, range and angle data from the high-angle director above, as well as ship's course, speed and gun ballistic data to aim the 4-inch anti-aircraft guns. The other midshipmen had similar assignments throughout the ship, John Austin was in charge of the after

HACP, Peter Gyllies was in the Air Defence Position above the bridge, Bob Davies was a Fire Distribution Officer for one of the after 20mm Oerlikon anti-aircraft guns and, finally, Bruce Dowling was in one of the 15-inch gun transmitting stations in the bowels of the ship.

At 1045 *Repulse* detected incoming aircraft to the south west on her radar and they became visible fifteen minutes later. The Navigating Officer, Lieutenant Commander Harold Gill, took the conn* on the bridge and would control the ship's manoeuvring under Tennant's close direction. The first attack soon began with *Repulse* the target. Nine bombers approached *Repulse* at a height of 10,000 feet in close single-line-abreast formation from the starboard bow.† As such Guy's HACP team were immediately put to the test. *Prince of Wales* and *Repulse* opened fire with their 5.25-inch and 4-inch guns respectively. The aircraft dropped their bombs with great accuracy. Seven bombs near missed the ship's port side and another one on the starboard-side. One bomb penetrated the deck near the port aircraft hangar and exploded on, but did not penetrate, the armoured deck. This started a fire and caused casualties in the Marines' messdeck. There was a lull of about twenty minutes, which allowed the fire to be largely brought under control. The sailors jettisoned the remaining Walrus aircraft into the sea.

The next raid approached and was much bigger. In the flagship, one officer on the bridge commented that, judging by the aircraft's approach, they were about to be subjected to a torpedo attack. Phillips refuted the assertion, stating the Japanese had no torpedo aircraft about. In her consort, the calm and professional demeanour that characterized *Repulse*'s bridge was about to be tested. The low-flying aircraft were too many to count and were the main strike package of torpedo bombers. Formations headed for both capital ships. There was no interest in the

---

* 'Having the conn' on the bridge is to give steering and engine orders for the ship. In a warship it is usually done by the Officer of the Watch, but in more demanding situations by the Navigating Officer or the Captain.

† As would be soon learnt the standard Japanese standard bomber formation was nine aircraft.

destroyers. The lookouts calmly reported the successive formations to Tennant who gave directions to his navigator to alter course towards the aircraft once Tennant deemed the aircraft were committed to their attack heading. In this way the ship presented the smallest aspect to the incoming torpedoes. Jock Hayes, who looked down on the bridge from the flag deck, said that Tennant, at this moment of great trial for the ship, was brilliant in his handling of *Repulse*.[30]

Tennant, mindful that this could be a long day and ammunition had to be conserved, ordered the Gunnery Officer to delay opening fire until he deemed the aircraft were in range. The resulting barrage was impressive if not particularly accurate. Both ships sorely lacked smaller calibre rapid-fire guns that could hit the aircraft before they released their torpedoes at 2,000–3,000 yards. For their part some of the aircraft machine-gunned the ships' upper deck gun crews as they overflew. By the end of the raid *Repulse* had evaded twelve torpedoes. Tennant judged the Japanese attacks as 'magnificently carried out'; only one attacker had got 'cold feet' and released his torpedo early.[31]

While Guy and others were involved in the anti-aircraft defences, hundreds of men were in stations below decks manning systems that might not be used or were involved in ensuring the machinery plant responded to the demands of the bridge. These men heard and felt the thuds of the guns, the heeling and shudders of the ship's evasive actions.

Whilst *Repulse* emerged unscathed, the *Prince of Wales* suffered a torpedo hit which dramatically reduced her manoeuvrability. Leach indicated this by hoisting the 'Not Under Command' shapes from the yardarm. There was not the same lull as between the first and second attacks. No sooner had *Repulse* gathered herself together than the third raid arrived. This was another high-level bombing attack with *Repulse* the intended target. The ship manoeuvred hard during the attack and no further hits were received.

Tennant now closed *Prince of Wales* to offer assistance. The battleship was restricted to 20 knots and still not fully manoeuvrable. Tennant asked his signal office what signals Phillips had sent to Singapore and was astonished to learn there had been none.[32] Tennant immediately signalled to the Singapore headquarters that 'Enemy Aircraft Bombing' Force Z with a position. This news was relayed to the air force. Air Vice Marshal Conway Pulford* received the signal just 25 minutes after Tennant had sent it. Pulford ordered fighters to be immediately launched. This took no more than six minutes to occur. They would be on top of Force Z forty minutes later.

A fourth attack was now detected with eight aircraft approaching low on the starboard bow. The Japanese tactics were now different for at three miles they split into two formations. Tennant judged the right-hand formation would attack first and altered course towards them as they released their torpedoes at a range of 2,500 yards. In the din of the guns and close-range pom-poms it was hard for Gill to give orders down the voice pipe to the helmsman.† These torpedoes were evaded. The left-hand formation which seemed to be heading for *Prince of Wales* altered course at just 2,000 yards. One of the torpedoes hit *Repulse*'s port-side. It was the twentieth torpedo that had been launched at the battlecruiser.

Despite the hit, the embattled *Repulse* could still do 25 knots and this speed would be needed as a fifth attack was about to commence. This time torpedo bombers approached low from multiple directions, which meant Tennant could not comb the tracks of every torpedo. Another torpedo hit *Repulse* near the gunroom and jammed the rudder. It was now only a matter of time. Three more torpedoes hit, two on the port side and one on the starboard. It was as one sailor wrote, 'her steering gone, her great heart torn'.[33]

At about 1225 Tennant, then made for him an 'exceedingly difficult' decision. He ordered over the main broadcast 'All hands on deck. Prepare

---

* Air Vice Marshal C.W.H. Pulford, CB, OBE, AFC was the Air Officer Commanding RAF Far East. He later died while marooned on Tjebier Island, near Sumatra in March 1942.

† Lieutenant Commander H.B.G. Gill RN would later be awarded a Mentions in Despatches 'for outstanding calmness in action under trying circumstances'.

to Abandon Ship. God be with you.'[34] Although Tennant had yet to receive any detailed damage reports, he knew the ship's construction so well, he was certain she could not survive so many torpedo hits. Fortunately, the main broadcast worked in most of the ship and this was credited with saving many lives. Another piece of luck was the order to the ship's company the day before to wear their life preservers at all times. The ship started to heel to port.

As Guy and his crew left their HACP compartment, Guy could feel the ship sinking. They found sailors moving towards external hatches in 'a very orderly fashion' and made their way up a couple of ladders. Guy eventually got out of the ship through a mess-deck scuttle (porthole). At this stage the ship was listing 30° and Guy slid down the ship's side and swam away as fast as he could.

As the sailors started to enter the water, *Repulse* was still menaced by Japanese aircraft. Bob Davies, having released his gun crew, strapped himself into the Oerlikon gun. Davies, normally quiet by nature, now yelled to those near him to keep clear of his weapon's arc of fire. He then opened fire on the approaching aircraft and continued firing even as the gun-mounting slowly submerged. Jock Hayes later wrote to Guy, 'How more brave can you be in the face of the enemy?'[35] Davies was posthumously awarded a Mention in Despatches.*

Bruce Dowling had been able to thread his way up through the ship

---

* The award of Mention in Despatches (MID) recognises a member of the armed forces whose name appears in the official report, written by a superior officer and sent to higher command, in which his or her gallant or meritorious action in the face of the enemy is described. A single bronze oak leaf device is worn on the ribbon of the campaign medal. Robert Davies' MID citation reads 'This very gallant officer was last seen firing an Oerlikon gun at the enemy aircraft when he and the gun mounting were slowly submerged. Under the Imperial honours system, actions of gallantry where the person is killed can only be recognised by a Victoria Cross or a MID. Vice Admiral Hayes maintained that Captain Tennant recommended Davies for a VC, but that Vice Admiral Sir Geoffrey Layton, (Commander-in-Chief, Eastern Fleet) would not support it. Layton is reported to have said 'in a disaster of such magnitude, decorations cannot be entertained'. In 2013 Davies' heroism was reviewed for a possible award of a Victoria Cross for Australia, but it was deemed that based on the documented evidence the MID was the appropriate award.

only to find himself on the listing upper deck looking down to a perilous drop in the ocean. As he pondered what to do, 'someone gave me a mighty shove and the next thing I knew I was down there covered in thick oil'.[36] In contrast, Peter Gyllies, who was an accomplished swimmer, executed a perfect swan dive off the air defence position to the considerable appreciation of the sailors in the water.

Musician Maurice Pink[*] was typical of many who struggled to find his way in darkened disorientating passageways, often in parts of the ship they rarely if ever entered. He and a group of sailors groped their way forward until a young Australian voice ahead of them with a torch told them to follow him. Exits to the other decks were blocked by debris from the multiple explosions. 'I felt sure I was going to die.' But the midshipman knew of a ladder that led up to the Captain's day cabin. From there, was a hatch that gave access to the upper deck. He calmly directed the men up and out of 'the black innards' of *Repulse*. They had made it in the nick of time, as the ship began to sink.[37] In the confusion of the moment Pink thought the midshipman was Guy. Bruce Dowling also thought he saw Guy save some sailors in another part of the ship. On both incidents Guy has affirmed he was not the rescuer. In the former case, the Australian midshipman was John Austin.

Among the general movement to leave the ship, there were acts of self-sacrifice. Down below in the forward part of the ship, a medical party tending the wounded from the first bomb hit elected to stay with the stretcher cases to the end.[38] They were to be among the 508 *Repulse* men who lost their lives. For those leaving the ship there was the danger of cutting one's feet on the barnacled hull, being caught in the still turning propellers, as was the unfortunate fate of some marines, or being sucked under when the ship finally went down.

On the bridge, Tennant bade farewell to his men. He momentarily thought about remaining on the bridge but looked down to the forecastle

---

[*] Maurice Pink would later become Chairman of the HMS *Prince of Wales* & HMS *Repulse* Survivors Association.

and saw Commander Dendy mustering sailors on the starboard-side. Tennant decided to join them. He walked down what was once a vertical part of the ship. He got as far as the 'B' Gun deck before the 'sea came up and swallowed me'.[39] The ship rolled over and sank at 1233, no more than seven minutes since the order to come on deck.

As the men entered the water *Repulse* disappeared stern first below the surface. The survivors gave a cheer for their old ship. The battered *Prince of Wales* would not last much longer. She had received three more torpedoes. But the '*Prince*' did remain afloat long enough for the *Express* to come alongside to take off many of the crew assembled on the upper deck. At 1320 she rolled over and sank taking Phillips and Leach with her. At about this time the RAAF 'Buffalo' fighters of 453 Squadron arrived overhead and chased off the last of the Japanese aircraft. They would remain to cover the rescue operations by the destroyers.*

The scene in the water was one of utter desolation with thick oil, flotsam and jetsam as well as the dead. The living looked desperately for floating objects to hold onto or get into. Some of the stronger swimmers helped others and one officer was seen blowing up the lifebelts of some of the struggling sailors. Only a few ship's boats had managed to be launched from *Prince of Wales*. Guy later remarked that 'the sea always looks very untidy when something's sunk'.[40] Among Tennant's personal papers is a handwritten account of his time in the water. He recalled being sucked down by the sinking ship but did not struggle. He wrote,

> I remember wondering whether if it was worth holding my breath and then decided I would. After a bit I realised the water was getting some light into it. After what seemed like a long interval I suddenly bobbed up to the surface in swirling water and heard a shout from a fellow in a Carley

---

* If Phillips had signalled for fighter protection when the Babs reconnaissance aircraft arrived that morning, the fighters would probably have been overhead at around 0746. If he had waited until he received the report of the attack on *Tenedos*, they would have arrived at 1140 which was before the damaging last raids.

float about five yards away saying 'Here you are Sir, come on.'[41] (Tennant was still wearing his steel helmet).

As with all the Australian midshipmen, Guy was a good swimmer and made some distance from the ship. This was aided by *Repulse*'s momentum through the water even though she was sinking. As Guy orientated himself he saw a destroyer, which was *Electra*, about 1,000 yards distant and struck out for her. In doing so he tried to avoid the large areas of oil in the water.* About him were other men holding onto bits of debris and so on, all endeavouring to make towards *Electra*. As he and others reached the ship's side the task of getting onboard now became clear. Guy later explained,

> ... 'being picked up by a destroyer' is a great phrase that's used, yes we were sunk and the destroyer picked up survivors and everybody dismisses it. It was great and fine and they went on home. Well, being 'picked up by a destroyer' is not quite as easy as that. You swim to the side of the ship. There's probably oil about which is covering you. There are lines, rope lines down the side of the ship and you try to hang onto one of these and get hauled up on board, which means that it's got to have a loop in it so you can hang onto it, or you put it under your shoulders somehow, or you scramble up the side in a scrambling net, which is a rope net down the side of the ship, or you go up a little ladder up the side of the ship vertically. The ship is moving in the swell. So all this makes it slightly difficult when you're in the water, you're not feeling terribly good, actually to get yourself up on board. So being picked up by a destroyer isn't one of those clear-cut things where you're lifted out of the water so to speak.

---

* The oil from the ship was a major hazard for the survivors because if swallowed it could prove fatal, it also greatly irritated eyes and eyelids. Some survivors reported it to be a muscle relaxant.

On deck *Electra*'s crew struggled to get all the survivors inboard with the decks becoming ever more slippery from the oil covered survivors. Space within the ship and on deck quickly filled. Some able *Repulse* sailors took over gun positions to free *Electra* sailors to help with the rescue. *Electra*, *Vampire* (with Tennant onboard) and *Express* were fortunately not subjected to further air attack and scoured the scene of debris and floating bodies for survivors.

One by one the destroyers left for Singapore with *Electra*, as senior ship, the last to go after three hours of search. *Electra*'s ship's company couldn't do enough for the survivors. Tots of rum and mugs of tea were passed around and some men were given showers and some clothing. Among the 500 picked up by *Electra* were Bruce Dowling and Jock Hayes. On passage to Singapore Hayes was found by one of *Electra*'s sailors and ushered into the sickbay. There was Midshipman James Bremridge who had a stomach wound from a Japanese machine-gun bullet. Hayes later wrote,

> I asked to be alone with him and took his hand. He gave
> a brave smile which knifed into my heart and conscience
> for any previous admonishment I had to bestow. He held
> on to my hand with a firm little grip as though trying to
> express the last tangible feeling in the young life he must
> have known was slipping from him. I have never before or
> since seen death, or the awareness of death, in that moment
> of truth so transform youth to man, suddenly adult, brave
> and silently perceptive of the tragedy in which we were
> both enmeshed.[42]

Guy and the other *Repulse* midshipmen then went below to comfort their friend. *Electra*'s doctor later remarked that the uncomplaining patients were 'probably the bravest patients he had ever treated'.[43] Bremridge died of his wounds in Singapore. *Electra*'s Gunnery Officer,

Warrant Officer Timothy Cain, wrote 'Captain Tennant had every reason to be proud of his ship's company: they were "knit-together" well, and were an example to us all.'[44]

The destroyers arrived individually through the night. The cruiser *Exeter* had earlier secured alongside and her sailors set up a reception area with tea, sandwiches and clothing. The warm showers helped get more of the oil off survivors, but it would take weeks to remove it from their pores. Tennant, with a bandage around his head, addressed *Repulse* survivors in the nearby gym telling them that despite the loss of their ship they should be congratulated for having done their job. He ordered a 'splice the mainbrace', which was a rum ration and was cheered by his crew for the last time. Petty Officer Charles Rogers stood next to a bedraggled group of boy seamen who then asked him whether they could have a tot. He replied 'Certainly, you can have rum like anyone else. You were in the action.' He then kept a weather eye on them as they had their first tot.[45]

Tennant told Jock Hayes that the midshipmen from both ships were of no use in Singapore and to get them away in *Exeter* so that they could continue their training.* The following morning after Guy and the other midshipmen went to the clothing store and received a suitcase and a couple of changes of working uniform, they were told to join *Exeter* that afternoon. Among the officers was a most welcome and familiar face. He was Lieutenant Commander Skipwith who had been one of the Year officers at the Naval College and survived the *Prince of Wales* sinking. *Exeter* sailed later that day for passage to Colombo through the Banka Straits.

On arrival in Colombo the midshipmen were billeted out to expatriates to allow them to recover from the sinking. Guy, John Austin, Bruce Dowling and Peter Gyllies stayed with the Urquhart family who

---

*   The *Prince of Wales* midshipmen stayed in *Exeter* and some became Japanese prisoners of war after her sinking. For Tennant himself, as the senior surviving officer, it was decided he would compile a report on the loss and fly to London to brief Prime Minister Winston Churchill and the Admiralty. The extensive papers include numerous first-hand accounts of the action. See 'Loss of HM Ships *Prince of Wales* and *Repulse*', ADM 199/1149 (UKNA).

showed them great kindness. One evening they were taken for dinner to Columbo's luxuriant Galle Face Hotel. Dressed in their 'survivors rig' of open neck shirts and slacks they drew the attention of other diners who wore dinner jackets. Guy and the others felt totally out of place in this environment not just due to their attire but also because of their state of mind following the loss of their ship.

After four days the midshipmen took the train to the Trincomalee naval base. There they joined *Revenge* three days before Christmas. In these desperate times she was one of four old Royal Sovereign class battleships* that had joined the Eastern Fleet to provide some defence for Ceylon and India. The Fleet was commanded by Vice Admiral Sir Geoffrey Layton who had relocated from Singapore.

For Guy the difference between *Revenge* and *Repulse* was stark. The change seemed mainly due to the cramped living environment onboard. The battleships were designed for service in home waters and therefore had limited fresh water. After they joined *Revenge*, which was the 'Trinco' guardship, they sweltered in harbour for the next seven weeks. Other factors and personalities played their part. It was common knowledge that one of the senior officers was having an on-going sexual relationship with a sailor, which in Guy's view typified the breakdown of discipline and cohesion in the ship.

The contrast between the ships was also typified by the management of the very small gunroom with now a large number of midshipmen. The sub-lieutenant of the gunroom had a hyphenated surname which he clearly felt raised him above everybody – a view not shared by anyone else.[46] He had placed a partition in the gunroom to divide the thirteen midshipmen from the small number of acting sub-lieutenants. There were other strictures of the sort that had been abolished in *Repulse*. To Guy, petty gunroom rules and practices which lacked common sense bred resistance. Eventually, some balance was reached, but for Guy fond memories of *Repulse* remained. On a positive note the eight other

---

* The battleships were *Ramillies*, *Resolution*, *Revenge* and *Royal Sovereign*.

midshipmen were from the RN Reserve of differing backgrounds and were a good bunch. Guy and the other midshipmen tried to keep their perspective and they understood that while their conditions in the gunroom were uncomfortable, sailors were enduring much more arduous conditions both in their ship and in the Fleet more generally.

In being assigned duties Guy was asked if he would go to the forward HACP position as in *Repulse*. Not keen to be in an enclosed compartment at Action Stations, he requested to be assigned a duty on the upper deck in the air defence position and the gunnery officer was happy to oblige. While in port, the midshipmen patrolled the harbour in boats armed with depth charges on the stern against possible midget submarine attack.* This at least relieved the tedium. While onboard *Revenge* the midshipmen had to complete their training, which would culminate in a Midshipman's Board before a Captain.

On 2 February 1942, while *Revenge* neared the end of her Trincomalee guardship duties, the aircraft carrier *Indomitable* arrived in port with her screening escorts. She was among the much-needed Eastern Fleet reinforcements that would eventually include her sistership *Formidable* and the famous battleship *Warspite*. Among *Indomitable*'s escorts was HMAS *Napier* and soon a boat brought Guy's classmates David Hamer, Maurice Molony and Audley Parker to join *Revenge* in preparation for their Midshipmen's Board. One outcome of their arrival was Maurice Molony taking the lead in the destruction of the hated gunroom partition. Its removal went uncommented upon and was not replaced. Guy's glum assessment of *Revenge* is reinforced by David Hamer, who later wrote that the battleship was 'a most frightening ship'.[47]

In March 1942 Admiral Sir James Somerville took command of the Fleet and was rightly concerned about the safety of Trincomalee as a base. He therefore moved his Headquarters to Mombasa and had

---

* The Japanese Navy did eventually conduct a midget submarine attack in the Indian Ocean. It was conducted on Diego Suarez harbour in Madagascar against *Ramillies* on 29 May 1943. The battleship was damaged and a tanker sunk.

Adu Atoll in the Maldives as a forward anchorage. The Japanese did not suspect this little visited atoll was being used for this purpose and it remained unmolested. Somerville split his force into two with the carriers and *Warspite* the nucleus of a fast group (Force A) while *Revenge* and her sister-ships were the centre of the second more vulnerable group (Force B). When Admiral Nagumo Chūichi and his powerful carrier force entered the eastern Indian Ocean, the Eastern Fleet soon lost the two heavy cruisers *Cornwall* and *Dorsetshire*, and then *Hermes* and *Vampire*, in separate attacks by Japanese carrier-based aircraft. Guy sensed considerable anxiety onboard *Revenge*, for it was clear that if the Japanese carrier force had forayed further into the Indian Ocean they would have likely sunk a 'basketful' of ships, including his own.[48] Somerville's overriding aim was to keep the remaining Fleet intact until the Japanese onslaught had run its course. Soon afterwards the old battleships steamed to the safety of East Africa.

Despite the tensions, there were however some light-hearted moments. While on watch on the bridge as an assistant officer of the watch, Guy was told to find the navigating officer who was needed on the bridge. Both the captain and the navigating officer had each a sea cabin near the bridge. Guy fruitlessly sought the Navigator in his cabin and then in inspiration thought to try the heads (toilet) that both officers shared. He banged on the locked heads door, calling for the Navigator. The fatherly tones of Captain Morgan* replied, 'No my boy. I'm quite alone.'[49]

In June the midshipmen successfully sat their Midshipmen's Board when the ship was at anchor in Kilindini Harbour. The midshipmen were each examined on subjects including navigation, gunnery, torpedo and communications. All seven Australians passed the Board. Of his time in *Revenge* Guy would later rate it as 'the most unhappy period' of his naval career and said,

---

* Later Admiral Sir Llewellyn Morgan, KBE, CBE, CB, MVO, DSC (1891–1969). His rejoinder to Guy came from a famous anecdote earlier told by Admiral Sir William Pakenham.

... there was no sort of get up and go in the ship. Everything was flat. I think in modern day analysis morale was rock bottom. There didn't seem to be anybody to inspire anybody in the matter of leadership and enthusiasm and getting a job done. But the dear old ship was never really meant to cruise around the tropical oceans. So it was just damned uncomfortable and a dreadful situation for all on board.[50]

All the midshipmen thankfully left *Revenge* for England. After passage in the troopship *Empire Woodlark* from Kilindini to Cape Town they were to embark in either of two ships, the Cunard liner *Athenia* and the smaller and slower *Almanzora*. During their short stay in Cape Town Guy and the other old *Repulse* hands advised the others who had not yet been to England to spend any spare money on tinned food to bring along. Guy was in the group assigned the *Almanzora* and they found the ship largely full of families being evacuated from Burma.

Their return to England was in circumstances not envisaged when they set sail from Rosyth just eight months ago. Before them was the prospect of promotion to Acting Sub-Lieutenant and attendance on the Sub-Lieutenants' courses in England. On completion, Guy and his classmates would be scattered among the Fleet to obtain their primary qualification – the Bridge Watch-keeping Certificate. They would then finally be fully qualified, albeit relatively inexperienced naval officers.

4

The Lucky Ship:
HMAS *Shropshire*

Then up spoke our Commander,
The Captain's right hand man;
'There cometh flying fighting men,
From far away Japan.
They do their best to sink us,
and dive through fearful odds –
For the Glory of Bushido,
and the fame of Shinto Gods.'

Horatius Mk. II[1]

I

Guy Griffiths returned to the UK in July 1942 and, after a couple of weeks leave, joined ten of his Naval College classmates for the Sub-Lieutenants' Course.* Normally of nine months duration, it had been truncated to just over three. The training provided everyone some welcome time ashore and the chance to share war experiences. In addition to the death of Bob Davies, Guy's class had also experienced the loss of Lyster Tatham. He died in the Mediterranean onboard the destroyer *Kandahar* when she

---

* Those other class-mates attending the course were Austin, Dowling, Gyllies, Hamer, Molony, Parker, Russell, Thompson, Thrum and Willis. In Guy's group were Dowling, Hamer & Willis.

sank after hitting a mine whilst trying to rescue survivors of the stricken cruiser *Neptune.*[*] David Manning, who had withdrawn from the Naval College at the end of the first year, re-joined the Navy in 1940 and was serving as an able seaman in *Perth* when she was lost in the Battle of Sunda Strait on 1 March 1942. His fate was unknown.

With seamanship already completed in *Revenge*, the Sub-Lieutenants' Course covered navigation, signals, torpedo, gunnery and anti-submarine warfare. The modules were conducted at various training establishments in southern England. There were about a hundred officers in the course and so they were split into smaller groups that rotated between each module and its respective training establishment. On successful course completion they would be confirmed as sub-lieutenants. There was a considerable financial and career incentive to do well. If an officer achieved First Class passes in all the modules he could 'gain' up to eighteen months seniority as a Lieutenant. Lesser results generated smaller amounts of 'time gained'.

During the torpedo module, the class was billeted in Brighton at either the Roedean School for girls or West House, the Saint Dunstan's hostel for blinded veterans. Both institutions evacuated their previous occupants to safer locations. Guy was billeted at Roedean and in his dormitory a buzzer above each bed was still labelled, 'If you want a Mistress during the night, press this Bell.'[2] It no longer produced the desired effect. For many years afterwards, as a result of its wartime role, Roedean was the only girl's school that gloried in having an Old Boy's Association.

In a more serious vein, for Guy and his classmates their stay in Brighton proved that the war was never far away. One of the features of Saint Dunstan's was that it had large glass windows. Its design was to help increase light and visibility for the partially blind. This created a real vulnerability in any bombing raid. So it proved in August 1942 when a

---

[*]   In all 837 men were lost when both ships sank on 19 December 1941. *Neptune* had only a sole survivor; *Kandahar*, just 73 men.

nuisance raid by Focke-Wulf 190 fighters who dropped bombs near Saint Dunstan's, blowing out the glass. Guy's classmates Parker and Thompson were both casualties. Parker was on the dangerously ill list for some time and while he made a made a limited recovery his future seagoing service would be confined to taking passage home. Thompson's injuries were even more serious and involved nearly a year's treatment in UK hospitals followed by further convalescence in Australia. He was then discharged 'Physically Unfit for Naval Service' in 1944.

One of the interesting wartime advances in warship design was the location under the open bridge of a small compartment that was equipped with a plotting table. Through a rudimentary electro-mechanical device, the ship's course and speed could be fed into an illuminated central marker that moved under the plotting table's paper sheet. The changing position of the ship, combined with other ships in company and submarines manually plotted, gave a clearer representation of the tactical picture. In some ships, radar displays were co-located in this compartment and relevant radar information was also transcribed onto the plot. This innovation was the genesis of the complex operations rooms used in modern warships. On Guy's course, students were exposed to this new way of viewing operations. Guy's technical aptitude led him to naturally to embrace these developments. For many more senior officers, however, the place to spend their time would remain the bridge for many years to come. Another glimpse of the future of naval warfare was the increasing importance of aviation at sea. Although discussion of aviation was rather cursory, Guy and most of the course had their first experience of flight in a twin engine bi-plane, the de Havilland DH.89 'Dominie'.

On completion of the course Guy was destined to join the replacement ship for *Canberra*, which had been lost in the Battle of Savo Island. *Canberra*'s loss had further depleted the Australian Squadron's six cruisers to just three.* This critically reduced Australia's contribution to the war effort. Britain, conscious of Australia's plight and with arguably

---

*   The RAN's cruiser losses were *Sydney, Perth* & *Canberra*.

higher priorities for its manpower, offered as a gift *Shropshire*, which was a near sister to *Canberra*.[3] She was gratefully accepted. The original intent, which was strongly supported by Prime Minister John Curtin and agreed to by King George VI, was for the ship to be renamed *Canberra*.[4] It was then learnt the US Navy was to name one of their new Baltimore class heavy cruisers *Canberra* in a generous and unexpected honour that recognized Australia's loss. It was therefore decided for *Shropshire* to retain her name.

Shropshire was undergoing a major refit and would not commission into the RAN for some months. In these circumstances Guy was determined to continue his training and he asked to be temporarily posted to a destroyer operating in local waters. His other classmates destined for *Shropshire* – John Austin, Bruce Dowling, Audley Parker and Greg Thrum also went to small ships. This would hopefully allow them to gain their Bridge Watchkeeping Certificates before joining *Shropshire*. While waiting for his posting Guy stayed once more with the Logue family. In a letter to her son Laurie, Myrtle Logue wrote:

> Guy Griffiths came home in a flat spin and he was due to join his ship in Scotland the following day, and he had just come to town from holidaying on the south coast, so I concocted a dinner and we said goodbye to him. You will remember the nice looking young lad who was sunk in the *Repulse*.[5]

The ship Guy joined on 5 January 1943 was the destroyer *Vivien* of the Rosyth Escort Force. She was of World War I vintage and had been converted to a fast escort, losing some of her torpedoes for greater anti-aircraft armament and depth charges. Conditions were cramped and austere and Guy had to bunk down on the wardroom settee. *Vivien* had taken part in the Norwegian Campaign and now was on the east coast convoy beat. She was commanded by Lieutenant Commander Roland

Leonard, who earlier in his career had wanted to be a submariner, but now he hunted them. The officers in escorts, such as in *Vivien*, were a mix of RN officers like Leonard; Royal Navy Reserve officers, who usually had joined pre-war and came from the merchant marine, and Royal Navy Volunteer Reserve officers who joined for the hostilities and came from diverse backgrounds. It was said tongue in cheek, that RNR officers were seamen but not gentlemen, RNVR were gentlemen but not seamen, while RN officers were both (or neither). Guy found *Vivien* to be a well-run and happy ship.

Vivien had experienced an eventful time in the war to date, tangling with Heinkel bombers and shooting one down. Leonard's predecessor, Lieutenant Commander Stephen Beattie, had ten months earlier earned a Victoria Cross commanding the destroyer *Campbeltown* in the Saint Nazaire raid. The east coast convoys were strategically important. London only held a fortnight's stock of coal and largely depended on colliers to maintain supplies from the northern coalfields. *Vivien* escorted the convoys between Rosyth and Sheerness, a distance of about 800 kilometres (450 nm). As one convoy veteran wrote of the colliers, 'these blackened humble little servants of local trade suddenly found themselves in the front line of the war at sea'.[6]

To fulfil the duties of an Officer of the Watch (OOW) and obtain a Bridge Watchkeeping Certificate, Guy had to take charge of, and be able to manoeuvre, *Vivien* day or night and in company with other ships. This would bring together all his training to date as well as the specific knowledge of *Vivien*, such as her weapons fit, machinery arrangements and handling characteristics. Coming on watch Guy would be briefed by the off-going OOW of the tactical situation, convoy details, navigational situation and machinery state. Also on the bridge would be three or four sailors keeping lookout and standing ready to send or receive light or flag signals. *Vivien* had an open bridge and so, at this time of year, all the bridge staff would invariably be in duffle coats and any other warm gear they possessed. The gyro compass pelorus at the centre of the bridge was where the OOW would invariably stand. Surrounding the pelorus were rudimentary but effective voice pipes to such compartments as the wheelhouse and the captain's cabin. The OOW had also to periodically duck into a protective shelter to maintain the navigation position of the ship on the chart. At night, the Captain would write instructions in a Night Order Book detailing any course, speed or other changes and on what occasions he needed to be called. As Guy had become somewhat familiar with on his recent course, *Vivien* possessed two rudimentary radar sets, of the type Guy had encountered on his recent course, predominantly for surface detections, and a plotting table located below the bridge. Sailors manning the plot could pass information to the OOW by voice-pipe. Despite these radar sets, the OOW invariably based his navigation on pelorus bearings of coastal landmarks, or lights or on sightings of celestial objects with a sextant. In the North Sea, with its currents, tidal streams and often poor visibility there was frequent uncertainty about the ship's position.

Above and behind the bridge was the gun director which in the normal defence watch state reported to the OOW. *Vivien* recently been retrofitted with the new Type 285 gunnery radar. There was also a sonar compartment and an operator who would also pass information on any sonar contacts. When in convoy the Captain was invariably on the bridge in his chair watching proceedings or taking a short nap. But the OOW was left to run the ship whether the Captain was on the bridge or not. He had to maintain concentration and vigilance for four, and sometimes six, hour watches. In *Vivien* Guy usually had two watches off before returning to the bridge for his next watch. Even in a small destroyer like *Vivien*, the responsibilities for the safety of the ship and her 110 men, as well as executing tactical instructions, were significant. This was particularly so for a 19-year-old such as Guy. A young officer was judged to be competent to be a qualified OOW based on the subjective assessment of the Captain. He had to be comfortable that if he was asleep in his bunk all would be well, or if things were starting to go awry, the OOW would call him in adequate time.

Guy soon learnt that one of the more challenging tasks for *Vivien* and the other escorts was to encourage the old-time masters of the colliers to remain in a convoy for their collective protection. He soon gained considerable respect for their seamanship skills in the blustery winter conditions of the North Sea. Guy settled in quickly in *Vivien* and within three months had gained his Bridge Watchkeeping Certificate. During his time onboard only one of the convoys *Vivien* escorted was subjected to Luftwaffe attack. The main threat was deemed the E-boats which required a vigilant lookout. Guy impressed Leonard during his short time onboard. On leaving *Vivien* in March 1943 Leonard described Guy as,

> A brisk, smart young officer who will do very well. He takes charge naturally and firmly (as one who has plenty of confidence in his own judgment) and is himself well disciplined. He is keen and very energetic. Well-mannered and of good appearance, he is physically strong.[7]

Guy's experience in *Repulse* and the even more hands-on duties in *Vivien* had convinced him that gunnery should be his chosen specialisation. Leonard helpfully recommended him for this specialisation. That training would be in future, but for now he could look forward to joining his first RAN ship.

II

On 17 April 1943 *Shropshire* commissioned into the RAN with little ceremony, still in refit in Chatham. Her new Commanding Officer was Captain John Collins, probably the most famous RAN officer at that time.* Collins was a member of the first class to enter the Royal Australian Naval College and had brilliantly commanded the cruiser *Sydney* in the Mediterranean earlier in the war. Most notably Collins was the victor in

---

* Later Vice Admiral Sir John Collins, KBE, CB, RAN (1899–1989).

the Battle of Cape Spada in which the Italian cruiser *Bartolomeo Colleoni* had been sunk. Collins had been in command of *Shropshire* for just ten days and had expedited the commissioning into the RAN because as an RN ship she was still issuing the rum ration and he was keen to dispense with this practice before the main draft of RAN sailors arrived.[*]

Guy joined *Shropshire* on 25 June. Also to join were John Austin and Bruce Dowling, Audley Parker, Colin Russell and Greg Thrum. Not all would stay in *Shropshire* and most, including Guy, hoped to be posted to a destroyer on arrival in Sydney. These newly promoted sub-lieutenants found a very experienced ship's company leavened with enthusiastic young sailors. There was a sizeable contingent from the old *Canberra* as well as from the first commission of *Perth*. The Commander was David Harries, who had commanded a RN minesweeping flotilla earlier in the war and most recently had been Australia's Naval Attaché in Washington. Impressively, in the wardroom there were four officers with the Distinguished Service Cross (DSC),[†] including *Perth*'s commissioning Gunnery Officer Lieutenant Commander Warwick 'Braces' Bracegirdle.[8] He had served in the cruiser in the Mediterranean and had experienced German 'Stuka' dive-bombing attacks and was particularly seized about *Shropshire* being proficient in air defence. *The Sydney Morning Herald* wrote:

> Captain Collins, who distinguished himself in the *Sydney*, should command her, and that her company should include officers and men who have served bravely on all seas, will enhance, if possible, the confidence and pride with which the public will follow the career of the *Shropshire*.[9]

Guy and the other sub-lieutenants were to keep watches on the

[*]   The RAN had a beer rather than a rum issue.

[†]   The Distinguished Service Cross in the British Imperial honours system was awarded during World War II to officers of the rank of up to Commander in recognition of an act or acts of exemplary gallantry during active operations against the enemy at sea.

bridge and were also assigned secondary jobs with the various department in the ship, as well as Action and Defence watch positions typically associated with the gunnery systems. The sailors who kept lookout on the bridge soon got to know the performance of the OOWs. Able Seaman David Mattiske later remarked that 'I had complete confidence in all our movements when Guy Griffiths was OOW.'[10]

In assembling *Shropshire*'s gunnery department, Bracegirdle had used his Navy Office contacts to build a strong team. Key among them were Lieutenants Ian 'Dusty' Rhodes, Ron Major and Harold Hardiman, Warrant Officer Gunner Bill Perren, Chief Gunner's Mate Arthur Cooper and the Gunner's Mates Norbert 'Nutty' Ferris, George Cheadle and Joe Feltham. They were a group from which Guy would learn a lot both about his specialization and also about leading sailors. 'Dusty' Rhodes was one of six Royal Australian Navy Volunteer Reserve (RANVR) officers onboard. All greatly impressed Guy with their capabilities and their at times different ways at looking at things.

From the outset *Shropshire* was a happy and well-run ship. In no small measure this was due to Collins' professionalism and demeanour. Bracegirdle later wrote that Collins was 'regarded onboard as "a fighting captain" which gave everyone great confidence'.[11] Guy thought that Collins, as a gunnery specialist, would be a distinct advantage for *Shropshire*'s impending service against the powerful Imperial Japanese Navy.

Although 14 years old, *Shropshire* now had the latest generation of radars. This included the Type 291, whose rotating aerial could, in the hands of skilled operators, be tilted in such a way that it could detect aircraft over land. This made her particularly useful in tracking aircraft and controlling friendly fighters to counter air attacks. More mundane, but very significant, was the introduction of 'cafeteria style' messing into *Shropshire* and the RAN. This replaced the old system of a sailor collecting the food for his mess mates from the galley and it being eaten in their messdeck. Cafeterias were being introduced into some of the newer RN ships, but some of the *Shropshire*-bound men had been exposed to it on passage to Britain and were determined that *Shropshire* incorporate the innovation. Guy felt the new cafeteria greatly contributed to the morale and well-being of the sailors. Its operation was overseen by Chief Petty Officer Cook 'Otto' Smith and the cafeteria soon became known as 'Otto's Grotto'.

The scale and thoroughness of *Shropshire*'s work-up in Scapa Flow pleasantly surprised Collins. There was particular emphasis on air defence and in one exercise twelve torpedo bombers conducted mock attacks on the ship, whilst *Shropshire* was allocated four Seafire fighters to control. The ability of the cruiser to vector friendly fighters to defend the task group was a new capability and one that would be invaluable in the Pacific War. Tragically, one Seafire crashed near *Shropshire* killing the young pilot.

Whilst in Scapa Flow *Shropshire* was inspected by King George VI, accompanied by Admiral Sir Bruce Fraser, the Commander-in-Chief of the Home Fleet. Guy was selected to be Officer of the Day on the Quarterdeck and as such in charge of the piping party on the quarterdeck for the Royal visit. In the Piping Party was the ship's Commissioned Bosun Arthur 'Jenks' Jenkinson who could remember King George V coming onboard the battlecruiser *Australia* at the end of the Great War. 'Jenks' was an outstanding seaman who revelled in seamanship, particularly on the forecastle with its associated anchor-work. When Guy eventually became *Shropshire*'s Forecastle* Officer, he, like the younger sailors, learnt much from 'Jenks' as well as marvelling at his extensive salty vocabulary.

With her work up complete, *Shropshire* was ready to re-enter the war. She left Scapa Flow on the inauspicious Friday 13th August, but this omen was mitigated by a telegram from the King wishing them a safe passage home.† By this time Guy, John Austin and Bruce Dowling had been away

---

* · The forecastle or fo'c'sle of a ship is the forward part of a ship.

† There is an apocryphal story that during the 19th century the Admiralty, in an attempt to dispel sailors' superstition about Friday the 13th, decided to commission a ship named HMS *Friday*. Her keel was laid on a Friday, she was

from Australia for over two years. *Shropshire* would be part of the dozen escorting warships for the 19-ship troop convoy, KMF.22, taking soldiers to the Mediterranean for the invasion of Sicily. The convoy departed Greenock on 17 August 1943 and once into the Atlantic it was shadowed by German aircraft. For such a valuable convoy the small aircraft carrier *Hunter* was assigned to the escort and her Seafires and Swordfish were reassuringly active in deterring German air and submarine attack. About 400 miles from Gibraltar *Shropshire* detached from the convoy.

Shropshire made a rapid homeward passage via the familiar ports to Guy of Freetown, Cape Town and Durban. The South African reputation for generous hospitality was maintained with over 300 men being invited to Sunday dinners by Cape Town families. Alongside in Durban were the Australian destroyers *Nepal*, *Norman*, *Napier* and *Quiberon*, which were all serving as part of the British Eastern Fleet. In *Norman* was David Hamer who was serving as her Gunnery Officer. *Shropshire* finally arrived in Fremantle on 24 September. *The West Australian* newspaper reported that *Shropshire* was, following her refit, 'now one of the most formidable fighting ships of her size'.[12] Whilst alongside Guy learnt from Commander Harries that he would remain in *Shropshire*, along with Austin and Dowling.

On 2 October 1943 *Shropshire* arrived in her new home port of Sydney and was met by the Governor-General Lord Gowrie, Prime Minister John Curtin, other dignitaries and, most welcoming of all, the families of the ship's company. The ship would be alongside for a month for a short refit in which time the men could take keenly anticipated two weeks leave. For Guy his return to the Hunter Valley was long awaited. To his family he had left them as a teenager and returned as a young man.

Back onboard *Shropshire* the refit of the ship was greatly hampered by a labour dispute at the dockyard. For the ship to sail Collins had his engineering sailors undertake much of the work which resulted in the ship

---

launched on a Friday, and she set sail on her maiden voyage on Friday the 13th. She was commanded by under Captain James Friday. She was never seen again.

being 'black-banned'.* Despite these hindrances *Shropshire* was prepared for her part in the war against Japan. The dockyard workers' actions were 'an alarming revelation'[13] to Guy and left an indelible impression on him. Destined not to sail with the ship was Bruce Dowling who had blood poisoning after treading on a rusty nail. Instead, he would join *Australia*.

III

In early November 1943 *Shropshire* joined the Australian–US Task Force 74 off the North Queensland coast. It consisted of *Australia*, the destroyers *Warramunga* and *Arunta* and the US destroyers *Bagley*, *Helm* and *Ralph Talbot*. It was commanded by the Commander of the Australian Squadron, Rear Admiral Victor Crutchley,[†] an RN officer and a VC winner, whose leadership had come under question following the disastrous Battle of Savo Island. *Australia* was commanded by John Collins's classmate the equally brilliant Harold Farncomb.[‡] The two officers were considered the preeminent RAN captains then at sea. The strengthened and reconstituted TF.74 would serve in the US 7th Fleet under the Commander South West Pacific Force, Vice Admiral Arthur 'Chips' Carpenter.

While the Japanese offensive had been decisively checked by the US victory at the Battle of Midway in June 1942, a clear Allied war strategy in the Pacific had yet to emerge. There were two almost competing approaches; the first, a western thrust under General MacArthur's direction. This would involve the US 7th Fleet conducting amphibious landings along the northern New Guinea coast and then west into the Dutch East Indies to yield locations for airfields preparatory for the retaking of the Philippines. In the second thrust, further north-east under Admiral Chester Nimitz, the US 3rd and 5th Fleets would involve

---

* A black-ban was a form of protest, short of a strike used by unions. It involved refusing to supply labour in response to an action.

† Later Admiral Sir Victor Crutchley VC, KCB, DSC, DL (1893–1986).

‡ Later Rear Admiral H.B. Farncomb CB, DSO, MVO, RAN (1899–1971).

island-hopping amphibious operations with an inexorable path to the Japanese home islands. The issue was finally resolved in discussions between President Roosevelt, Nimitz and MacArthur in July 1944. Both forces would advance and combine for the Philippines operation and then on to Japan. This approach was endorsed at the Allied leaders' Octagon Conference in Quebec on 11 September 1944. For their part, the Japanese, much weakened after Midway, would attempt to deplete the Americans by dogged resistance in the islands. They still harboured the hope of a decisive sea battle near the Philippines. This strategy would be in the face of ever-growing US naval and air might, and, unknown to the Japanese, the Allied reading many of their coded signals.

On 7 November 1943 TF.74 arrived in Milne Bay, in eastern New Guinea for a final period of training and briefings before commencing operations. Milne Bay had rapidly developed into an important RAN forward base that provided logistical, engineering, ordnance and training support to all ships. Already, mainly Australian troops had conducted a bloody campaign involving the recapture of Buna, Lae, Salamaua and Finschafen along the Rau coast. MacArthur now envisaged a series of amphibious landings further along the coast of northern New Guinea. Before these could occur, it was vital to neutralise the Japanese air threat from Rabaul. To that end the western half of New Britain was secured from the Japanese and Rabaul neutralised, isolated and pounded by repeated air attacks. The New Britain operation was called 'Dexterity' and involved landings first at Arawe (Operation 'Director') on the south-west coast and then at Cape Gloucester on the western tip of the island. TF.74's first operation was to be Operation Dexterity. It was further strengthened towards the end of the month by the US cruisers *Boise*, *Nashville* and *Phoenix*. In the coming months these ships and the USN's different way of doing business proved a revelation to Guy.

On the evening of 29 November, at the outset of Operation Dexterity, the destroyers bombarded the Japanese airstrip at Gasmata. On 15 December the US 112th Cavalry Regiment was successfully landed at Arawe with covering fire from the ships. This landing was followed on Boxing Day by the larger Cape Gloucester assault which was supported by an intense bombardment from Crutchley's cruisers. The Japanese tried to repel the landings with two raids each of about 70 aircraft. These were initially reported by the intrepid coastwatchers ashore and then *Shropshire*'s tilting Type 291 air search radar detected inbound aircraft when they were still over land. Only a handful got through the alerted protective fighter screen with 64 Japanese aircraft were destroyed on D-Day.[14]

As part of his professional development, Guy would be rotated to different Action Stations of increasing complexity over his time onboard. His first was as officer-in-charge of one of the four 8-inch gun turrets. He was there to lead and to learn. As Guy later wrote, 'The real man in charge was Gunner's Mate Petty Officer Cheadle who was a turret expert. He was positive in his command of drills which were absolutely essential in all 8-inch turrets.'[15] Cheadle exemplified the disciplined leadership and attention to detail that Guy admired in the Gunnery Branch. This cramped space with the tropical sun beating down on the turret was a physically draining post. But the turrets were the ship's raison d'être and there was great teamwork shown by the 20-man gun and magazine crew.

The next operation to secure the Vitiaz Strait between New Guinea and New Britain involved the 2 January 1944 landing at Saidor on the New Guinea north coast. In addition to its airstrip, the capture of Saidor frustrated any evacuation of the 12,000 Japanese soldiers remaining in New Guinea. Originally, all these operations were to be a precursor to the capture of the now besieged Rabaul. But the Quadrant Conference had wisely opted to by-pass the Rabaul bastion with its increasingly fortified 100,000 strong garrison. This decision saved many lives.

After the New Britain operations, Crutchley returned with his cruisers to Milne Bay and there had a meeting with Vice Admiral Thomas Kinkaid,* MacArthur's new naval commander. After discussion of future

* Later Admiral T.C. Kinkaid, USN (1888–1972).

operations, *Australia* and then *Shropshire* returned to Sydney for leave and maintenance. On 7 February *Shropshire* sailed with Crutchley and Admiral Sir Guy Royle, the RAN's First Naval Member, embarked for a revealing inspection of the Australian Naval Squadron and the forward bases. The tour underscored that operations involved weeks at sea, with ships being fuelled and stored underway. This mode of operation was new to the RAN. It was clear also that the squadron was transformed. It had gone from a defeated force at Savo Island that operated with the USN in a clunky manner, to one totally integrated with the Americans. The squadron was now adept in modern communications, the use of radars, new tactics and procedures as well as in underway replenishment techniques. The RAN ships, while much better equipped with anti-aircraft weapons, still lagged behind the Americans in this area. This effort represents one of great, but unsung achievements of the RAN. It was a period of war-driven innovation that Guy enthusiastically embraced. He later recalled,

> ...the tactical formations were different, the communications were slightly different – we had voice communication between ships, which was a big breakthrough instead of flag signals and there was a new language; the Americans used different phrases meaning exactly the same thing and quite succinctly saying it, but just in a different manner. And so I think in a way the advantage was that it opened our mind to a new way of operating the Navy.[16]

Royle was left in no doubt that the two bugbears for the Australian Squadron were mail and food. Both were supplied by an inexperienced and inadequately resourced RAN logistics organisation. Guy recalled,

> If mail reached us it seemed to be purely by accident that it eventually got there. I would like to think that somebody had been beavering away at it, but the capability of getting

the mail from A to B to the ship up on deployment didn't seem to exist and it was a very ad hoc arrangement and I imagine it gave a lot of headaches to the people trying to get the mail to us.[17]

The issue of mail and newspapers was raised by successive commanders of the squadron as well as ships' captains. A three-month delay was not unusual and one captain lamented the arrival of newspapers that would interest only historians or shopkeepers in need of wrapping paper.

In regard to food, none of the RAN ships had sufficient refrigeration space for the amount of food needed for long periods at sea. The staples were 'bully' beef and dehydrated or tinned vegetables which had, according to Guy, the twin characteristics of being neither nutritious nor attractive. But all things are relative, and Guy later recalled the story told to him by Petty Officer Yeoman Ernie Boston, who had served in the cruiser *Sydney* when she defeated *Emden* in 1914. Among his many sea stories was when *Sydney* reached Gibraltar and embarked casks of salted beef date stamped '1815'. Boston said, 'You could boil it, you could bake it, you could fry it, you could tow it astern, but you just couldn't eat it.'[18]

IV

The next strategically important operation was the seizure of the Admiralty Islands. Initially, a reconnaissance in force it was staged on 29 February 1944, but it was soon decided to hold the ground and the reconnaissance became an invasion. The landings were closely supported by T.F.74's destroyers which hotly engaged artillery at ranges as short as 3,000 yards. Over coming days Crutchley brought *Shropshire* and the other cruisers into the fray to silence stubborn Japanese resistance. The whole-hearted naval support earned the appreciation of the hard-pressed US soldiers and marines ashore. The prize was of great strategic significance.

Seeadler Harbour on Manus Island, with its large anchorage, became the subject of immediate and colossal infrastructure development. A base for over 37,000 personnel was quickly established and a double airstrip constructed. Most critically, two battleship-capable floating docks were towed in sections from the US while repair ships arrived to facilitate even substantial battle repair. These facilities provided the springboard for future operations and the forward base for TF.74.

In coming months Manus Island was a welcome rest and recreation port after long periods of sea time. There were sporting facilities, beaches and a bar. This allowed sailors from both navies to meet socially which developed into frequent inter-ship visits. In *Shropshire*, the men sweltered in non-air-conditioned compartments while in contrast the newer US cruisers were air-conditioned, well-armed and equipped with modern conveniences, including ice cream machines. Guy enjoyed getting to know the Americans and their ways. This professional curiosity, combined with his sociable nature would lead him to form life-long friendships with two American officers, Lieutenant Fred Hip and Warrant Officer Ira Bonnett from *Nashville*. At the time Guy was the Sub-Lieutenant of the Gunroom, and there developed a routine when both ships were in Manus of Guy going over to *Nashville* for a meal and a movie, with Hip and Bonnett coming to *Shropshire's* gunroom for a beer. The latter was unavailable on the 'dry' USN ships.

The final operation to neutralise the Japanese XVIII Army in New Guinea was at Hollandia. On the early morning of 22 April 1944, 158 ships steamed purposefully towards the cloud-shrouded coast. In command of the amphibious force was Rear Admiral Daniel Barbey, known to the Australian sailors as 'Uncle Dan' or 'Dan Dan the Amphibious Man'. Among his ships for the first time were the RAN's *Kanimbla*, *Manoora* and *Westralia* now converted from Armed Merchant Cruisers to Landing Ships–Infantry. Rear Admirals Crutchley and Berkley commanded TF.74 and TF.75 respectively, each with a mix of cruisers and destroyers to support the three simultaneous landings at Aitape, Humboldt Bay and

Tanahmerah Bay on a front of about 240 km. The warships opened up an intense bombardment at 0630 with air support was provided by the US 5th Army Air Force. Judging by the Japanese reaction, surprise was complete. Even though Hollandia proved unsuitable as a bomber airfield location, the operation was a major blow against the Japanese. Of the 11,000 Japanese in the area nearly 3,500 were killed.

At Aitape Guy was struck by another example of the different approach the Americans had to matters. One of *Shropshire*'s boats, fitted with the infernal Kitchener rudder, became stranded on the beach during a transfer of personnel. Hours were spent trying to retrieve the boat. Some USN officers watching this effort came down and suggested leaving the boat and on *Shropshire*'s return to Manus Island going to the boat pound and just picking up an LCM (landing craft mechanized). This *Shropshire* duly did and found the LCM to be in Guy's view 'heaven' with its powerful engines, manoeuvrability and functional design. It was a real boon to the ship.

These operations were TF.74's last under Admiral Crutchley. 4 February 1944 marked a significant milestone in the RAN's development. On that day the War Cabinet decided it was time, with the end of Crutchley's tenure, for an Australian to assume command. Captain Collins, who had already served as a non-substantive Commodore in the Dutch East Indies and with his outstanding war record, was the logical choice. What is more the War Cabinet agreed to extend Admiral Royle's tenure as First Naval Member by a further year with the plan for Collins to be promoted to Rear Admiral and succeed him as professional head of the Navy. As part of the command changes it was decided Captain Farncomb would relieve Collins in command of the Australian Squadron when Collins replaced Royle. In the meantime, Farncomb would be given command of a RN aircraft carrier.[19] In implementing this scheme, on 9 March Captain Emile Dechaineaux, formerly in *Warramunga*, took command of *Australia*, and on 6 May 1944 Collins was replaced in *Shropshire* by another classmate Captain Harry Showers.

The World War II Campaign in the Western Pacific

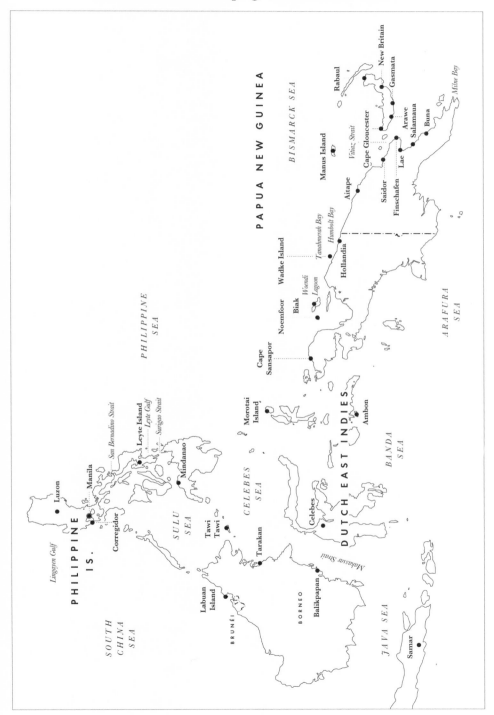

Guy had found Captain Collins to be 'a likable character and he always seemed friendly to junior officers, assuming we were doing our duty properly'. Critically for Guy, Collins had possessed the ability to lead and 'weld the ship together'. For his part Collins was impressed by Guy and wrote that he was a promising young officer who was 'capable, reliable, with a good power of command, excellent physique and a pleasant manner and should do well. One of our better products.'[20]

Captain Showers had already distinguished himself in the war by playing a pivotal role assisting the Free French assume control of New Caledonia when he commanded *Adelaide*. Most recently, he helped save his last command, the cruiser *Hobart*, when she was torpedoed off Espiritu Santo. Showers soon demonstrated himself to be a capable and even-tempered cruiser captain.

On 13 June Collins, now a Commodore First Class, became Commodore Commanding Australian Squadron embarked in *Australia*. Collins' first operation was the landing at Noemfoor about 160 km west of Biak. Over seventy ships and landing craft embarked 14,000 troops for the Biak assault, which overwhelmed the opposition. In the prelude to the Philippines campaign there was a landing on Morotai Island in the Maluku Islands. Once again, the landing was important to provide airstrips for future operations. These airstrips would be vital in both the American-led Philippines and Australian-led Borneo campaigns. The opening bombardment by TF.74 on 15 September 1944 was accompanied by an eruption of nearby Mount Halmahera.

After the Morotai operation Captain Showers' short tenure in command came to an end. He was to be promoted to Commodore 2nd Class to become the Second Naval Member, responsible for the critically important area of personnel for the Navy. When Showers left *Shropshire* by US PT boat in Woendi Lagoon there were three lusty cheers from the ship's company. Also at the end of the Morotai operation, Guy had a change of Action Station to the much more responsible position of Portside Air Defence Officer (ADO). He joined Lieutenant James

Osborne, a 36-year-old RANVR officer, who coordinated the starboard side. In peacetime, Osborne farmed a property near Gundaroo on outskirts of Canberra. Guy appreciated his steady country attitude to matters and thought him a 'marvellous character'.[21] For his part James Osborne was reassured by Guy's 'coolness and efficiency'.[22] In these critically important positions they soon worked very well together and became firm friends.

The ADOs were located port and starboard on the Air Defence Platform above and behind the open bridge. From these elevated and exposed vantage points they allocated anti-aircraft (AA) guns to targets. To assist in this there were six lookouts who each had a stand with binoculars. When an aircraft was spotted they could mechanically indicate its bearing and angle from the horizon to the 4-inch gun directors and the guns would be slewed to the target. For the smaller calibre guns such as the pom-poms, 40mm and 20mm the ADOs would direct them via the gunnery broadcast system. Some mounts, such as the pom-poms, had sailors to act as local directors which helped the ADO during multiple aircraft attacks.

A key modification to *Shropshire* that Bracegirdle had initiated during the refit before entering RAN service was the fitting of a radar-equipped anti-aircraft director for each of the 8-inch gun turrets. This modification had been fitted to some RN cruisers and enabled the turrets to individually engage aircraft with 'barrage fire'. In this mode, the shells had a time-mechanical fuze which was set to explode the rounds at 3,000 yards from the ship. This would put up a 'wall' of fragments and smoke which should deter or damage incoming aircraft. This was a novel tactic that Guy and the rest of the gunnery department looked forward to trying out.

Because of the wartime losses among RAN captains, Showers' relief was sourced from the RN. He was Captain Godfrey Nichols who, like Showers, had specialised in navigation. So far in the war Nichols had commanded the light cruiser *Galatea* in the Mediterranean and most recently was the Deputy Director of Naval Intelligence. This had given him a very good overview of the war at sea in all the theatres. In that position Nichols had cheerfully demonstrated an ability to take 'readily to unfamiliar duties for which his previous service in no way fitted him'.[23] This flexibility was ideally suited to commanding an Australian ship in the Pacific. The men in *Shropshire* found that Nichols had a professional air, positive attitude and calm demeanour. The news of a new captain is well captured in Ron Russell's post-war poem *Memories of HMAS Shropshire* when he wrote,

> One day the buzz went round the ship,
> we've got a brand new skipper,
> A decent cove, but Oh by jove,
> the bloke's a bloomin kipper
> But Captain Godfrey Nichols, RN
> (now in God's home port)
> was a thorough going gentleman
> and really quite a sport.[24]

Guy later remarked that Nichols 'expected and received the best input from the ship's company'.[25] Above all it was Nichols' trust he clearly placed in the experienced *Shropshire* team that would earn him great respect and affection from his men.[26] All boded well for the ship. This was just as well, for Nichols had, in Guy's words, 'arrived just in time to jump in at the deep end'.[27]

V

On 13 October 1944 T.F.74 sailed from Hollandia escorting a large convoy towards the first landings in the Philippines. As multiple convoys converged on the landing areas over 650 ships dotted the wide expanse of ocean. The Australian Squadron's contribution to the Philippines campaign was to be more than just cruisers and destroyers. In Collins' national, but not tactical, command were the amphibious ships *Kanimbla*,

Manoora, *Westralia*, as well as the frigate *Gascoyne* and the sloop *Warrego* which had been modified as hydrographic vessels. They were augmented in this vital role by the small Harbour Defence Motor Launch *1074*. With a complement of a dozen sailors and a speed of just twelve knots, *HDML 1074* had a rough passage and when left astern on the transit had the indignity of being rammed by a US warship when her recognition coded signal was misinterpreted. Despite a damaged bow *HDML 1074* carried on. Guy was greatly impressed by both courage and seamanship displayed by her crew.

TF.74 remained part of Admiral Kinkaid's 7th Fleet and most immediately came under the command of the Commander Fire Support Group Vice Admiral Jesse Oldendorf.* Also in support of this vast operation was Admiral 'Bull' Halsey's 3rd Fleet whose carrier-borne air wings had already begun attacking Japanese positions. It was anticipated the Japanese response to the operation would be intense, for their High Command saw the Philippines campaign as critical. The Commander-in-Chief of the Imperial Japanese Navy, Admiral Toyoda Soemu said in his post-war interrogation,

> Should we lose in the Philippines operations, even though
> the fleet should be left, the shipping lane to the south would
> be completely cut off so that the fleet, if it should come
> back to Japanese waters, could not obtain its fuel supply. ...
> There would be no sense in saving the fleet at the expense
> of the loss of the Philippines.[28]

The Philippines was the last opportunity for a 'general decisive battle' and Toyoda's staff had formulated Plan Sho-Go 1 to concentrate their remaining ships to defeat US naval forces before they reached the Japanese mainland. The likelihood of Sho-Go's success was doubtful. Over three days in June during the Battle of the Philippine Sea, the

---

* Later Admiral J.B. 'Oley' Oldendorf, USN (1887–1974).

Japanese had lost three aircraft carriers, and more significantly over 430 carrier-borne and 200 land-based aircraft. The Japanese Navy had been reduced to four naval task forces. The first was in home waters with three aircraft carriers still awaiting replacement aircraft.

The three other Japanese formations that would be involved in Sho-Go 1 were two formations to the south west in Brunei and one from Formosa (Taiwan). The southern groups were Vice Admiral Kurita Takeo's powerful Central Force of 5 battleships, including the 18-inch gunned behemoths *Yamato* and *Musashi*, 12 cruisers and 15 destroyers and Vice Admiral Nishimura Shōji's Southern Force, comprising the battleships *Yamashiro* and *Fusō*, the heavy cruiser *Mogami* and 4 destroyers. Vice Admiral Ozawa Jisaburō commanded the Northern Force consisting of 4 aircraft carriers and 2 battleships. Significantly, Ozawa's force was not fully complemented with aircraft. The three formations would converge on the Philippines to give battle.

On the passage to the amphibious landing area, 'Braces' Bracegirdle assembled his Gunnery Department on the 4-inch gun deck for one of his signature briefings. Bracegirdle was in Guy's judgement an outstanding Gunnery Officer who was highly respected. The more Guy worked for him, the more he realized Bracegirdle was 'right on the button' with his judgments.[29] Bracegirdle's candid and compelling briefing style ensured his sailors were kept in the picture and well-motivated. This particular briefing was in Guy's view, a vintage performance. Bracegirdle announced that *Shropshire* was 'going into Tiger Country' and that the Japanese would put up stiff opposition. Therefore the guns crews had to give the performance of their lives to protect their ship. Any aircraft detected late was to be engaged by gun crews firing on their own initiative. If Bracegirdle's prediction about the impending action was to be proved correct, then Guy as the port side ADO, would have 'a ringside seat'.[30]

An incident on the early morning of 20 October says much about Nichols and *Shropshire*. The bombardment of Leyte Island was set to begin at dawn. As *Shropshire* closed the coast in the gloom of the early hours, lookout Able Seaman Mattiske reported seeing the phosphorescent wake of a horned floating mine caught in *Shropshire*'s port paravane sweep.[*] It was tangled in the wire about twenty feet from the ship abreast the bridge and had enough explosive to blow a hole in the ship's side. As nothing could be done until first light, and it was going to be a long day, Bracegirdle, who was on watch as the Principal Control Officer, ordered some damage control precautions and evacuated sailors from the general area. He only then called Captain Nichols who peered over the side to view the mine, still in his pyjamas. Complimenting the lookout and satisfied with the measures put in place, Nichols calmly returned to his bunk behind the bridge.

Discussion ensued about how best to deal with the mine, including rigging some sheer legs and slowly hauling it out of the water. It was settled upon to try and get it to float free of the ship. Guy as Forecastle Officer fortunately had assisting him the very experienced Bosun 'Jenks' Jenkinson. Once the ship's company were closed up at Dawn Action Stations preparations were made to cut the paravane wire. Guy had the wire taken to the capstan and also got two sailors to tie together some boat hooks to gingerly fend off the mine.[†] Looking down at the sinister object Guy ordered the wire to be slowly hauled in a short distance to encourage the mine to become dislodged. Fortunately, it did exactly that and floated down the ship's side. The stern lookout threw a lifebuoy and smoke float adjacent to the mine. The presence of the mine and smoke float was then announced on TBS. One of the ships astern exploded the mine with a round from a 40mm Bofors gun.

The amphibious assault was preceded by a heavy bombardment from the battleships, cruisers and destroyers. The first of two waves of landing craft hit the beach about 0900. In all 70,000 troops were to be landed

---

[*]   A paravane was a torpedo-shaped float streamed by wire on either side of the bows of warships to counter sea mines. The wire may have a series of blades to cut the mine's wire allowing it to float to the surface to be destroyed.

[†]   A capstan is a mechanical device used onboard ships for chiefly hauling in anchors. Its rotating drum can also be used to haul in wire and rope hawsers. There are usually two capstans on a forecastle.

on Red and White beaches in the vicinity of Tacloban on Leyte Island. By midday *Shropshire* had completed her bombardments. In the mid-afternoon she contributed to the air defence while ready to support the army if needed. At around 1630 a Japanese torpedo bomber passed astern of the ship and the cruiser *Honolulu* was struck by a torpedo. Smoke billowed from the ship and she developed a discernible list. That afternoon General MacArthur waded ashore at Red Beach and made a brief speech opening with the words 'People of the Philippines, I have returned'.[31] The ships remained in Leyte Gulf overnight. In *Shropshire* personnel tried to relax in their action stations. Through the night, intermittent explosions and tracer could be heard and seen ashore.

Early the following morning, the 139th anniversary of the Battle of Trafalgar, *Shropshire*'s radar detected aircraft coming from the west. They were quickly reported to all ships by radio. At 0600 *Shropshire* opened fire on a 'Val' dive bomber that passed very close astern of her and passed down her starboard side. At only about 15 metres off the sea the aircraft, which had been hit several times by *Shropshire*'s guns, appeared to be clearing to the west but then wheeled round and flew towards *Australia*, coming up her stern. A couple of Bofors and Oerlikons scored further hits on the Val, but the pilot, in possibly the first suicide attack of the war, continued on and deliberately struck *Australia*'s foremast and bridge.* This started a large fire. Because *Australia* was to starboard of *Shropshire*, Guy did not witness the impact, but shortly thereafter saw the conflagration on *Australia*'s bridge from his ADP vantage point.

In *Australia* were Guy's classmates Bruce Dowling, David Hamer and Colin Russell. Both Hamer and Russell were clear of the bridge. Hamer had been standing on one of the rear 8-inch gun turrets and saw the aircraft almost at eye level heading towards the ship. Bruce Dowling,

---

* There is debate about whether *Australia* was the first victim of a kamikaze attack. The Val that attacked *Australia* was from the 6th Flying Brigade, Imperial Japanese Army Air Force, and did not come from the newly formed dedicated Imperial Japanese Navy Special Attack Unit. It appears that the pilot, perhaps believing his damaged aircraft would not reach base, decided to conduct a suicide attack on *Australia*.

however, was in charge of the 8-inch gun director located behind the bridge. The resultant flames poured through the apertures of the director. Fortunately, Dowling was nearest to the open hatch and, when fire engulfed the director, he was blown out and fell to the deck below. He was the only one of the director crew to survive the inferno. Dowling was blinded for some days and had severe burns that covered his face and body. His war was over, but a long and immensely painful battle had just begun.

On the bridge itself many suffered fire and blast injuries. Sailors took Commodore Collins, Captain Dechaineux and the other survivors below for treatment and removed the dead from the forward superstructure. Dechaineux, with a serious stomach wound and burns, was critically injured, but his few words were about the welfare of his men. *Australia*'s captain died later that day. In all 30 men were killed and 64 injured. Collins was lucky to survive. He was seriously burnt, had a broken back and ribs, an eye injury, a punctured lung, concussion and various 'gunshot' wounds. After the attack Admiral Kinkaid, who had seen the hit from his nearby flagship, came across by boat with his doctor to survey the scene onboard. He discovered Collins on the wardroom deck among the wounded. Kinkaid determined that *Australia* was in no fit state to continue the fight and ordered her and the torpedoed *Honolulu* to be escorted to Manus Island.

The remaining Commodore's staff were transferred to *Shropshire* and Captain Nichols became acting Commander TF.74. Realistically, there was only one officer suitable to replace Collins in command of the Squadron and that was Farncomb. He was ordered to hand over command of the aircraft carrier *Attacker*, then in UK waters, and in November 1944 he flew home to then join the patched-up *Australia* in Espiritu Santo.

The deliberate crashing of an aircraft into *Australia* presaged a campaign that would be called kamikaze,* but initially these pilots were

---

* Kamikaze is usually translated as 'divine wind'. Kami is the word for god, spirit, or divinity while kaze is 'wind'.

called 'suiciders'. In *Shropshire* the fiery hit on *Australia's* bridge shocked many sailors. Recalling this, Guy said,

> We were surprised that there were people who would do this, because you couldn't imagine it happening from our own side. But everybody realised that the Japanese were a different culture and that's what they were doing and you had to accept it. You couldn't say, 'I think this is "offside", I don't think you should do this. You're breaking the rules of war.' If there are any rules once war's declared, the rulebook seems to fly out of the window to be dropped by the wayside.[32]

On 22 October the ships were subjected to further air attacks. *Shropshire* was targeted by one Val and both ADOs directed fire which drove it off. While there was a lull in the afternoon, the battle was about to enter its critical phase. That same day the Japanese Central and Southern Forces sailed from Brunei. The Southern Force shaped course to pass through the Surigao Strait en route Leyte Gulf. Admiral Oldendorf received periodic intelligence of Nishimura's progress, which was impeded by damaging US air attacks.

The following morning the ships in Leyte Gulf were again attacked by Japanese suicide aircraft. Fortuitously, one that was undetected until too late flew over *Shropshire* heading for a larger ship. For about 75% of the time during the Leyte Gulf operation *Shropshire* was at action stations and during lulls men would try and rest in place. At about 1615, while some of the men were having an early dinner, two Japanese aircraft approached TF.74 and all ships opened fire. *Shropshire's* radar then detected a further five aircraft closing the ship. Fortunately, these were intercepted by fighters. After that action *Shropshire* closed to within 3,000 yards of San Joaquin village to bombard Japanese positions before having a relatively quiet night patrolling the Gulf.

On 24 October the ships were subjected to the largest air attack yet. *Shropshire's* radar detected nearly 100 aircraft closing from Luzon to the north west. US carrier aircraft intercepted the bulk of the raid before they could reach the transports, but about 20 penetrated this first line of defence. *Shropshire* then directed the close-in fighters which shot down 8 more. At 0835 a Zero got through and headed straight towards *Shropshire* but was driven off by 4-inch gunfire. The ship was then subjected to high-level bombing from two aircraft with bombs exploding 500 yards on the port side and 200 yards ahead.

Then came possibly the most dangerous attack for *Shropshire*. Around twenty aircraft approached from the port bow and beam to attack the cruiser and other ships. Guy directed his side's AA defences. All the TF.74 ships were also opening fire. One Landing Ship Tank was struck by a kamikaze and later sank. *Shropshire* remained unscathed. They had to endure two more large raids during the day but most aircraft were expertly intercepted by the carrier-based fighters which flew from the escort carriers east of Samar Island.

VI

At dusk on 24 October Admiral Oldendorf directed his forces to counter the approaching Admiral Nishimura's Southern Force. The timing was fortuitous in that the Japanese air attacks in Leyte were daytime only and, all things going well, Oldendorf could deal with the Southern Force and return to Leyte before first light. Oldendorf's force of 6 battleships, 8 cruisers including *Shropshire,* supported by 28 destroyers and 39 patrol torpedo (PT) boats* were deployed to Surigao Strait to block entry into Leyte Gulf.

Using his overwhelming numbers Oldendorf would have first the

---

* Oldendorf's battleships were *Maryland, Mississippi, Tennessee, California, Pennsylvania* & *West Virginia*. His cruisers were *Louisville* (flagship), *Portland, Minneapolis, Shropshire, Denver, Columbia, Pheonix* & *Boise.* The destroyers were divisions drawn from Destroyer Squadrons (DESRON) 54, 24 (including *Arunta*) & 56.

PT boats and then the destroyer divisions successively attack from the flanks as the Japanese proceeded up the Surigao Strait. Among the destroyers was *Arunta* and she would lead one division into the attack.[*] At the northern end of the Strait and steaming across Nishimura's path would be Oldendorf's battleships and cruisers. This would create a classic 'crossing the T' situation whereby Oldendorf's ships would be able to fire simultaneously at the approaching enemy, but only the lead Japanese could return fire.[†]

In *Shropshire* Nichols prepared the ship for the action. There was intense anticipation within the ship at the prospect of the rarest of all battles, a fleet engagement against battleships. For this action Guy was not to be an ADO. Instead, he was to be the Rate Officer in the 8-inch gunnery control team led by John Austin as the 8-inch Control Officer. Guy's role involved observing the fall of shot on the enemy ship and, if necessary, ordering corrections to bring the shots in line with the target – not easy in a night action. Located just below the director, Guy would have a visual view of the impending action. In another example of the confidence Nichols had in his team, Lieutenant John Riley the Action OOW had been lent to the depleted *Australia*, and so Nichols let his assistant, Midshipman Rothesay Swan, fill the role. Swan was told that 'all I had to do in times of action was carry out the orders of the Captain and Navigator'.[33]

In glassy seas the Japanese Southern Force steamed through the night at 20 knots. There was no turning back. As the two forces drew inevitably towards a titanic battle, the advances in the war since the Battle of Savo Island were to be starkly demonstrated. In particular, improved training and radar technology had now given the Americans and Australians a decided edge in night fighting.

---

[*]   A Destroyer division normally consisted of 4 or 5 ships with two divisions comprising a Destroyer Squadron.

[†]   The most famous 20th Century example where the 'Crossing T' manoeuvre was executed was the Battle of Tsushima in 1905. The Japanese Admiral Tōgō Heihachirō used it to devastating effect against the Russian Fleet commanded by Admiral Zinovy Rozhestvensky.

Over three hours from 2036, the PT boats conducted a series of attacks against the Japanese. They, however, steamed on unscathed through the smoke, starshell and searchlights. At 0230 the five ships of DESRON 54 launched torpedo attacks from both sides of Nishimura's formation. Forty-seven torpedoes sped towards the Southern Force. Nishimura's flagship *Yamashiro* was struck by a torpedo but continued on. Less fortunate were the destroyers *Michishio*, which was stopped and left sinking, and *Yamagumo* which blew up, lighting up the horizon for the waiting cruisers and battleships. Unknown to Nishimura, the battleship *Fusō* had also been hit by one or two torpedoes. From *Shropshire*, Guy saw the large explosion astern of *Yamashiro*. The stricken *Fusō* had broken in two, releasing large amounts of oil which caused an extensive fire on the water. Both sections of the hull sank within forty minutes, with only ten sailors surviving out of 1,900 men.

The next attack was by DESRON 24, again in two divisions. The eastern attack of three destroyers missed their targets. The other division of three destroyers led by Commander Alfred Buchanan in *Arunta* launched fourteen torpedoes with one striking *Yamashiro* slowing her down to five knots for a short period. In the final destroyer attack, by DESRON 56, two more torpedo hits were made on the battleship.

During these actions the Oldendorf's battleships and cruisers were slowly steaming on a course perpendicular to the Japanese path to 'cross the T'. One group of cruisers lay between the approaching Japanese and Oldendorf's battleships while *Phoenix* (Rear Admiral Berkley embarked), *Boise* and *Shropshire* protected the western flank.

Shropshire's radar team first detected the Japanese ships at about twenty miles and could see the fast-steaming destroyers conducting their attacks. At 0353, as the destroyers peeled away, Oldendorf's cruisers and then battleships finally opened a devastating fire. In the words of one *Shropshire* sailor 'all hell broke loose'.[34] *Shropshire* opened fire three minutes later using her radar to determine the *Yamashiro*'s range. The Americans had 'flashless' ammunition which meant no light was emitted when the rounds left the guns. Unfortunately, *Shropshire* did not have such ammunition. For Guy this meant he had to quickly adjust his eyes to the varying light conditions to be able to observe the fall of shot. Usefully, though, each of the ships had different coloured tracer in some shells for identification. *Shropshire's* colour was yellow.

In the engagement the 8-inch guns' crews worked up to firing eight broadsides every two minutes. This was the greatest rate of fire they ever achieved. In all *Shropshire* fired thirty-two broadsides – a total of 214 rounds. For Guy in observing *Shropshire's* shellfire and deciding whether to apply any corrections he had to differentiate the shells from his own ship from those of others hitting or straddling the *Yamashiro*. But measuring the expected time of flight of *Shropshire's* rounds helped in identification. In a stroke of good fortune, at one point, *Shropshire's* rounds arrived on target simultaneously with those of a US ship. The explosion of the US rounds hitting the target illuminated *Shropshire's* off target yellow rounds and allowed Guy to order a small correction. It was not possible to assess how many times *Shropshire* hit *Yamashiro*, but in all she straddled the battleship sixteen times.

Both *Yamashiro* and *Mogami* sustained fearful punishment. At 0419 the battered *Yamashiro* rolled over and sank taking Admiral Nishimura and most of her crew with her. The battered *Mogami* retired only to be sunk by carrier aircraft the next day. The Battle of Surigao Strait was the last battle in history between battleships. Guy later said his lasting memories of the action were 'the incredible sight of the tracer from the six battleships, eight cruisers and some twenty destroyers all firing at the Japanese ships coming up the Strait… the impressions were indelible.'[35] It was *Shropshire's* and *Arunta's* finest hour and the only time RAN ships engaged battleships.

Meanwhile to the north, Kurita's Force had sailed northeast to pass south of Mindoro with the aim of passing through the San Bernadino Strait. Success in this mission would be assisted if the US 3rd Fleet became focused on the Ozawa's force heading south from Formosa. While in part this occurred, Kurita lost two cruisers and the mighty *Musashi* to submarine and air attack. On the morning of 25 October on clearing the San Bernadino Strait, Kurita encountered the escort carrier force of Rear Admiral Clifton Sprague.* The Battle of Samar was one of the most remarkable engagements of the war. Kurita with his overwhelming force should have wreaked havoc on Sprague's small carriers, but was repulsed by the heroic efforts of the destroyer escorts and the hurriedly rearmed carrier aircraft. Sprague lost one escort carrier and three destroyer escorts, while in the repeated air attacks Kurita lost three cruisers.

The Battle of Leyte Gulf was a disaster for the Japanese. They suffered heavy losses in ships, aircraft and personnel. Its navy never recovered. For the Allies there was still more to do to secure the Philippines. Manila was yet to be liberated and airfields in the north had yet to be secured so the US could direct its full might against the Japanese mainland.

VII

After Leyte Gulf *Shropshire* returned to Manus Island for rest and maintenance. Bracegirdle, armed with two cases of whiskey from the Wardroom, 'negotiated' a weapons upgrade for the ship. Twelve 20mm gun mountings were replaced with thirteen 40mm guns, which had much greater range and stopping power. Wisely, Captain Nichols informed Navy Office of the upgrade as a *fait accompli* the following month.[36] *Australia,* repairing at Espiritu Santo, also fitted additional 40mm guns but not as extensively as *Shropshire.* In another welcome innovation RAN ordnance experts had conducted trials and approved for use USN 8-inch shells for the RAN cruisers. This not only eased resupply but gave them access to flashless ammunition.[37]

The next amphibious landings were to be on the Philippines' largest and most important island of Luzon. Instead of a direct landing in Manila Bay to retake the capital, it was decided to go ashore on the

---

* Later Vice Admiral C.A.F. 'Ziggy' Sprague, USN (1896–1955).

central west coast in the relatively lightly defended Lingayen Gulf. Two landing sites were intended at the southern end of the Gulf, one near the town of Lingayen and the other near San Fabian. The intent was for the four divisions of the US 6th Army to push south to secure the roads south towards Manila.

From 31 December the first of the 650 ships of the invasion fleet steamed towards Lingayen Gulf. Admiral Oldendorf's Bombardment and Fire Support Group included 6 battleships, 12 small aircraft carriers, 8 cruisers and 48 destroyers. Among them were *Australia*, *Shropshire*, *Arunta*, *Warramunga*, *Gascoyne* and *Warrego*. At about midnight on 2–3 January the force passed through a now quiet Surigao Strait to provide escort and be in position for the initial survey and bombardment. For this operation Guy remained at his old action station of Portside ADO. At dusk on 3 January two Japanese aircraft closed the ships. *Shropshire*'s port pom-pom and Bofors engaged one, which crashed into the water 50 metres from the portside. The portside batteries opened up again and drove the other away.

On 4 January as the Fleet steamed up the west coast of the archipelago, Japanese air activity continued to build, presaging a titanic air battle once Lingayen Gulf was reached. In the afternoon a kamikaze hit the escort carrier *Ommaney Bay* causing a major blaze. Soon after the sun had set another 'aircraft' was detected and *Shropshire*'s port AA weapons, as well as those of other ships, opened fire. It turned out to be the planet Venus. As Guy later remarked, 'one could not say the lookouts were napping'.[38] At about 2000 a large explosion was heard astern as the *Ommaney Bay* blew up and sank.

On the afternoon of 5 January, as the ships steamed by Manila Bay, Japanese aircraft tried to break through the umbrella of sixty American fighters that protected the armada. Most were intercepted, but at 1700 *Arunta* was missed by a kamikaze, but damaged by its bomb that fell close by. Soon after, six Japanese Vals, flying low, evaded American fighters and passed astern of *Australia* with one slamming into the escort carrier *Manila Bay*. The fires were extinguished and she resumed flying operations a couple of days later. Despite concerted anti-aircraft fire, one Val, after gaining height, executed a steep dive and hit portside midships of *Australia*. The aircraft's fuel started a blaze and its bomb also detonated causing death and injury among the gun crews. *Australia*'s third funnel and crane were also damaged. The fire was quickly doused by a hose team despite exploding ammunition around them. In the attack twenty-five men were killed, including all of the aft portside 4-inch and eight of the forward 4-inch gun crews. Some bodies were never found, either obliterated or blown overboard. Among these missing men was Guy's classmate Colin Russell. Sailors from some of the smaller calibre guns courageously backfilled the 4-inch mounts, while others from the 8-inch magazines took over the smaller calibre guns.

The following day, 6 January, saw the pre-landing bombardment commence within Lingayen Gulf. *Australia* was not assigned specific targets, but rather was to respond to any targets of opportunity. One Japanese battery opened fire and was promptly silenced by *Australia*. To the west, *Shropshire* was assigned targets on Poro Point. At midday the battleship *New Mexico*, which was steaming ahead of *Shropshire*, was attacked by a suicider. Although *Shropshire* managed to take off her tail, the aircraft still struck the battleship's bridge. It killed thirty-one men including her captain and Winston Churchill's liaison officer to General MacArthur, Lieutenant General Herbert Lumsden. Lucky to escape uninjured was the Commander-in-Chief of the newly formed British Pacific Fleet, Admiral Sir Bruce Fraser, who was also onboard to witness operations.

Shortly after this hit, *Shropshire* was successively attacked by two Japanese aircraft. Guy saw the first of the 'Zekes' come head-on out of the sun presenting only the radial engine and wings to his guns. As the guns opened fire, Guy recalled, 'The result seemed inevitable, but then he altered direction slightly and passed within a few feet of the ADP, just over the Bofors on B turret and crashed in the sea just off the starboard bow.'[39] The second aircraft was also shot down within yards of the ship. Less fortunate was the destroyer-transport *Brooks* which was struck by a suicider, *Warramunga* going to her aid.

Throughout the day low-flying suiciders came from the coast to attack the ships. At 1725 a Val headed towards *Australia* from her starboard quarter. Despite a barrage of fire the aircraft struck the starboard side between the two 4-inch mounts. Aviation fuel ignited over the deck and the aircraft's bomb exploded. Once again the fire was quickly put out, but there was a heavy toll on gun crews. All of the rear starboard 4-inch gun crew were lost as well as some of those manning the forward mount. In all, fourteen were killed. Within a couple of days both 4-inch mounts would be made serviceable. In the meantime *Australia* maintained her station.

An hour later *Warramunga* reported that an aircraft was diving towards the cruisers. Acting Temporary Leading Seaman Roy Cazaly,* was doing some maintenance on *Shropshire*'s port pom-pom and saw the aircraft heading for the bridge. He quickly swung the mount around and gave a burst of fire that tore off its wings. The aircraft exploded near the port side to the relief of the bridge crew. Cazaly's single-handed actions were recognised with the award of a Distinguished Service Medal.

The following day both cruisers stood ready to engage any Japanese artillery fire from the shore. *Shropshire* was straddled once and returned fire to silence the shore position. While that day was relatively quiet for air attacks they would resume in earnest on 8 January. After standing offshore overnight the ships steamed into the Gulf. Shortly thereafter three Val dive bombers flew towards *Shropshire* followed by two American Wildcat fighters. One Val passed down *Shropshire*'s starboard side hotly followed by a Wildcat. Both planes were shot down but, to the great relief of all, the American pilot was safely recovered. Soon after another suicider was engaged by Guy's crews and hit the sea 200 yards on the port side of *Shropshire*.

---

* Leading Seaman Roy Cazaly was the only son of the famous Australian Rules footballer of the same name.

The raid was far from complete. Just after the second suicider was destroyed, a twin-engine 'Dinah' bomber made a run from astern of a line of battleships and cruisers. *Australia*, last in line, opened a concerted fire. The aircraft was repeatedly struck by fire from *Australia* and a low flying Wildcat. The Dinah hit the water twenty yards from *Australia* but carried on to strike the ship's side. Gun crews aft were drenched with high octane aviation fuel which fortunately did not ignite. Before these men had time to hose the fuel off their clothes a second Dinah made an almost identical run on *Australia*. This was also hit many times before striking the ship's side below the bridge. Its bomb blew a thirty-five square metre hole in the hull which resulted in a 5° list. One of the propellers landed on the upper deck amid other shrapnel but miraculously there were no injuries.[40] Minutes later the escort carrier *Kadashan Bay* also had a hole blown in her side by a suicider. Undeterred by her repeated strikes *Australia* continued her bombardment duties. In contrast to *Australia*'s experience, some of the suiciders appeared to shy away from *Shropshire*'s barrage fire. Tokyo Rose would later accuse the ship of using 'flame throwers' against aircraft.

On the morning of 9 January, the landings of 68,000 troops took place. *Kanimbla*, *Manoora* and *Westralia* were among the ships disgorging their precious cargo. Both *Shropshire* and *Australia* took part in further bombardments. Such was the effectiveness of the three previous days of bombardment and air strikes that there was virtually no opposition. Suicide air attacks continued, however. Just after 1300 two 'Judy' fighters came in low over land and both were engaged by the warships. The first passed by *Australia* and struck the battleship *Mississippi* at her waterline to little effect. The second flew towards *Australia*'s bridge being repeatedly hit as it did so. The suicider narrowly missed the bridge but its wing tip grazed the Type 273 radar and part of the foremast. The fighter then crashed into the top of the forward funnel and passed over into the water. No other warship had been subjected to, or indeed survived, so many suicide attacks. With black humour Captain Armstrong in *Australia* later memorably signalled to Nichols in *Shropshire* 'We catch 'em – you shoot 'em'.[41]

Indeed, the charmed *Shropshire* was only one of four battleships or cruisers that had not been hit by suicide aircraft.* Importantly, the Army secured the town of Lingayen and its intact airstrip by dusk. At day's end the damaged *Australia* and *Arunta* were ordered to retire south to San Pedro Bay along with other seriously damaged ships. It was clear *Australia* would need to return to Australia; she was effectively out of the war. Before she left, Farncomb and his staff shifted across to *Arunta* for transfer to *Shropshire*.

It was during the Lingayen Gulf battle, as Guy witnessed the air battle going on around him, that he got a hankering to become a pilot. He went to see the Commander, who by this stage was George Oldham. He was a great character, who had himself been an Observer (air navigator) in the Fleet Air Arm. His advice was clear, 'Oh no, Griffiths, I wouldn't advise that. I think you've been selected for gunnery and you stick to that, that's a good thing to do.' So, Guy did not go flying and did not regret that decision.[42] In later years, however, Guy lamented not acting upon the advice of the ship's instructor officer, Lieutenant James McCusker, to study, even part-time, for a university degree.

On 22 January Commodore Farncomb and his staff joined *Shropshire* in a much quieter Lingayen Gulf. Farncomb had a reputation for his bravery, fierce intellect and sternness. He was known in the Squadron as 'Fearless Frank' and Guy, while having had little dealings with Farncomb, had immense respect for him. Also joining the ship during this period were twenty-one British soldiers who had been prisoners of war captured in Singapore. They had been liberated by US Rangers ashore and were now treated with great hospitality in *Shropshire*.

In Lingayen Gulf the air attacks had now largely disappeared. Unknown at the time, the Japanese had relocated their remaining Kamikaze aircraft to Formosa for homeland defence. As Commander Task Unit 77.3.5 Farncomb had in addition to *Shropshire*, *Arunta* and

---

* The other ships were the battleships *Pennsylvania* & *West Virginia* & the cruiser *Portland*.

Warramunga; the US heavy cruisers *Portland* and *Minneapolis* and the destroyers *Conway, Eaton, Braine* and *Frazier.* On 6 February TU.77.3.5 finally left Lingayen and sailed for Manila. They had weathered the kamikaze storm. The dogged defence of ships had involved long and wearing hours at action stations. During one night watch Bracegirdle noted Guy's waning attention and over the intercom from the Bridge to the ADP came 'God is watching, Griffiths'.[43] As more ships were struck by 'suiciders' so grew their psychological effect on the ships' companies. Guy reflected,

> As the operation went on in Leyte Gulf, there were other suicide attacks and it became the norm so to speak during Leyte Gulf and it increased markedly at Lingayen because their airfields were somewhat closer. There was a resignation. I don't mean people were resigning but they were resigned to accept this form of attack. It gave way to some fear because any aircraft attacking the ship you immediately assume that of course if you didn't shoot it down it's going to crash inboard. Quite a number were attacking *Shropshire.* We were lucky; they steered away if they didn't like our air defence, steered away and went to other ships and that happened quite a number of times. On the other hand, we shot down quite a number of aircraft as well.
>
> So, there was a determination that tended to increase the accuracy of fire by better aiming. But you had the attacks coming at the same time that people were at their action stations, battle stations for prolonged periods, everybody was tired and weary, so it really was drawing out every ounce of energy that a crew had to keep up the work of defending the ship during the daylight hours.[44]

When TU.77.3.5 arrived in Manila the capital was still being cleared of Japanese who were not finally subdued until 4 March. Heavy fighting was also underway at Corregidor on the tip of the Bataan Peninsula. On 16 February Farncomb's heavy cruisers were called in to assist Admiral Berkey's force in bombarding the Japanese fortified positions. The use of 8-inch semi-armour piercing shells finally had the desired effect on the cliff fortifications. At the same time the men had a close view of the historic recapture of Corregidor, which included a large-scale drop of paratroopers. After the Corregidor operation *Shropshire* was overdue for a refit in Sydney.

The RAN's action in the Philippines Campaign is one of its finest achievements. While the heroics of *Australia*'s ship's company gained deserved national attention, the performance of *Shropshire*'s men was quite outstanding. Such was the ship's contribution that Admiral Kinkaid wrote to the Commander-in-Chief US Fleet, Admiral Ernest King in Washington, specifically about *Shropshire*'s achievements with her 8-inch director controlled barrage fire.* Kinkaid gave a Commander 7th Fleet Commendation to the ship.[45] For his part Admiral Oldendorf was particularly complimentary of *Shropshire*'s peerless radar detections close to land and her estimations of aircraft height which repeatedly alerted the carrier-based fighters and gunnery teams in the Task Force. The thorough setting to work and training on her radar sets from the outset paid off handsomely.

Besides the material and tactical contributions to *Shropshire*'s deeds, Captain Nichols later highlighted the stability in the composition of the ship's company for the preceding six months which enabled them to develop as a tight team. This was critical in their ability to perform the demanding 'snap-shooting' against the suicide aircraft.[46] Guy believed *Shropshire*'s achievements would have gained much greater historical prominence if the ship had been renamed after an Australian city and her performance repeatedly celebrated by future ships of that name.

In the resulting awards and decorations, sixteen were awarded to

---

* The barrage fire tactic was to be used in the RAN fleet for the next 40 years.

Shropshire officers and sailors. Among them Captain Nichols received a Distinguished Service Order and Bracegirdle a bar to his DSC.* Guy was also awarded the DSC. In Captain Nichols' nomination of Guy he commended his 'marked leadership, ability and courage as Air Defence Officer during the Lingayen operations when subjected to suicide bombings by Japanese aircraft.'[47] The nomination was specially recommended by Commodore Farncomb. The DSC would mark Guy out for the rest of his career for his 'valuable services in action'.[48] Guy found the ADO role the most difficult duty that he undertook during the war and said simply that he and James Osborne 'managed to do the best we could in that time'.[49] Guy was at pains to make the point that his DSC really reflected the outstanding performance of *Shropshire's* gunnery team. Also awarded a bar to his DSC was Lieutenant Ron Major who led the ship's radar team. In Guy's estimation, Major was a 'key man' in *Shropshire's* success through his sheer wizardry in estimating aircraft height and colourfully leading his team of ten officers and sailors in their vital work.[50] Also among DSC recipients were classmates John Austin for his performance in the Battle of Surigao Strait and David Hamer for his ADO duties in *Australia*.

Shropshire sailed south to Manus Island where she briefly exercised with the Philippines-bound *Hobart*, now operational after her torpedo hit. On 16 March *Shropshire* finally arrived in Sydney for a well-earned leave and maintenance period. Joining *Shropshire* whilst she was alongside was Guy's classmate Peter Gyllies, who would also join the Gunnery Department.

VIII

While the main American effort following the Philippine campaign was to be the landing on Iwo Jima, two other operations were mounted. They were the retaking of Borneo, which would secure oil and rubber supplies,

---

* A bar to an award is when the recipient receives the same award for a subsequent deed. A rosette is affixed to the medal ribbon.

and the mopping up of Japanese positions in New Guinea. In Borneo the first of the Codename 'Oboe' series of landings by Australian troops had already successfully taken place at Tarakan (Oboe 1) on 1 May. The next operations would be in the north on Labuan Island (Oboe 6) near Brunei slated for 10 June and involving the Australian 9th Division, and in the south at Balikpapan (Oboe 2) programmed for 1 July with the Australian 7th Division.

At the beginning of June, *Shropshire* sailed from Sydney to bolster the Australian Squadron for these operations. Her shakedown was truncated to ensure she could take part. On 14 June *Shropshire* joined *Hobart* and *Arunta* in the southern Philippines and Commodore Farncomb transferred to *Shropshire*. After early Australian success on Labuan, the Japanese resistance had hardened and the Squadron steamed to support the 9th Division. That afternoon *Shropshire* closed and fired upon Japanese strongholds to telling effect, killing a hundred Japanese, but tragically also two Australian soldiers. Further bombardments took place the following day before Japanese resistance ended.

At the end of June the amphibious, bombardment and aircraft carrier groups converged on Balikpapan. On the afternoon of 27 June, *Shropshire* and *Hobart* closed the Klandasan beaches and commenced the initial bombardment whilst the destroyers *Arunta*, *Hart* and *Metcalf* provided anti-submarine protection. After nearly four hours of deliberate bombardment Farncomb withdrew his ships into the Makassar Strait. The ships returned each day for a further bombardment and to protect the amphibious fleet, which included, once again, the trio of *Kanimbla*, *Manoora* and *Westralia*. On the eve of the landing, Japanese positions were subject to further Allied air attacks. On the morning of 1 July, with General MacArthur witnessing operations from the US cruiser *Cleveland*, the 7th Division made their landings. The approach channels which had been swept for mines were marked with small buoys and the well-practiced landing craft were for the most part able to hit the beach such that the troops landed dry shod.[51]

The Japanese resistance was initially light as were the Australian casualties. The warships remained offshore for nine days providing round the clock bombardment support as well as harassing fire to wear down the enemy. A feature of the Balikpapan operation was the accuracy of the naval gunfire in dealing with Japanese positions, a testament to the expertise the ships had developed since 1942. For most ships of the Australian Squadron, 9 July represented the day they fired their last rounds at the enemy. That evening *Shropshire* weighed anchor and steamed to a well-earned break in the Philippines. On 21 July 1945, after nearly seven months of arduous service, Farncomb was relieved by Commodore Collins, who had recovered sufficiently from his wounds.

IX

After resuming command, Collins called on Admiral Kinkaid. Among the matters discussed was the Australian Squadron's part in the invasion of Japan. The overall campaign was codenamed Operation 'Downfall'. It was divided into two large operations, Operation 'Olympic' – the invasion of Kyūshū and Operation 'Coronet' – the invasion of Honshū. The Australian Squadron would take part in Olympic, which was set to land troops ashore on 1 November 1945. It was to be undertaken by Admiral 'Bull' Halsey's 3rd Fleet and would be the largest amphibious operation in history. The Australian Squadron would join a fleet comprising seventeen aircraft carriers, eight battleships, twenty cruisers and seventy-five destroyers. Collins' ships would once again be part of the inshore bombardment force. The defence of Kyūshū was expected to be intense. In addition to the envisaged 9,000 kamikaze aircraft there was also the prospect of attacks from human torpedoes and suicide boats. Collins was conscious of the unique and conspicuous appearance of his three-funnelled cruisers, which would no doubt draw particular kamikaze attention[52]. Once ashore the US troops would have to face a determined Japanese 16th Army, fighting for the first time on their own soil.[53]

To prepare themselves for Olympic, the Australian Squadron was based at Subic Bay just to the north of Manila. It was, however, to be spared the rigours of this final operation. On 6 August the men were astounded to hear a new and most destructive bomb had devastated the Japanese city of Hiroshima. After a call for Japan's surrender went unheeded, a second atomic bomb destroyed Nagasaki on 9 August. Six days later the Japanese announced their unconditional surrender. On hearing the news Guy went for a walk on the upper deck and thought after all these years of only knowing war, 'I wonder what happens to me now.'[54]

To celebrate the occasion, Captain Nichols invited 400 RAN and USN officers from the Task Force for a party on the quarterdeck. It was a great event with free-flowing beer and gin. Two *Shropshire* stokers had purloined some officers' uniforms and joined the party. Inevitably, they stood out and the following day went before the Commander's disciplinary table. The Commander was by this time James 'Copper' Morrow who asked the sailors whether they enjoyed the party. When they responded that they had a great time, Morrow said he was pleased, 'but it cost each officer 35 shillings – so you are each fined 35 shillings'. Guy, thought the punishment perfectly blended justice, humour and sensitivity to the occasion.

To the satisfaction of all it was decided the Squadron would be present in Tokyo Bay for the surrender. This brought forward the shift from Kinkaid's 7th Fleet to Halsey's 3rd Fleet. Collins paid farewell calls on both Kinkaid and General MacArthur. The General told Collins the Squadron's departure from his command was like a death in the family.

Commodore Collins's ships – *Shropshire*, *Warramunga* and *Bataan* – sailed out of Manila Bay on 25 August passing Corregidor and Bataan at sunset. Clearing the Philippines there were two days of clear blue skies and calm weather as the squadron relaxed for the first time at sea in five years. After rendezvousing with *Hobart* on passage, on the morning of 31 August, Collins, flying his broad pennant in *Shropshire*, led his ships in line astern into Tokyo Bay. In contrast to the sunny passage, the weather was grey and threatening which added to the atmosphere.

As the ships entered port numerous white flags could be seen fluttering from buildings and hill tops. This gave the men their first sense of victory. The desolation of the port, the city and shipping became all too apparent. As the Australian Squadron threaded its way to its assigned anchorage the sailors saw before them a mighty armada of over 250 warships. Overhead there were large formations of aircraft regularly flying over the vanquished city. Among the battleships were Halsey's flagship, *Missouri*, where the surrender would take place; *South Dakota* wearing the flag of Admiral Chester Nimitz and *Duke of York* with Admiral Sir Bruce Fraser embarked. There was a sense of great pride among the squadron sailors at being part of this final act to the war. To the men in *Shropshire*, Commodore Collins later wrote, 'It's a far cry from No. 3 Basin, Chatham Dockyard, to Berth D.60 in Tokyo Bay, but here we are, and still rather bewildered by the sudden realisation of our dreams.'[55]

The following day Commodore Collins met the other members of the Australian Delegation for the surrender. It was led by General Sir Thomas Blamey and comprised Lieutenant General Frank Berryman and Air Vice Marshal William Bostock, while the Navy was represented by both the Acting First Naval Member, Rear Admiral George Moore and Collins. From an early hour on the day of the Surrender Ceremony a stream of boats made their way to *Missouri*. As the dignitaries assembled, hundreds of bombers and fighters swept overhead in waves of omnipresent power. Guy captured the mood onboard *Shropshire*,

> I think by the time we got to Tokyo we'd been out of action ... the war had ceased and so everybody's fully relaxed and marvelled at the show of strength that was presented to the Japanese on that particular day when the surrender was signed. The sky was covered with aircraft from shore bases, bombers, heavy bombers, and naval aircraft. The

surface ships stretched all the way around Tokyo Bay, so many battleships and aircraft carriers present. And also, of course, what we didn't see were the number of aircraft carriers at sea flying their squadrons over Tokyo Bay as a show of strength. It was a very awe-inspiring scene, really, that particular day.[56]

As the ceremony got underway sailors around the assembled armada listened to proceedings via a radio broadcast. They could hear MacArthur in his distinctive voice act as master of ceremonies and call forward each national delegation. The national representatives saluted MacArthur and then their head signed the instrument of surrender. With MacArthur's words 'These proceedings are now closed' six years of war came to an end. Soon thereafter the sun broke through the diminishing clouds. Privileged to be part of the ceremony, Commodore Collins thought 'It was a pity that every man in the Squadron could not have been there to see the late "world conquerors" stand so abjectly, waiting to be allowed to sign the surrender document.'[57]

During the port visit Guy and some of the other officers took a tram which was surprisingly still working, into Tokyo from the port. For the thirty-minute journey all that could be seen were completely flattened homes and other buildings. Devastation was complete.

Whilst the armada was at anchor, the British escort carrier *Speaker*, with 445 former internees and prisoners of war, including some *Perth* survivors, left harbour. She steamed close by Commonwealth warships as she did so. Sailors gave a loud cheer to the former prisoners on *Speaker*'s flight deck to wish them a safe voyage to Sydney. It was a moving occasion for Guy and all concerned.

For the RAN the war had resulted in the loss at sea of over 2,100 men and nineteen ships. After the surrender some ships would remain as part of the occupation force but most would go to their home ports. *Shropshire* was one of the lucky ones, destined to arrive in Sydney before

Christmas, collecting some soldiers in Wewak along the way. But Guy's return to Australia was to be even more expeditious. While he wondered in Subic Bay what was to become of him, the Navy had a plan. He was to attend his keenly sought after gunnery specialization course which started in the UK in January 1946. So Guy was given passage to Sydney in the British destroyer *Wakeful* to enable him to take leave before starting the next phase of his career. Also taking passage in *Wakeful* was the war correspondent George Johnston, who would later achieve international fame with his novel *My Brother Jack*.

In *Shropshire* Guy had witnessed how a happy, well-led ship could sustain herself for long periods of arduous sea duty in the face of a most determined enemy. That outstanding leadership came from the top, and Captain Nichols was to be a shining example to Guy for the remainder of his career. Guy would later remark that Nichols was a 'marvellous character and the ship's company never forgot him'.[58] For his part Nichols wrote that Guy was 'an outstanding young officer who had carried out his duties conscientiously. Zealous, loyal and cheerful he knows how to handle men and they trust him.'[59] This assessment highlighted the other admirable attribute of *Shropshire*, which was the positive relationship that existed between her sailors and officers.

In 1941 Guy and four fellow midshipmen sailed in the Shaw Savill & Albion Line refrigerated cargo ship *Karamea* to Britain. (Green Collection)

In 1881 Guy's paternal grandfather Dr Ernest Griffiths arrived in Australia in the clipper *La Hogue*. (State library of Victoria)

Guy aged five years old. (Griffiths Collection)

The *Caerphilly* homestead in 1931. Guy and his sister Dorothy with croquet club out front with their mother Lewie among those on the verandah. (Griffiths Collection)

The *Wilderness* winery. Young Guy is the tallest among the children out front. He was fascinated by the machinery associated with wine production. (Griffiths Collection)

PHILLIP YEAR. 1937.

F. K. M. Thompson, J. S. Austin, G. R. Griffiths, G. J. Willis, M. L. Molony, L. J. Tatham, B. Dowling,

J. D. Goble, G. B. Thrum, R. I. Davies, Lieut. Comdr. H. C. Wright, P. Gyllies, H. J. Bodman, D. J. Hamer,

D. W. Manning, J. C. W. Kennedy, A. I. Parker, C. N. Russell.

The Phillip Year at the Royal Australian Naval College. (RAN)

Left
Guy & classmate John Austin at Foster on holiday with John's family. (Griffiths Collection)

Below
Guy's Term following their 1940 graduation with the much-liked Commander Alexander Loudon-Shand. *L to R:* Hamer, Molony, Tatham Guy, Thrum, Gyllies, Austin. (Griffiths Collection)

Above

The battlecruiser HMS *Repulse*. She was a happy and efficient ship but 'her back end would waggle like a duck'. (PA Images)

Left

Captain William Tennant of HMS *Repulse* his was the finest captain Guy served under during his career. He is seen here later in the war as a Vice Admiral.

Guy and fellow former HMS *Repulse* midshipmen at Trincomalee.
(Griffiths Collection)

Guy (1st left, centre row) on his Sub-Lieutenant's Courses at Whale Island in August 1942. (Griffiths Collection)

The destroyer HMS *Vivien*. Guy qualified as an officer of the watch in her.
(LCDR J.E. Manners RN)

King George VI arrives to inspect HMAS *Shropshire*. Guy is the officer saluting at
the left of the photograph. (RAN)

HMAS *Shropshire* in action (RAN)

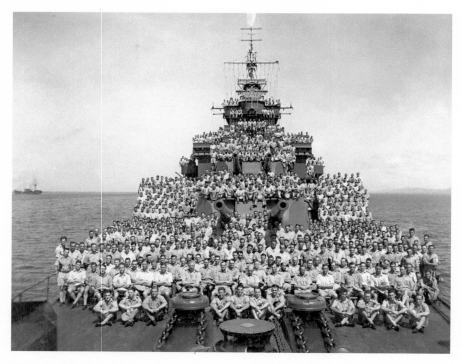

HMAS *Shropshire* ship's company. Guy is on the far right, second row. (RAN)

5

The Korean War

The bitter sea wind froze
even the truth into tears

From *'The Winter Sea'* by Kim Nam-Jo

I

In the last months of World War II the RAN had in commission 337 ships and 39,650 men and women in uniform. The vast majority of the men and all of the women had joined the Navy for the hostilities only. A demobilisation program soon got underway, led by one of Commodore Collins's classmates Captain James Esdaile. It was a complex undertaking which had to balance the still operational requirements of providing ships in Japanese and other Pacific waters with the personal, social and financial imperatives to release personnel expeditiously back into civilian society. Within five years the size of the Fleet had shrunk to 75 ships and fewer than 10,000 men. The demobilisation program was inevitably a blunt instrument and some policy mistakes were made such as the disestablishment of the Women's Royal Australian Naval Service.*

Some of the men who had joined for the war took to naval life and were successful in remaining in the Service. But this was only about 2% of the war volunteers. Equally, some of the career officers who had

---

* By 1948 with personnel shortages the WRANS was re-established.

passed through the Naval College had had their fill of the sea after five years of war. Once again this was a small number. In Guy's class Robert Davies, Colin Russell and Lyster Tatham had been killed. Another three classmates were invalided out of the service. They were Bruce Dowling, following his severe injuries from *Australia*'s first kamikaze attack, Keith Thompson as a result of the raid on Saint Dunstans, and David Manning, who had firstly survived *Perth*'s sinking and then extreme rigours of the Japanese prisoner of war camps.

There were twenty-two officers on the 1946 Long 'G' Course. All were RN except for a couple of Canadians and two Australians, Guy and David Hamer. The two course instructors were the very personable Lieutenant Commander James 'Fish' Dalglish and the more rigid Lieutenant Commander Michael Pollock. The former was the son of Australian-born RN Rear Admiral Robin Dalglish who returned to Australia to command the Squadron in the interwar period. Pollock, who earned a DSC as Gunnery Officer of *Norfolk* in the engagement with the German battlecruiser *Scharnhorst,* would go on to become First Sea Lord.* Guy found his classmates to be a very pleasant group and formed a lifelong friendship with David Williams, who later became Second Sea Lord.† The course began in the magnificent environment of the Royal Naval College at Greenwich. Although Guy found himself close to the nightlife of London, the city was still blighted by the significant damage to buildings and infrastructure.

The commencement of the course in January, coincided with the inaugural sessions of the United Nations General Assembly and the Security Council. These were to occur in London.‡ Among the many events held to mark these historic occasions was a formal dinner in Greenwich's Painted Hall to be hosted by Prime Minister Clement Attlee.

---

*   Later Admiral of the Fleet Sir Michael Pollock, GCB, LVO, DSC (1916–2006).

†   Later Admiral Sir David Williams, GCB (1921–2012).

‡   The UN General Assembly first met in the Central Hall while the Security Council met in Church House, both near Westminster Abbey.

In addition to cabinet ministers, Guy and his class were among those who also attended to help host the delegates and their entourages. The Naval College staff had gone to great lengths to decorate the hall with palms from Kew Gardens and other sources. After dinner the course members were joined by some of cabinet ministers for songs around a piano. The pianist was the First Lord of the Admiralty, Albert Alexander, while the lusty voiced Foreign Secretary, Ernest Bevin, provided an inexhaustible repertoire. Towards the end of the night David Hamer hatched a plan which was executed with five RN accomplices. It was to spirit a three-metre Lord Howe Kientia palm to the top of the chapel's high dome. It was an undertaking requiring both ingenuity and alcoholic fortification. The following morning the palm, which as it turned out was the personal property of the Keeper of Greenwich Parks, was plain for all to see, as was its demise in the cold night. The dead plant took much longer to recover gingerly from the roof. As is traditional with such high jinks, the Naval College Commander soon called for the culprits, who duly confessed and received a severe remonstration. But unusually they were then directed to take one of six tightly rolled scrolls which contained their individual punishment. Four had each to obtain botanical information about palms from the gardens at Woking, Reading and Kew. Another had to write an apology to the unappeased Keeper. David Hamer had by chance received the more taxing punishment of having to write a 1,000-word essay on the introduction of palms into England. He achieved this with the willing assistance of the Natural History Museum staff, who may have thought the Navy was once again thinking of sailing to the South Seas in search of rare specimens.

Professionally, the course delved deeper into ballistics and the technical aspects of gunnery than Guy had hitherto experienced. In the first three months the students immersed themselves in maths, physics, chemistry, radar theory as well as the new fields of nuclear, biological and chemical warfare at sea. This involved academic study from which there had been a long wartime hiatus for all course members. Guy found it 'blew the cobwebs from his brain'.[1] Once when he complained to his countryman about this aspect of the course, David Hamer offered to help by breezily rattling off twenty or so formulae one had to remember. In Guy's mind there was no need to guess who was going to top the course.

After the Greenwich primer, instruction commenced in earnest in the hallowed ground of the Gunnery School HMS *Excellent* at Whale Island, Portsmouth. Home to RN gunnery since 1830, it combined gunnery with parade training, which to many were inseparable. Drill and appearance were of high priority. All the students wore white gaiters whilst the instructors wore black. Fortunately for Guy, he was comfortable and confident on the parade ground, which spared him from some of the agonies a few of his classmates experienced. Whale Island exemplified why specialist training for RAN officers was conducted with the RN. Virtually every fire-control system in the Fleet was installed at the School, as well as guns up to 40mm. For larger guns the class would be an assigned a gunnery training ship. This array of training equipment and the required training staff was beyond the RAN's means.*

The sea time was in a cruiser where Guy and other students were assessed in their conduct of surface and anti-air gunnery firings. There were also modules in various army and naval training establishments in southern England. The course allowed plenty of time for sport and Guy played cricket, hockey and rugby as well as taking part in cross-country running and sailing.

Prior to the summer break in the course, one of the staff at Australia House suggested that Guy stay at the Lygon Arms Hotel in the heart of the Cotswolds. The famous establishment still extended free accommodation to Commonwealth servicemen as part of a 'hospitality scheme'. Guy and Canadian classmate Hal Lawrence arrived at the village of Broadway and were soon directed to a grand hotel dating back to the 1300s. Famous

---

* Specialist warfare officers training for RAN officers continued with the RN until 1984. The author attended the last course.

102

guests included King Charles I, Oliver Cromwell and most recently King Edward VIII. The hotel boasted stable-like garages for the wealthy clientele's limousines. Above each garage was accommodation for the chauffeur. It was in these humbler quarters that the Commonwealth servicemen stayed. It was both modest and marvellous at the same time. The manager of the Lygon Arms was an Australian, Douglas Barrington. He had himself been on the Long Gunnery Course in 1945 and benefited from the 'hospitality scheme'. At war's end Barrington left the Navy and secured a position at the hotel. For Guy and Hal, the stay was memorable both for the enjoyable walks in the beautiful countryside but also to the friendliness of locals and guests. The Lygon Arms Hotel was to become Guy's home away from home with Guy and the Barringtons becoming firm friends: so much so that Guy would become godfather to their daughter, Prudence.

In March 1947 the class undertook their final written and practical examinations. Guy passed the course, although both he and his instructors thought he should have done better. He was judged, however, with experience to have the potential to be a first-class gunnery officer. Instead of returning to Australia, Guy was initially offered a two-year exchange position as gunnery officer of a minesweeping squadron based in the Persian Gulf. Guy later reflected that the minesweepers 'had small pop guns and so on, but having served in the tropics for most of World War II, the thought of going to the heat of the Persian Gulf in non-air conditioned ships really didn't attract me'.[2] Instead Guy was appointed to the Gunnery School at HMS *Drake* at Devonport (Plymouth) as the Parade Officer. He stayed at *Drake* until February 1949. Guy earned a reputation as a very smart and capable officer, who was a strict but impartial disciplinarian and who got good results. Personally, Guy found this period of his career to be very happy and it allowed him to explore the West Country while still not aware of his strong familial connections to that part of England.

II

During World War II the potency of aircraft in the war at sea had been repeatedly demonstrated and in 1947 the Australian Government approved the RAN's proposal to acquire two aircraft carriers for the post-war Navy. Fortuitously, the RN had some now surplus light fleet carriers that were in advanced stages of construction. These were offered to Commonwealth and other navies on attractive terms. The two carriers allocated to Australia were the newly commissioned HMS *Terrible* and the yet to be completed *Majestic*. They were to be commissioned into the RAN as *Sydney* and *Melbourne*, respectively.

On completion of his posting at *Drake*, Guy was to join *Sydney*, then based at Devonport in Plymouth, to take passage home as an OOW. When Guy arrived to join the ship, she had just commenced running sea trials in Scottish waters and so he was accommodated in the aircraft carrier *Glory* that had been used as an alongside accommodation ship for *Sydney* personnel. *Sydney* returned to Devonport on 11 April for Guy and the remaining members of the ship's company to join. The ship sailed the following day. As *Sydney* went down the English Channel the air wing flew on to join the ship. It was the 20th Carrier Air Group (CAG) which consisted of Sea Fury fighters (805 Squadron) and Firefly reconnaissance aircraft (816 Squadron). Fifty-two aircraft were embarked and just over half of the pilots were from the RN.

The Commanding Officer of *Sydney* was Captain Roy Dowling who had commanded *Hobart* in the later stages of the war. Guy found among the wardroom some familiar faces. Guy's classmates Audley Parker and Jim Willis were onboard as were Neil McDonald and James 'Red' Merson from the Naval College class above. Some, like Guy, would only remain onboard for the passage home.

Because of the shortage of specialist naval aviation officers and sailors, the RAN recruited 438 former RN personnel, as well as gratefully accepting additional men on loan. One ex-RN sailor had second thoughts and deserted prior to sailing. He was 'replaced' by a stowaway. There was another personal dimension: that of the wives and families. Many of the former RN sailors' families sailed separately to Australia. They were joined via passenger ship by about 150 brides who came had married *Sydney* officers and sailors during their time in the UK.[3]

The passage to Sydney took about a month with the ship transiting the Suez Canal. *Sydney* received warm welcomes in Fremantle and Melbourne. Guy found this passage a fascinating glimpse into the new carrier Navy. Prior to *Sydney*'s arrival in her new home port on 28 May 1949, the ship anchored in Jervis Bay for 'Operation Decanter'. This was to transfer the aircraft and the associated aviation stores by lighter ashore and then onto the nearby new Naval Air Station at Nowra. Guy had spent less than six months in Australia since he graduated from the Naval College in 1940. The unspoilt surrounds were something of a revelation and it made Guy appreciate that as a result of his extensive overseas naval service he had 'lost the feel of the country and its beauty'.[4]

After a short period of leave Guy returned to Flinders Naval Depot (*Cerberus*) to join the staff of the Gunnery School. The Gunnery Officer for whom Guy would work was Lieutenant Commander Tim Synnot; Guy had not really had much contact with him in the Service but he had a fine reputation. Guy was pleased to find some old *Shropshire* sailors among the staff. Training establishments more strictly enforce rules than at other bases. *Cerberus* was no different and Guy had to be one of the benchmarks for drill and discipline as he had been at *Drake*. Guy by now was 26 years old and cut an impressive and, at times, intimidating figure. On one occasion the graduating 1946 Entry midshipmen had just received their injections prior to sailing to the UK to continue their training. Feeling more relaxed they thought they would march, rather than 'double'* along a direct route past the sailors' accommodation block near the parade ground to their quarters. In one of the many arcane rules

---

* Doubling or Double Marching is essentially a moderate jog in step at about 180 paces per minute.

Cerberus seemed to delight in, the road was out of bounds to midshipmen. Out of nowhere came a thundering voice to 'stop that squad'. Across the parade ground was Guy. After counselling the squad leader, Midshipman 'Toz' Dadswell, Guy had him take his squad at the double, back to use the correct route. A sailor serving at *Cerberus*, Seaman Francis Crowley, wrote to Guy over four decades later that,

> Most of us were very nervous about going near your cabin, as we were told that you were a martinet, who read Nelson every night! And a Whale Island Gunnery Man, who was Navy Right Through, and I know that you were, and I am very proud for you, for that. You are and were a 'Real Naval Officer'.[5]

This appreciation was in part echoed by Tim Synnot who thought Guy was a hardworking and promising officer but who required more leadership experience.[6] While Guy's time at the Gunnery School helped his readjustment to Australia, from a professional point of view he really needed to consolidate his specialist gunnery training with a sea posting. Ideally, this would be in a ship with a significant gunnery armament. After just six months ashore Guy returned to sea. Unexpectedly, it was a return to *Sydney*.

Guy joined the flagship on 26 January 1950. She had just begun a work-up with the carrier air group off Jervis Bay. Captain Dowling was in his last three months of command and a new Executive Officer, Commander Victor Albert Trumper Smith, had just joined. 'VAT' Smith came with a considerable reputation. He was an experienced naval aviator, who had led a torpedo attack on the German battlecruiser *Scharnhorst* and been shot down twice in the war.[*] More recently he had also been involved in some of the planning for the new Fleet Air Arm. Of more immediate import to Guy and the other officers was that Smith was a

---

[*] Later Admiral Sir Victor Smith, AC, KBE, CB, DSC, RAN (1913–98). His uncle was the great Australian cricketer Victor Albert Trumper.

serious-minded Executive Officer who was keen to ensure *Sydney* was a taut ship. Among the pilots was Guy's classmate John Goble, who gave Guy his first flight from the carrier in a Firefly.

The duties of a gunnery officer in a light fleet carrier were more than met the eye. These extended beyond being responsible for the ship's gunnery armament of thirty 40mm Bofors. Guy was also responsible for the provision of ammunition stores for the carrier air wing and also kept bridge watches. Gunnery Officers are also responsible for the parading of the ship's guard and other ceremonial matters.* Guy insisted on a very high standard of dress for the flagship's guard to the personal challenge of its members. One of them Petty Officer Bill Ritchie was surprised one day when Guy noted his tie used the Windsor knot, the most symmetrical of tie knots. Guy asked him to teach him how to tie it. Guy's attention to his dress and appearance set the example for others to follow and he always impressed 'the birdies'. Indeed, it was rumoured among the aircrew that Guy changed his immaculate white uniforms three times a day.[7] In turn Guy found his life in an aircraft carrier fascinating. Guy enjoyed the company of the 'birdies' and shared a cabin with the Sea Fury pilot Lieutenant 'Jock' Cunningham. He soon gained insight into the intricacies and the potency of seaborne air power. This reinforced his views on the strategic and tactical advantages of aircraft carriers that he had developed in World War II.

Sydney, after visits to the southern state capitals, undertook along with *Australia,* the destroyers *Warramunga, Bataan* and the frigate *Murchison* a series of very successful port visits and exercises in New Zealand waters with the RNZN. A vivid memory for Guy was the dwarfing of the carrier in the majestic fiord of Milford Sound. Tragically, the cruise also saw the first deaths of *Sydney* ship's company. Three senior sailors died in a vehicle accident involving their jeep near Whangaruru when returning from repairing a diverted aircraft.

---

* Typically, major ships, such as aircraft carriers, would parade a Guard for a ceremonial port entry (normally comprising a Sub-Lieutenant or Lieutenant, a Petty Officer and 12 sailors) or as a Guard of Honour for the formal VIP visit (varied in size but for the Sovereign it comprised 102 officers and sailors).

On 22 April 1950, *Sydney* received a new commanding officer, Guy's old commander from *Shropshire* Captain David 'Darbo' Harries. Since that time Harries had gone on to successfully command *Hobart* and *Australia*. In Guy's assessment, Harries was conservative, competent and a man of few words who soon enjoyed the considerable respect of the ship's company. Some of the officers thought he should smile and drink a bit more. But as Guy remarked, 'he was not that sort of character. He just got on with things.'[8] Harries was exacting and his nickname, 'Darbo', was in reference to a well-known jockey, because Harries was 'always on your back'. Importantly, Harries was a good judge of people and would give them more responsibility if they had the potential to take it. Guy prospered under that approach.[9] 'VAT' Smith's assessment mirrored that of Guy and thought Harries was a first-class Captain who 'understood people far better than they realised and always had the wellbeing of his ship in mind'.[10] Harries would join Tennant and Nichols in Guy's triumvirate of great sea captains. The first major activity under Harries' command was on 7 June when *Sydney* left Australian shores once more to return to the UK to collect the Navy's second Carrier Air Group, the 21st, which was destined for the yet to be completed *Melbourne*.* So for the fifth time in his short naval career Guy took passage to England.

Two weeks after *Sydney* left Australia, the North Korean army invaded South Korea. This came after nearly two years of a generally unsuccessful North Korean-backed insurgency in the south. Within a week Australia was able to offer the destroyer *Bataan* and the frigate *Shoalhaven* to support a hastily assembled United Nations organised force under US leadership. A role in this conflict for the RAN's sole aircraft carrier was not immediately obvious.

On arrival in Portsmouth sixteen aircraft of the new CAG flew over the ship in welcome. *Sydney* spent six weeks working up the air group in UK waters before steaming home. During one of the extended periods

---

* The 21st Carrier Air Group consisted of 808 Squadron (Sea Furies) and 817 Squadron (Fireflies).

alongside Guy and number of officers organised a ski trip to the Austrian resort of Kitzbühel for any members of the ship's company who wanted to try their hand at skiing. To elicit interest Guy gave some ski instruction in *Sydney*'s hangar. The response was enthusiastic and a full bus took the journey to the continent. For most it was their first time on skis. Once at the resort many of the men surprised other skiers with their enthusiasm by practising on their skis in front of the lodge before breakfast. One of the contingent was Lieutenant Arthur 'Nat' Gould, who was formerly in the RAAF during the war. His service included teaching Russians to fly Hurricanes on the Eastern Front. One evening Guy and 'Nat' were having après ski drinks and struck up a convivial conversation with the Austrian barman. 'Nat' and the barman soon worked out that they were both flying fighters on the same part of the front at the same time but on opposite sides. For Guy the 'ski bug' had well and truly bitten. He found skiing both challenging and 'good for the soul' with the week away being a complete break from the Navy. Guy was also convinced of its value to the Navy for it allowed officers and sailors to mix informally and thereby enhance their interrelationship. This, in his view, was much more effective with skiing than with most other sports because the interaction was for a week and not just for the duration of a game.

One of Guy's duties onboard was snotties' nurse. There were five midshipmen, all from the 1946 Entry, who had earned Guy's ire at *Cerberus*. They joined Sydney in inauspicious circumstances. Their train arriving too late for them to join the ship in Plymouth, they had to relocate to Torquay where they finally joined *Sydney*. They soon learnt that Guy, VAT Smith and the Captain had high standards in all things naval, especially punctuality. Whether Guy intended it or not, the midshipmen viewed him with considerable trepidation and generally tried to keep out of his way.

On 26 October *Sydney* sailed from Portsmouth, with the ship returning to Australia in December with fifty-eight aircraft and associated stores which would fully provision the new Fleet Air Arm.

During this deployment Guy and the other members of the ship's company had followed as best they could the deteriorating developments in Korea. Surprisingly, there was an important role for navies. Along the mountainous Korean peninsula the coastal strips on both coasts were the arteries of the divided country. This characteristic enabled naval forces to both support the hastily assembled UN troops and to interdict North Korean forces and supply lines. Over time a naval concept of operations emerged whereby USN and RN aircraft carriers would operate off both coasts while cruisers, destroyers and frigates from a variety of countries would conduct shore bombardments as requested by the army ashore. The role of carrier-borne aircraft would prove particularly important with often quicker response times to support troops than land-based aircraft based from further to the south or in Japan. Initially, the RAN provided a destroyer and a frigate, but by early 1951 the British experienced problems maintaining a continuous presence of a light fleet carrier off Korea. In April 1951 Australia was asked if *Sydney* could fill a gap in coverage and relieve *Glory* from September to January 1952.

On 14 May 1951 a signal was sent ordering the formation of the 'Sydney Carrier Air Group' which, for Korean operations, had three squadrons instead of the usual two.* This would ensure there were sufficient aircraft and aircrew for sustained operations. The CAG would be commanded by the very experienced Commander Mike Fell RN, who had led an attack on the German battleship *Tirpitz* during the war.† Fell greatly impressed Guy not only for his 'smooth as silk' demeanour but for the way he developed the CAG into a high-performance team. Three quarters of the aircrew had World War II experience and they included three fighter 'aces'.[11] The work-up of the ship and her air group began in July off Jervis Bay, but due to the adverse weather was moved north to Hervey Bay. For Guy, the preparations and work-up had been particularly hectic in ensuring the diverse array of air ordnance was embarked.

---

* The Sydney Carrier Air Group consisted of 805, 808 & 817 Squadrons.
† Later Vice Admiral Sir Michael Fell KCB, DSO, DSC and bar (1918–76).

The Naval Campaign in the Korean War

CHINA

Yalu River

Island of Yang-Do

NORTH
KOREA

Yang Do

*SEA
OF
JAPAN*

Wonsan

Pyongyang

Ch'o Do • Sariwon

Wollae Do

Yangyang

38°N

Seoul

Inchon

*YELLOW
SEA*

YongDoc

SOUTH
KOREA

Pusan

III

Sydney sailed for Korea in company with the destroyer *Tobruk* on 31 August 1951. The ships went via New Guinea where a flight flew over Rabaul at the request of local authorities, as the township had been subject to recent civil unrest. The passage was punctuated with a regular flying program to maintain proficiency, whilst Guy organised aircraft to tow sleeve targets to practise his 40mm gun crews. These activities did not go without mishap and one Sea Fury ditched as a result of engine failure whilst a sailor fell overboard from a gun sponson. Fortunately, both pilot and sailor were recovered.

During the passage Guy and fellow ski enthusiasts Lieutenant Commanders Geoff Hood and Philip Stevenson met in Guy's cabin to discuss how to foster the sport in the Navy. They concluded that on return to Australia they should explore the idea of creating a Navy ski club and perhaps most ambitiously, build a Navy ski lodge at one of the country's fledgling ski fields.

Both ships arrived earlier than planned in Yokosuka on 19 September because of the desire to take on fuel and be ready to return to sea in the unsettled typhoon season. They were greeted by a comically dressed USN band and half a dozen geisha girls in a small boat. During the short visit, Guy and other members of the ship's company had the opportunity to tour nearby Tokyo which was starting to recover from its wartime ordeal.

Yokosuka was not to be *Sydney*'s base for operations, however, and the ships sailed on to Kure. On 27 September *Sydney* and *Tobruk* arrived and immediately commenced busy handovers with *Glory* and *Anzac* respectively. Conveniently, the aircraft carriers were berthed either side of a floating pontoon. This helped facilitate the transfer of items ranging from aircraft to stores as well as the interchange between the men. Once the handovers were complete, *Glory* and *Anzac* sailed for Sydney and much needed refits. An important addition for *Sydney* was a USN Dragonfly helicopter complete with aircrew for search and rescue duties.

Also in Kure was the aircraft maintenance carrier *Unicorn* wearing the flag of Flag Officer Second-in-Command, Far East Station, Rear Admiral Alan Scott-Moncrieff.* Arriving later that day was the Commander-in-Chief Far East Station, Vice Admiral Sir Guy Russell.† Captain Harries called on both admirals. Significantly, Scott-Moncrieff also commanded the UN Task Group of which the Australian ships would be part. The British concept of operations was for *Unicorn* to station herself in either Kure or Sasebo to await the Commonwealth light fleet carrier. Damaged aircraft could be transferred to *Unicorn* for repair and spare aircraft were also kept to replace any lost aircraft. It proved an excellent arrangement.

The routine for the light fleet carriers was to conduct thirteen-day patrols off the Korean coast. This would include two days transit and another day midway through the patrol for fuel and ammunition resupply at sea. *Sydney* would eventually conduct seven such patrols. Her aircraft would be used offensively to interdict road, rail and sea transport which included destroying tunnels and bridges. They were also to provide spotting information for ships conducting shore bombardment as well as undertaking photo reconnaissance. *Sydney*'s patrols were synchronised with the American escort carrier USS *Rendova*‡ to ensure one of the carriers was always on task.

The first patrol was off Korea's east coast and commenced on 4 October. It soon gave *Sydney* a flavour of the operations. One aspect of the UN mandated force was its multinational composition and there were warships from the British, Canadian, Dutch, New Zealand and US navies in the formation. Among the latter was the battleship *New Jersey*. *Sydney*'s aircraft launched forty-seven sorties on the first day and they varied from defensive patrols, bombardment spotting for *New Jersey* and air attacks on enemy positions. In coming days there were further such sorties, as well as attacks on North Korean junks operating inshore. Some

---

*   Later Admiral Sir Alan Scott-Moncrieff, KCB, CBE, DSO and bar, (1900–80).

†   Later Admiral Hon. Sir Guy Russell GBE, KCB, CB, CBE, DSC (1898–1977).

‡   Later replaced by the escort carrier USS *Badoeng Strait*.

of shore targets were identified by a small commando group codenamed 'Kirkman' operating southeast of Wonsan. The sorties were often in the face of enemy flak and sixteen aircraft were hit by ground fire with one Sea Fury having to ditch on 5 October.

As the tempo and *Sydney's* efficiency grew it was not unusual for the ship to launch around fifty to sixty sorties in a day. This translated as a very busy time for Guy's air armament supply parties who had to arm the aircraft with bombs, rocket and cannon ammunition. In the first twenty days of flying they provided over 520 bombs, 4,100 rockets and 260,000 cannon rounds.[12] Fortunately, Guy was blessed with a keen and motivated group of sailors, ably led by very experienced former RN air ordnance warrant officers, Bill Baylis and 'Chuck' Churcher.

At the end of her successful first patrol *Sydney* entered Sasebo. Not long into the visit Typhoon Ruth bore down on the harbour. The ship and its aircraft were secured as much as was possible in the face of this severe storm. Although Sasebo had been rated a typhoon anchorage by the old Imperial Japanese Navy, the port was not devoid of potential dangers. The anchorage was crowded and not all ships were able to secure to typhoon-proof buoys. There was a risk that even if *Sydney* rode out the storm, other ships would break free from their buoys or drag their anchors and collide with her. Therefore at about 1500 on 14 October Captain Harries decided to take *Sydney* to sea.

Harries and his navigator, Commander Hinton Shand, RN skilfully threaded their way through the harbour and then proceeded out to sea. By the time Guy took over as OOW for the First Watch (2000–2359) *Sydney* was in mountainous seas which were streaked with foam. At times, when *Sydney* was in a trough the crest of the next wave was at the height of the bridge. To minimise damage Harries adjusted course so the ship kept the swell on the starboard bow. Frequently, water swept down the flight deck from larger waves. Guy was impressed with the calmness and teamwork displayed by Harries and Shand.

Despite the heavy lashings that secured the aircraft on the flight deck, the waves still washed some aircraft overboard and heavily damaged others. Winds neared 200 km/hr at the storm's peak. Sea and rainwater flooded into the ship and there were a few small electrical fires that were quickly extinguished. The Dutch destroyer *Van Galen* and the Canadian *Sioux* had also proceeded to sea. *Van Galen* in particular took a fearful battering in the heavy seas and remained close by *Sydney* in case she did not ride out the storm. The eye of Typhoon Ruth passed over the area in the early hours of 15 October and that afternoon a battered *Sydney* returned to a devastated Sasebo. In port a dozen ships had been driven ashore or sunk and 200 people died. Nationally, Typhoon Ruth killed 1,294 people and destroyed 34,000 buildings. Captain Harries later observed that 'this typhoon was a most unpleasant and unforgettable experience which I have no desire to repeat'.[13]

After repairing storm damage, *Sydney* commenced her second patrol on 18 October. This time it was on the west coast and with an increased intensity. Once again some targets were identified by a clandestine commando unit, in this case codenamed 'Leopard'. By this time the aircrew had learnt to adapt their attack techniques and soon became adept at placing bombs into tunnels and at the key structural points of bridges. The sorties were not without loss and in two days, 25–26 October, three aircraft were lost to enemy flak. Fortunately, the first Sea Fury pilot, Lieutenant Colin Wheatley, was soon picked up by a helicopter. The second Sea Fury pilot, Sub-Lieutenant Noel Knappstein, crash landed on a Han River mudflat and enterprisingly sold his aircraft to local villagers before being rescued by the frigate *Amethyst*. The last of the trio, a Firefly, was downed by flak when attacking a tunnel near Sariwon on 26 October. The aircrew avoided capture and *Sydney's* Dragonfly helicopter was despatched to conduct the hazardous rescue at dusk. It was a near thing in many ways with a North Korean soldier being killed by the helicopter aircrew just as the downed aviators were taken onboard.

Not all were so lucky. On 5 November 805 Squadron's senior pilot, Lieutenant Keith 'Nails' Clarkson, was lost when his Sea Fury failed to recover from a dive when hit by flak. During the deployment *Sydney* had been conducting a radio telephone trial with Overseas Telecommunications, which enabled telephone calls at sea. Captain Harries had authorised aircrew to make such calls home to sustain their morale and Clarkson had only spoken to his wife the night before his death.

On 7 December, five other aircraft were hit by flak; three managed to return safely, one crash landed with the pilot rescued, but less fortunate was Sub-Lieutenant Dick Sinclair. His Sea Fury took an enemy round in the oil cooler that soon started a fire as he sped from the coast. He was killed when his head struck the tail fin while bailing out of his burning aircraft. The dangers of flying were brought home to *Sydney*'s ship's company when Sinclair's body was recovered onboard and he was later buried at sea in a moving ceremony on the snow-dusted flight deck. Guy greatly admired the skill, courage and morale of the aviators, particularly in the face of the determined ground fire and mounting losses. He also considered that Commander Fell magnificently led them through these travails.

During her penultimate patrol, *Sydney*'s aircraft conducted determined sorties to cover the evacuation of ninety hard-pressed 'Leopards' from Yong Do.* The following day, 2 January, Sub-Lieutenant Ron Coleman in a Sea Fury was lost when his aircraft became separated from a formation over the Yellow Sea. Three days later, Lieutenant Peter Goldrick was able to land his flak-damaged Sea Fury on *Sydney*'s deck despite a .303 bullet wound to his right arm. In perhaps a reflection on the bureaucracy of the day, Navy Office decided to cease Goldrick's flying pay as he was temporarily unfit to fly. To the satisfaction on all onboard *Sydney*, Harries successfully had this dull-headed decision overturned.

Sydney returned to Kure on 9 January. This port visit allowed Guy and five other ski enthusiasts the opportunity to travel 150 kilometres from the port to Dōgoyama Kogen, a small and undeveloped ski-field.

---

* 'Do' translates from Korean as 'island'.

Dōgoyama more than made up for its limitations with regular dumps of powder snow as weather fronts came across from Siberia.

In her last patrol, *Sydney* experienced the grimness of the Korean winter with snow and ice covering exposed aircraft and ship's fittings. On some days flying was impossible due to gales or snowstorms. In the breaks in weather sorties were conducted against North Korea's infrastructure, with ten aircraft receiving flak damage in return for their efforts. During all these patrols a portion of *Sydney*'s 40mm armament was manned. In the wintery conditions, for those assigned to the mounts it was an arduous and thankless duty. This was particularly so as the Navy had very poor cold-weather clothing. As one aviation sailor said, 'they (the gun crews) were the people we really felt for'.[14] For his part Guy, wherever possible, had an aircraft tow a sleeve target to practise their proficiency in the unlikely situation of an air attack when offshore. Fittingly, one of *Sydney*'s last missions was to provide spotting information to *New Jersey*, which was also leaving the Korean theatre. The last day of flying was on 25 January, with *Sydney* handing over to *Badoeng Strait*.

Sydney's Korean deployment was a successful one and the sole one by an Australian aircraft carrier in war. In 64 days on station her aircraft flew 2,366 sorties and in one 24-hour period she flew 89 sorties, which was a record for a light fleet aircraft carrier. The work rate was high for all onboard when on patrol. Most pilots were flying two sorties a day and nearly 40% of the aircraft returned unserviceable, placing great strain on the maintenance crews. In the end *Sydney* suffered 3 pilots killed and 10 aircraft lost with aircraft hit by flak on 99 occasions. *Sydney* had, however, significantly disrupted the movement of North Korean forces as well as supporting UN troops on the ground. Of his service in *Sydney* during the Korean War, Guy later recalled,

> ... it was good to be able to see this actually in action and how it operated and learn about the whole business of air power at sea. Well perhaps not the whole business, but our

capability such as we did have with our relatively small 20,000-ton aircraft carrier. But the pilots demonstrated great courage and professionalism.

On return to Australia and on leaving *Sydney*, Captain Harries wrote that Guy was 'quite definitely an outstanding officer'. He went on to write that Guy 'had maintained a high degree of enthusiasm with the gunnery department, a feat not easily achieved in a light fleet carrier … I shall be disappointed if he does not reach the higher ranks of the Service.'[15]

IV

After Guy's service in *Sydney* he returned once more to *Cerberus,* joining on 13 March 1952, this time as the deputy at the Gunnery School. Importantly, Guy was automatically promoted to the rank of Lieutenant Commander on 1 June, on reaching eight years seniority as a Lieutenant. His career aspiration at this point was, having attained his specialisation, to further consolidate at sea and then be competitive for promotion to Commander. Most of the sea commands in the Fleet were for officers of Commander rank and a successful 'drive' was a prerequisite to further advancement.

Guy was destined to serve at the Gunnery School until the end of November and in that time the Officer in Charge witnessed the rejuvenation of the school under Guy's 'boundless energy'.[16] Guy achieved this in part by being able to increasingly harness the strengths of the staff and mitigate where their weaknesses lay. Sport continued to play an important part in Guy's life. Significantly, in that year a meeting was held in Navy Office in Melbourne of those interested in creating a RAN Ski Club. The response was very positive and Guy became one of the six committee members 'to gather together all those in the Navy who have skied at one time or another, or who are interested in skiing in the future, for the mutual benefit and for the encouragement of skiing as a Naval sport.'[17] It was envisaged that club members would not only ski in Australia and in New Zealand but, on the Korean War veterans' recommendations, in Japan.[*] The following year a Commonwealth Navy Order formally promulgated the RAN Ski Club.[18] The slow search also began for a suitable site at a ski field where they hoped to erect a rudimentary prefabricated lodge.

The overhaul of the Gunnery School was timely, with the first post-World War II gunnery systems entering the Fleet in the new Battle class destroyers. Guy had continued to press for a sea posting in a ship with a substantial gun armament and his opportunity finally arrived when he was selected to replace Lieutenant Andrew Robertson, the Gunnery Officer of the lead ship of the Battle class, *Anzac*. She was then on active service off the Korean coast as part of the United Nations Blockade and Escort Force.

On 26 November 1952 Guy joined *Anzac* in Kure, where the ship was undertaking maintenance and a welcome break from her duties. The destroyer was the Squadron Leader and in command was Captain Galfrey Gatacre.[†] 'Gats' was famed in the Navy for being the navigating officer of the battleship *Rodney* when she took part in the sinking of *Bismarck*. A quietly spoken and highly professional captain, he ran a happy and hard-working ship. The wardroom had fourteen officers, among them was the Navigating Officer, Lieutenant Peter Doyle, with whom Guy would have to work closely when conducting shore bombardments.

Anzac had been deployed for three months and had settled into the operational tempo of the war. Her most notable action, which attracted global press coverage, was on 16 November, while at anchor protecting the Ch'o Do garrison, *Anzac* was fired upon by four 76mm mountain guns.[19] The guns, then 12,000 yards distant, were sited in caves, and in their third salvo had rounds falling around *Anzac*. In this perilous situation *Anzac*

---

[*]   Since that time the RAN Ski Club have frequently sent groups to ski in Japan.

[†]   Later Rear Admiral G.G.O. Gatacre, CBE, DSO, DSC & Bar, RAN (1907–83).

quickly slipped her cable leaving a buoy marking the anchor. Nearby shoals prevented *Anzac*'s quick seaward escape. Fortunately, in a spirited fight *Anzac*'s guns found the caves' entrances and the smoke and dust partly obscured *Anzac* from the North Koreans' view. A running duel ensued for nearly half an hour with *Anzac* firing 174 rounds with 50 enemy shells falling around the ship. Eventually, the shore guns were silenced but not before *Anzac*'s anchor buoy had been hit and sunk.[*]

The ship's company had recently been informed that *Anzac* would not be relieved until June 1953 and had adjusted reasonably well to the news. The following day the Minister for the Navy, William McMahon, visited the ship and later that afternoon *Anzac*, and the Dutch destroyer *Piet Hein,* sailed for their next patrol. In a freshening gale they rendezvoused on the west coast with *Glory* who was escorted by the US destroyer *Hickox.*

Guy found a gunnery department seasoned with World War II veterans. His Commissioned Gunner was Geoffrey 'Snow' Gafford. He had been part of the commissioning crew of the World War II cruiser *Sydney* and had been in her during her brilliant Mediterranean exploits. Such experienced personnel were to prove important for Guy. The original British Battle class was the final word in World War II design. But the RAN had decided to incorporate the more modern Mk.VI 4.5-inch gun turrets, the new Flyplane II fire control system, and the advanced 40mm STAAG mountings with their integrated radar systems. On paper the RAN Battles were very impressive ships and indeed they were when everything worked. But on a bad day they were diabolical. To complicate matters the manuals and other documentation were initially scanty or non-existent. Fortunately, the resourceful David Hamer was the commissioning Gunnery Officer of *Anzac*'s sister-ship *Tobruk* and he had written some of the missing manuals to the benefit of both ships. Guy later remarked,

---

[*]   Lieutenant Robertson was deservedly awarded the Distinguished Service Cross
     for this action.

119

The whole thing as a gunnery system was unreliable and relatively ineffective. We did bombardments and that was OK but we were fortunately never required in an air defence role and in those days one kept looking back at the experience you've had for a couple of years alongside the Americans in 1944–1945, when they were using their Mark 37 system and their single and twin 5-inch turrets. The accuracy of their fire and their output and their apparent reliability seemed very good. There we were in early 1950s, six years after the war with a new system which gave a lesser result.[20]

Guy soon saw action in *Anzac*. On 30 November the destroyer engaged enemy troops on the mainland who were suspected of preparing for an assault on the garrison on Sunwi Do. On completion the destroyer returned to *Glory*'s protective screen. Four days later *Anzac* engaged enemy troops north of Wollae Do. During all this the weather was near freezing, with gales and snowstorms. A welcome break in the routine was a week-long assignment with the inshore forces from 7 December, which generally involved evening bombardments of enemy positions. The ship then proceeded to Kure for maintenance and crew rest. The return to Korean waters soon reminded Guy of the harshness of the Korean winter he had experienced in *Sydney*. This was accentuated by the *Anzac* having an open bridge. Guy would later write,

Passing weather fronts invariably brought sleet and snow falls on both the west and east coast, and on the open bridge of the destroyer I clearly recollect that on the New Year's dawn the temperature was 8°F (−13°C).[21]

In conducting inshore operations in winter it was not uncommon to operate among pancake ice flows. Although the RAN's involvement in the war was in its second year, it had yet to issue adequate cold-weather

120

clothing. As a result crew members would wear a range of apparel with the thick US Army jackets the most prized. In terms of their diet, if it got particularly cold then the men were entitled to an issue of sardines and malted milk tablets. Guy would later assess it was the open bridge and the inadequate cold-weather clothing that were the greatest challenges of the deployment.[22]

Following the Kure port visit *Anzac* was reassigned to inshore operations on the east coast in the vicinity of Yang Do. A task unit of four, mainly American destroyers, was assigned to the area to prevent an invasion of the UN-held island and interdict the enemy supply lines on the mainland as well as to engage troop concentrations or artillery. As the US destroyers were commanded by officers of commander rank, *Anzac* was senior ship of the task unit.

Rear Admiral John Gingrich, USN* was in overall command of east coast operations and had been in the post for about six months. In that time he had addressed the tensions existing between his predecessor and his subordinate commanders, over the manner of the blockade and shore bombardment tactics. Gingrich placed greater priority on bombardments being observed by spotters and not conducted 'blindly'. This cut ammunition expenditure by half and reduced wear and tear on ships. Perhaps because of *Anzac*'s recent exploits, Gingrich impressed on Gatacre that his valuable destroyer was not to enter into any duels with mountain guns.

Anzac found operations with the US force a very different and 'refreshing' experience.[23] She joined three US destroyers, *McNair*, *The Sullivans* and *Evansville* who had to date interdicted some trains along the coastal rail-line. The threats to the ships could come from either North Korean aircraft, sea mines or the very numerous and active shore batteries. Christmas Day 1952 was spent at sea and the long refuelling evolution with *Mispillion* was given a festive air with Christmas carols being played on the tanker's loudspeakers.

---

*   Later Admiral J.E. Gingrich USN (1897–1960).

Once again at the end of this patrol *Anzac* proceeded into Kure for maintenance. As a break from the ship, personnel could avail themselves of either the Australian Army rest camp or USN facilities ashore. There were also waterfront bars, the traditional sailors' haunt. As a gauge of their popularity in the first six months of the deployment, 114 of *Anzac*'s 265 sailors had contracted some form of venereal disease.* This was not an abnormal proportion for deployed RAN ships at the time. *Tobruk*'s subsequent deployment for example had 155 cases[24] and Captain Harries had earlier lamented about *Sydney*'s high incidence that,

> I am convinced that nothing was left undone, either by disciplinary action within the regulations, education or exhortation, both ecclesiastical and secular, to reduce the incidence of Venereal Disease ... Unless there is a radical change for the better in the attitude of the Australian Sailor to promiscuous sexual intercourse and his light-hearted view of VD, the incidence of this scourge will, I fear, remain high in HMA Ships away from home waters.[25]

In her next patrol *Anzac* returned to the west coast and mixed screening *Glory* with bombardments of enemy positions. Often the spotting of *Anzac*'s fall of shot was undertaken by one of *Glory*'s aircraft. At times the extent of the coastal ice floes precluded destroyers getting close enough to conduct their fire support mission. During the patrol, ships cycled in and out of the formation and this included *Glory* which was replaced by the US aircraft carrier *Bataan*.

Whenever possible, Guy tried to organise anti-aircraft practices using a sleeve target towed by one of the carriers' aircraft. Over time he detected a flaw in the gunnery fire control system which gave inaccurate

---

* The total for the ten-month deployment would eventually be 204 cases of venereal disease of which 64 cases were repeat infections. These statistics were routinely reported in ships' monthly *Reports of Proceedings*. In some larger RAN and RN ships on deployment there would be a designated 'VD mess deck' for afflicted sailors to be temporarily accommodated.

ranging solutions. *Anzac*'s gunnery system was typical of increasingly complex equipment entering the Fleet. The delineation between the gunnery and the electrical departments had to break down if these complex systems were to be properly maintained and defects resolved. It was in this context that Guy encouraged the bridging of this gap between the two departments onboard to good effect. Fortunately for bombardments *Anzac*'s surface gunnery capability was unimpaired. On 16 March she was tasked to engage an enemy artillery battery on the mainland which was firing on friendly forces on Mu Do. The destroyer closed the coast at high speed and in the subsequent bombardment fired nine rounds which silenced the enemy.

On *Anzac*'s return to Kure on 5 March 1953, awaiting her was a new commanding officer. Captain Gatacre was to become the Australian Naval Attaché in Washington DC, and his relief was Captain 'Black Jack' Mesley. Guy had served with Mesley in *Shropshire* in the later stages of World War II. Relieving a captain during an operational deployment is not usual but it was, in part, necessitated by *Anzac*'s extended deployment. In Gatacre's final *Report of Proceedings* on leaving *Anzac*, he made the following observations that well captured the view of the naval war off Korea in the context of the Cold War,

> The experience of having taken part in naval operations in the Korean theatre is undoubtedly invaluable for officers and men. It provides an excellent, up-to-date, personal and unit operational training in many of the functions of naval forces in total, global war. It is of inestimable value that service in the Korean theatre affords the experience of being completely integrated with the units and forces of many members of the United Nations Organization. Of greatest value to more senior officers particularly, must be the friendships made with officers in the navies of the other nations of about one's own seniority. Those friendship will

always be ready to ripen with further association and could be a guarantee of harmony in the concept and execution of future operations by United Nations naval forces.[26]

In the case of Guy's future sea commands Gatacre's words were to prove only too true. The next patrol from 10–23 April was uneventful, with *Anzac* operating in the screen of the carriers *Bataan* and then *Glory*. This was a particularly useful settling-in period for the new captain. The highlight of the patrol was having the new Commander-in-Chief Far East Station, Vice Admiral Sir Charles Lambe* embarked for a day to view *Anzac* at sea.

After a welcome visit to Hong Kong, the next patrol, 12–26 May, was once again to join and command four US destroyers to defend the garrison on Yang Do and interdict enemy supply routes on the mainland. Early on Guy went ashore at Yang Do and spoke to the garrison commander who thought an invasion of the island was unlikely. Whenever a ship was assigned as the Yang Do guard ship she would watch for any small boat traffic and at night periodically fire starshell over the strait. During these periods off Yang Do *Anzac* bombarded enemy troop concentrations, and with the help of intelligence from the garrison, engaged enemy gun emplacements and caves. *Anzac* also unsuccessfully tried to bag a train coming out of a tunnel. As if to emphasise the dangers of operating inshore, Guy's 40mm gun crews also sank two floating mines.

During the patrol another incident occurred which demonstrated to Guy the hazards of sea command. On the evening of 19 May, *Bradford* closed a small contact steaming towards Yang Do. There was fog and *Bradford* called the unknown vessel on radio. Although a friendly sampan had been tracked leaving Yang Do earlier in the day and was thought still to be in the general area, *Bradford* did not receive a reply from the incoming craft and assessed it an enemy. *Bradford* opened fire and duly sank the craft. In the morning the survivors picked up by *Shelton* revealed that the

---

* Later Admiral of the Fleet Sir Charles Lambe, GCB, CVO (1900–60).

sampan was manned by South Korean soldiers who were returning to Yang Do with two captured North Korean soldiers. Nineteen men were killed in the incident. Captain Mesley held an investigation onboard *Anzac* the following day and he later wrote that the tragedy 'occasioned much thought and considerable worry to all Commanding Officers'.[27]

In a welcome break before *Anzac*'s final patrol the ship was sent to Tokyo to join the frigate HMS *Mounts Bay* for a four-day port visit to celebrate the coronation of Queen Elizabeth II. The two ships provided the physical facilities and personnel to raise the profile of the ascension to the Japanese government and public. Guy recalls successive ship tours and an endless round of social events by the Commonwealth diplomatic representatives and their Japanese hosts. This included an impromptu event by the New Zealand Legation to celebrate Sir Edmund Hillary's scaling of Mount Everest. After this successful visit *Anzac* sailed first to Kure and then Sasebo to materially prepare for a patrol off the west coast.

On 8 June *Anzac* sailed from Sasebo in company with newly joined aircraft carrier HMS *Ocean*. Once again the destroyer alternated between screening the carrier and patrolling inshore. Whilst operations continued with little variation, Armistice talks were known to be underway. Four days into the patrol *Anzac* undertook an unusual jackstay transfer with *Ocean*. It was for one of the carrier's sailors whose transfer to the RAN had just been approved. As the Armistice talks neared their end the British depot ship *Tyne* joined the force to help in the evacuation of UN held islands that would be returned to North Korean control. It was a daunting task involving nearly 40,000 people, but one in which *Anzac* would not take part as her time in Korean waters was up.* The ship left the UN Task Group therefore with mixed feelings. Her ship's company was happy to be finally heading for home but, as Captain Mesley wrote, *Anzac* was 'sorry we could not be there to finish the job in which we have taken an active part for the past nine months.'[28]

---

* The evacuation of thirteen islands between Paengyong Do & Yongpyong Do would involve the evacuation of 600 US, 1,500 ROK marines, 14,450 partisans and 24,000 refugees.

To prepare for the homeward voyage *Anzac* had one last port visit to Hong Kong. It was for a week and importantly it gave 'Jenny' and her side party the opportunity to repaint the ship. Jenny* and her younger competitor 'Suzie' were Hong Kong institutions. Their traditionally clad women would, from sampans, repaint ships' sides with brushes tied to bamboo poles, touch up the superstructure as well as selling various wares for the recompense of old rope and spent brass ammunition cartridges. The Executive Officer, the Gunnery Officer and their key senior sailors would negotiate the terms. Certain rituals were observed. On the ship's arrival Jenny and her girls would line up on the wharf with flowers for the captain. Newspapers would appear daily for the captain and the wardroom and at the end of the day Jenny would be driven to the naval base gate in the captain's car. The traditional ship's company photograph in Hong Kong would always have Jenny sitting next to the Captain. Over the years Jenny would follow the careers of many Commonwealth naval officers and Guy became one of those officers known to her. When the now refreshed and resplendent *Anzac* left Hong Kong a traditional firecracker farewell emanated from one of Jenny's sampans to ward off any evil spirits.

Anzac returned to Sydney on 3 July. Her nearly ten-month deployment was the longest for a Commonwealth warship in the Korean War. The following week the ship proceeded to Williamstown for a much-needed refit and progressive leave for the ship's company. In mid-September *Anzac* came out of dock and commenced a shakedown. The complex gunnery systems took Guy, his team and the dockyard staff considerable time to properly set to work. *Anzac* rejoined a Fleet, which for a unique window of time, had two operational aircraft carriers. Due to the delays in completing *Melbourne* the RN had temporarily loaned *Vengeance* which was commissioned into the RAN. *Anzac* had the opportunity to operate with both carriers off the Queensland coast. On 29 September forty aircraft from both carriers flew over Brisbane. Unbeknownst at the time,

---

* 'Jenny' was Mrs Ng Muk Kah, BEM (1917–2009).

it was the high-water mark for the Fleet Air Arm.

In early January 1954 Guy ended his posting in *Anzac*. He had become a capable and operationally experienced gunnery officer. Captain Mesley assessed that Guy was destined for early promotion to Commander. He had been concerned that Guy in dealing with subordinates had sometimes delivered criticism in a potentially destructive way. It was something he counselled Guy about and which the latter took onboard.

V

Guy's next sea appointment was to be gunnery officer of the much-awaited new aircraft carrier *Melbourne*. He was not destined to join the ship until November 1956. In the first instance Guy spent the remainder of January 1954 at *Albatross* and trained the Royal Guard for the visit of Queen Elizabeth in the following month. Guy then took passage in the P&O liner *Orion* for the UK where initially he, for the third time, would attend the Greenwich Naval College, on this occasion for the Royal Naval Staff Course.

The staff course was specifically designed to train officers to work in the Admiralty and on the staff of flag officers. Equally importantly the course broadened the minds of the lieutenant commanders and commanders who had spent the vast bulk of their career at sea. In Guy's case eight of thirteen years had been spent in ships since leaving the Naval College. Unlike the year-long army and air force courses, the RN staff course was only six months. This in part reflected the Navy's ambivalence to staff duties and that the course was not seen as a prerequisite for command. There were about forty students on the courses which typically included a smattering of British Army, Royal Air Force, Admiralty civil servants and a couple of RAN officers. A strength of the course was its emphasis on logically and analytically tackling problems and articulating recommended courses of action. Amongst the requirements was for the students to give thirty-minute presentations on various subjects. To Guy it was remarkable that it had taken so long in his career to be given this type of training and experience.

For Guy the staff course was a highlight of this phase of his naval career. The Director of the Staff College was the intelligent but prickly Captain David Luce,* whom Guy did not impress. He would have dealings with Luce later in his career. Guy found the studies both challenging and rewarding. He felt, however, that the course was increasingly less relevant to the RAN, which was now focused operations in the Pacific and working with the USN. In addition, only a handful of RAN officers received the benefit of the staff training each year, and Guy felt that an indigenous course was required, as was conducted by the Australian Army.

After a series of tactical and refresher courses, on 10 May 1955, Guy finally joined the stand-by crew of the Navy's newest aircraft carrier which was still known as *Majestic*. The vessel was then fitting out at the Vickers Shipyard in Barrow-in-Furness. The commissioning commanding officer was Guy's former captain of *Anzac*, Galfrey Gatacre. Guy was appointed as the Gunnery Officer and would also be the Assistant to the Executive Officer, who was Commander W.F. 'Bill' Cook. The main influx of ship's company came on 26 October when 600 officers and sailors arrived from *Vengeance* which had earlier returned to Portsmouth. She had reverted to the RN the previous day.

The Korean War demonstrated the stark performance differences between jet and propeller-driven fighter aircraft. Henceforth if the RAN was to possess aircraft carriers they had to be equipped with jet fighters. For some time the feasibility of modifying the two ships to embark jets hung in the balance. But by 1952 plans were finalised for *Melbourne* to receive the required angled flight deck, steam catapult and a mirror landing system. The angled deck allowed the faster jet aircraft to land without the risk of hitting aircraft about to launch on the catapult. The steam catapult gave the extra acceleration and power required for heavier and faster jet aircraft, while the mirror landing system provided a visual

---

* Later Admiral Sir David Luce, GCB, DSO & Bar, OBE (1906–71).

glide slope to assist pilots landing on deck. The plan was for *Melbourne* to enter service with these features and then *Sydney* would be retrofitted. While small for a carrier, *Melbourne* would be the world's first operational carrier to incorporate all three technical innovations. There were other advances that improved habitability such as being fitted with bunks rather than hammocks. Guy felt that all these advances gave *Melbourne* a modern feel.

The air group for *Melbourne* signified a shift towards the Cold War focus of anti-submarine warfare (ASW) rather than the offensive strike emphasis with *Sydney*. *Melbourne* would normally embark Sea Venom jet fighters to provide air defence of the fleet, 12 Gannet ASW aircraft plus a pair of Sycamore utility helicopters.*

On 28 October 1955 a renaming ceremony was held onboard *Melbourne* in Barrow-in-Furness. It was in the presence of the Australian High Commissioner, Sir Thomas and Lady White, the Second Sea Lord, Admiral Sir Charles Lambe and dignitaries that included the former First Naval Member and champion of aircraft carriers, Admiral Sir Louis Hamilton, and the future Governor of NSW, Roden Cutler, VC. In bleak weather the ceremony was held in the hangar and Guy commanded the guard.

For the next five months *Melbourne* and her CAG worked up off the British and French coasts, interspersed with a variety of port visits. The ship soon established a fine reputation. Guy took twenty-three officers and sailors to Hochsölden in the Austrian Tirol for ten days skiing. As with his expedition from *Sydney* it introduced many to the snow and the sport. Towards the end of the work-up *Melbourne* was visited in Portsmouth by the Duke of Edinburgh. He piloted a Whirlwind helicopter from Buckingham Palace to *Melbourne*'s flight deck and wore his RAN Admiral of the Fleet uniform for the first time.[29]

The early years of jet aircraft were to prove particularly dangerous

---

* Unusually for an aircraft carrier *Melbourne* was initially equipped with a hull-mounted sonar.

ones. This was soon brought home to *Melbourne* when one of its Sea Venoms clipped a house chimney while taking off at the Royal Naval Air Station Yeovilton. It crashed into a caravan killing the two aircrew as well as a mother and child. On 14 March *Melbourne* finally sailed from Greenock bound for Australia. The ship had embarked 39 Sea Venoms and 34 Gannets for the passage. They were tightly packed in the hangar and on the flight deck.

During the first leg of the passage, when off Cape St Vincent, the P&O Liner *Iberia*, with seventy *Melbourne* wives and families embarked, steamed close by the aircraft carrier for them to get an excellent view of *Melbourne* at sea. Ten days later *Melbourne* called into Naples to a warm welcome. A gala performance of the opera *Lucia di Lammermoor* was given in the ship's honour by the San Carlo Opera with the diva Maria Callas singing the leading role. Later 200 officers and sailors visited the Vatican and had an audience with Pope Pius XII. He told them that as seafaring men they went about the world seeing many lands, visiting many places and meeting many different peoples. This experience should have bred in them a breadth of vision and understanding which should transcend all petty jealousies, quarrels and misunderstandings.

The passage through the Suez Canal and the Red Sea was particularly hot and uncomfortable in the crowded ship with the two aircraft lifts the only open space for recreation. It was much worse for the engineers who manned the boiler and engine spaces. One stoker, Harry Lys, was carried out of the spaces unconscious with a temperature of nearly 42°C. He died three days later when the ship reached Colombo. Guy oversaw the ceremonial arrangements for Lys's burial in Kamate Cemetery, which over 200 members of the ship's company attended.

Even as *Melbourne* steamed towards Australia there were discussions within the senior Government and Defence echelons about the viability of RAN aircraft carriers in the face of budget cuts and the continued advances in aircraft technology that a small aircraft carrier would have less facility to accommodate. The decision not to modernise the *Sydney* reflected Defence's priorities. Guy felt that there was also the absence of a careful study of the strategic environment in which Australia was situated.[30] Periodic uncertainties about *Melbourne*'s future would haunt the ship for her entire career.

Melbourne arrived in Fremantle on 23 April 1956 to be greeted by one of the largest crowds seen in the port. *The West Australian* announced that it was 'A proud moment in our naval history' and that the *Melbourne* 'is the most modern fighting ship it is possible to conceive'.[31] Her presence was felt at Perth's Anzac Day March when with *Melbourne*'s guard commanded by Guy, a 600-strong contingent, accompanied by both her band and pipe band led the parade. After a lively passage across the Great Australian Bight *Melbourne* rendezvoused with *Sydney*, flagship of the Flag Officer Commanding HM Australian Fleet (FOCAF), Rear Admiral Henry Burrell.* *Melbourne* paraded a guard and band on the flight deck and fired a thirteen-gun salute to the flagship.

As expected, *Melbourne* received a very warm welcome in her namesake city. After a busy three days the ship sailed to join the Fleet in Jervis Bay and disembark her aircraft. On 9 May *Melbourne* entered Sydney Harbour as part of a Fleet Entry. At Garden Island the carriers were berthed stern to stern with a brow between the two ships. This was to allow the transfer of personnel, stores and other material associated with flagship role. In a short ceremony on 14 May Rear Admiral Burrell transferred his flag to *Melbourne*. Guy now became the Fleet Gunnery Officer in addition to his ship duties.

After a short docking and maintenance *Melbourne* went to sea in late July to work-up both the ship and her air group. The jet era had finally begun for the RAN. During the work-up it became apparent that the mirror landing system was a significant enhancement compared to the old 'batsman' system used in *Sydney*. Nevertheless, the dangers inherent in naval aviation once again materialised with the first loss of an aircraft from *Melbourne*. On the morning of 9 August a Sea Venom was launched,

---

* Later Vice Admiral Sir Henry Burrell, KBE, CB, RAN (1904–88).

only to roll to starboard and crash into the sea. After an intensive search it was clear both aircrew were lost.* Later that day the ship returned to the spot and conducted a memorial service, dropping two wooden crosses over the scene.

In September 1956 *Melbourne* began her first Asian deployment. Since Guy had last been deployed to the region there had been two important developments. The first was the creation in October 1954 of a British Commonwealth Far East Strategic Reserve (FESR). Australia, Britain and New Zealand stationed military forces in Malaya as 'a tangible Western commitment to the defence of Southeast Asia'[32] against communist aggression. The FESR had to be, 'equipped and trained to a level at least sufficient to enable it to participate in operations at short notice against forces of a first-class Asian power.'[33] In practical terms this meant a permanent deployment of about 4,500 Australian personnel from the three services, who needed an active training regime.† For the Navy, this involved the continuous commitment of two destroyers or frigates and an annual deployment of *Melbourne* to the region.

The other development was the 1955 creation of the South East Asia Treaty Organisation (SEATO).‡ This was an initiative on a broader scale, but with the same intent of countering communist expansion within the region. In the naval sphere, each participating country would take it in turn to sponsor an exercise. In 1956 Australia organised Exercise Albatross which practised naval forces in maritime trade protection in the South China Sea.

It was into this changed strategic environment that *Melbourne* deployed to meet both Strategic Reserve and SEATO commitments. She also served a diplomatic role of 'showing the flag' within the region. The

---

* The aircrew were Lieutenant Barry Thompson, RAN and Lieutenant Keith Potts, RAN.

† The other Australian forces were an infantry battalion and a fighter squadron, sometimes augmented by a bomber squadron.

‡ SEATO was disbanded in 1977. The SEATO members were Australia, France, New Zealand, Pakistan, the Philippines, Thailand, the UK & the USA.

modern Australian flagship had high profile visitors onboard including the President of the Philippines, the Prime Minister of Thailand and senior regional military commanders. This first deployment, with its mix of port visits and exercises, set a pattern that was to be largely followed throughout *Melbourne*'s 27-year operational life. *Melbourne* would become a regular visitor to the region and for a generation symbolised Australian engagement in Asia. In all *Melbourne* would deploy twenty-one times to Asia.

Guy performed very well in *Melbourne*, both as the Gunnery Officer and the Fleet Gunnery Officer. Sometimes officers of that specialisation are characterised as being 'seldom right but never doubtful'. One of the young pilots onboard, Lieutenant Neil Ralph,* wrote that Guy 'even then he attracted respect and did not behave as we were given to understand gunnery officers normally did. He was reasonable!'[34] For his part, Captain Gatacre maintained a high opinion of Guy, believing him to be an outstanding officer in all respects with a forceful personality and excellent manner. This view was shared by the FOCAF, Guy's old *Sydney* captain, Rear Admiral Harries, who rated Guy as the best Lieutenant Commander in the Fleet.[35]

Not surprisingly, in December 1956 Guy became the Admiral's Staff Officer Operations and Intelligence (later retitled to Fleet Operations Officer or 'FOO') and was promoted to Commander at the end of that month. In this role Guy was responsible for developing the overall Fleet program and overseeing the day-to-day activities of the ships when in company with the flagship. Depending on the Fleet program, FOCAF and his staff moved between the Fleet Headquarters at Garden Island in Sydney and the flagship, usually *Melbourne*. The first major activity for Guy was the Navy's support to the 1956 Olympic Games in Melbourne. *Melbourne* spent the duration of the XVI Olympiad in port, providing about 200 event marshals daily as well as supporting various ceremonial occasions during the Games.

---

* Later Rear Admiral N. Ralph, AO, DSC, RAN (1932–).

At the beginning of 1957 *Melbourne* prepared for a deployment, first to New Zealand, followed by her second Asian deployment. The RAN task group exercised once more with Commonwealth and US warships in a series of exercises, the preeminent one being the British sponsored Exercise Astra, practising convoy protection from Singapore to Bangkok. After a period of settling into the new role, Guy became a highly regarded FOO. He was seen as being professionally knowledgeable, quick thinking and hardworking, but at times impatient with those who did not keep up with him. In one encounter exercise against the New Zealand cruiser HMNZS *Royalist*, one of *Melbourne*'s aircraft had located a contact and identified it as the cruiser. In the operations room the staff thought the aircraft had misidentified *Royalist*. Listening to the discussion, Guy asked who the pilot was, and, when told it was Lieutenant Dadswell, said, 'Then it's *Royalist*.' It was.

During this deployment *Melbourne* called into Hong Kong for a maintenance period. It was at a party onboard that Guy, then 34 years old, met the tall blonde 24-year-old Carla Mengert, who worked at the West German Consulate. Her invitation came as a result of her sister, Irmstraud, who now lived in Hobart and who knew another *Melbourne* officer. During the ship's three-week port visit Guy and Carla saw each other enough to decide to maintain their friendship.

Although German by nationality, Carla had actually been born to German doctors resident in Java on Christmas Day 1932. The family was still there at the outbreak of World War II. Carla's older brother Hans had managed to get to university in Germany early in the war. He subsequently joined the Hitler Youth and then had to serve in the Reich Labor Service[*] before being conscripted into the Army. Hans was an infantry soldier in the elite Panzergrenadier-Division *Großdeutschland* which was involved in heavy fighting on the Eastern Front. It is believed Hans was killed in January 1945, just before his 19th birthday, as his unit

---

[*] During the war the Reich Labor Service supplied frontline troops with food and ammunition, repaired roads and airstrips. It also helped construct the Atlantic Wall, laid minefields, manned fortifications, and guarded vital facilities.

fell back into East Prussia.

While Carla's father was interned in India, Carla, along with her mother and sister, had remained in the Dutch East Indies and were later sent by the occupying Japanese to Shanghai where the girls were educated at the Kaiser Wilhelm School. It was a very strict institution which had its own branch of the Hitler Youth and was a focal point of the expatriate community. Carla's first glimpse of her 'homeland' was not until 1950 when her family was finally repatriated to a divided Germany.

Melbourne's 1958 program began with initial exercises in Western Australia, then her third Asian deployment with the largest SEATO Exercise to date. Ocean Link involved RAN, RN and USN aircraft carriers. Once again interlaced with the exercises were 'show the flag' port visits. Fortunately for Guy and Carla, this included another visit to Hong Kong. At the end of the Asian leg instead of returning direct to Australia, *Melbourne* visited Pearl Harbor and the home of the US Pacific Fleet for the first time. On return to Sydney, *Melbourne* went into refit and Guy left the Admiral's staff destined for his first posting to the RAN's strategic headquarters – Navy Office. In his 21-year career to date *Melbourne* was the first ship Guy had not served in during a war. During his time in *Melbourne*, Guy had prospered under Rear Admirals Harries, Gatacre and then Burrell. For the first time his qualities were assessed as those of a naval officer destined for the highest ranks of the Service.[36]

VI

When Guy joined Navy Office on 13 August 1958 it was still located in Melbourne. This was a 30-year hangover from when the nation's capital was temporarily Melbourne. Over the ensuing decades government departments slowly transferred to Canberra with the Defence departments amongst the last to go. They were slated to finally transfer in 1959. At the time of Guy's arrival, the Chief of Naval Staff (CNS) was Vice Admiral Sir Roy Dowling whom he had briefly served under during

Sydney's delivery voyage. In 1958 Navy Office had a staff of about 710 of whom only 17% were uniformed personnel.* The Navy, more than the other two services, relied heavily on public servants for its administration and technical support. Many of them had served long years in Navy Office, led by the Secretary of the Department who was the venerable Tom Hawkins. He had joined Navy Office as a clerk in 1915 and had served fourteen CNSs. Hawkins was a fount of knowledge but could be prickly if respect was not given him or work was not up to his exacting standard. To Guy, Hawkins was a remote, God-like figure who was the continuity expert within the naval bureaucracy.

Admiral Dowling's deputy was another familiar face to Guy, Rear Admiral Gatacre, while his classmate John Austin was also there. Navy Office was divided into branches and divisions that dealt with warfare, personnel, financial, logistics, engineering and administrative matters. It took Guy a while to understand how Navy Office worked as an organisation. This was in part because junior officers were never briefed on Navy Office and what it actually did.

Guy had been appointed the Deputy Director of Manning within the Naval Personnel Branch and was responsible for the drafting of sailors to the fleet as well as shore establishments. This was achieved by a drafting roster in which each rank and specialist category had a unique sea to shore ratio. Administration of the roster could have a significant impact on morale and retention. Guy was keen for the workings of his directorate to be transparent and be seen to be fair to sailors and so he wrote articles in the new *Navy News* explaining 'the mysteries of draft'.[37]

The Personnel Branch was led by the Second Naval Member, Rear Admiral 'Arch' Harrington. A future CNS, Harrington had a strong and somewhat unapproachable personality, exemplified by his carefully cultivated cheek-whiskers known colloquially as 'bugger's grips.' Nevertheless, Guy learnt that 'Arch' would support innovation, if its

---

* In 1959 when the RAN's naval strength was 13,000 it had a civilian workforce of 8,600.

proponent could robustly advocate for the proposal.

The senior civilian in the Personnel Branch was the very personable Bill Kenny, who had been in Navy Office since 1913. Guy's immediate superiors were Captain Eric Peel, who had distinguished himself commanding *Gascoyne* in the Philippines Campaign, and Commander Allen Dollard, who had achieved similar recognition in *Murchison* on the Han River during the Korean War.

In 1959 Carla came to Australia and on 1 August Guy and Carla were married in Sydney at the historic Saint Mark's Church on Darling Point. Allan Willis, brother of Jim, was Guy's best man. Carla and Guy spent their honeymoon skiing at Perisher Valley, staying at the Telemark Lodge which, inconveniently, had separate dormitories for men and women. Carla's mother, who had come from West Germany for the wedding, had helpfully brought skis and clothing for the bridal couple.

To many naval officers the move from sea to a desk with a largely civilian staff is a major transition. Guy's vigorous and assertive approach to matters while working well at sea required some adjustment in this new environment. To some senior officers, perhaps more acclimatised to the conservative Navy Office culture, Guy was seen as 'hot-headed', but his team worked and performed well under him. Professionally, Guy faced the challenges of manning the Fleet in an environment which had constrained funding for pay and conditions as well as having to maintain the National Service Scheme. The other overriding issue for Navy Office was its 1959 move to Canberra. This commenced in January and was undertaken in three stages with the Personnel Branch being among the second wave. The relocation was to the purpose-built Defence Headquarters which *Navy News* described as being the Australian equivalent to the US Pentagon building.[38] It co-located the Navy, Army and Air Force departments and a growing central Defence bureaucracy in a cluster of buildings on Russell Hill, two kilometres from the Parliament House. Guy approved of the move and felt the Navy was finally part of the Federal government organisation.

Canberra in 1959 was still a work in progress. Lake Burley Griffin had yet to be filled, the population was just 44,000 and the social circles were small. Indeed, by the time the Defence departments personnel and their families had relocated, they had increased Canberra's population by about 12%.[39] Carla and Guy enjoyed this new environment and like many newly arrived residents, lived in flats along on or near Canberra's main thoroughfare, Northbourne Avenue. Because of her previous employment at the West German Consulate in Hong Kong, Carla was able to secure a similar position at the West German Embassy. If you were outdoor-minded Canberra had its attractions with ready access to sporting facilities and the ski-fields in the winter. It was also during this period that Guy was initiated into the Freemasons at Lodge Caledonia of Canberra. This was at the encouragement of 'Snow' Gafford and some other naval members of the craft. Although he was unaware at the time of his family's long family association with the Freemasons, Guy felt aligned to its values of fraternity, benevolence, education and making 'good men into better men.'[40] Guy also enjoyed a camaraderie of like-minded men outside the confines of the Navy.

Guy served in Navy Office until February 1961. In his nearly three years ashore he had demonstrated an ability to work effectively in the less appealing, but necessary, Defence bureaucracy. Importantly for his future career prospects, his performance still marked him as an officer with very good potential to succeed in higher ranks. Guy's new posting was the one he most sought. After 24 years in the RAN Guy was given a sea command.

Left
Guy at war's end in 1945.
(Griffiths Collection)

Below
Guy in London in 1949.
(Griffiths Collection)

HMAS *Sydney* in Malta on her 1949 delivery voyage. (JA Mortimer)

Guy excelled in ceremonial duties. Here he is as the Guard Commander for the 1952 Trafalgar Day Ceremony at Como Park with the Governor of Victoria, General Sir Dallas Brooks. (Griffiths Collection)

HMAS *Anzac* in pancake ice off the Korean coast (RAN)

Guy (middle, 2ⁿᵈ row) and HMAS *Melbourne*'s ski party at Hochsölden in 1956.
(Griffiths Collection)

Left
Guy and Carla's
Wedding at St Mark's
Church at Darling
Point, Sydney on
1 August 1959.
(Griffiths Collection)

Below
Guy Jnr being
christened onboard
the equally new
HMAS *Parramatta*.
(Griffiths Collection)

Guy Snr onboard HMAS *Parramatta*. (Griffiths Collection)

HMAS *Parramatta* operating with Royal Navy ships during an exercise as part of the Far East Strategic Reserve. (RAN)

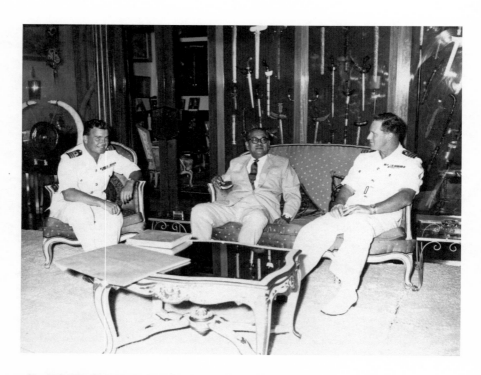

Above

Guy and Commander 'Red' Merson calling on Prime Minister Tunku Abdul Rahman Putra during *Parramatta* and *Yarra*'s 1962 deployment. (RAN)

Left

Guy as a Captain (Griffiths Collection)

The commissioning of HMAS *Hobart* at the Boston Naval Yard on 18 December 1965. (RAN)

The two commissioning captains – Captain Harry Howden of the first HMAS *Hobart* with Guy and Captain and Mrs Peel. (Griffiths Collection)

Left

The ship's company of HMAS *Hobart* exercising their Freedom of Entry to the City of Hobart for the first time. (Griffiths Collection)

Below

South Vietnamese Prime Minister Air Vice Marshal Nguyễn Kỳ and Madame Kỳ visiting HMAS *Hobart* during her preparations for her deployment to Vietnam. (Griffiths Collection)

6

First Command:
HMAS *Parramatta*

There is one who alone is ultimately responsible for the safe navigation, engineering performance accurate gunfire and morale of the ship. He is the Commanding Officer. He is the ship. This is the most difficult and demanding assignment in the Navy.

Joseph Conrad[1]

I

In February 1961 Guy arrived in Sydney to stand by the first of the new River class frigates, the *Parramatta*, then building at Cockatoo Island Dockyard. The ship was due to be commissioned mid-year after sea acceptance trials. *Parramatta* was lead of four ships that were based on the RN Type 12 'First Rate' frigates that were built as a response to the Soviet submarine threat. For the RAN they were the first ships designed from the outset to counter fast submarines. As part of their design the River class would be fitted with a pressurised citadel to allow them to operate in areas where there was nuclear fallout present. In time the ships would be fitted with the Seacat anti-aircraft and the Australian Ikara anti-submarine missile systems. But these were scheduled to be retrofitted to *Parramatta* after Guy's tenure in command.

As was the practice over recent years, warship construction was shared between Cockatoo Island (Sydney) and Williamstown (Melbourne) naval dockyards. The second ship in the class was *Yarra*, being built at Williamstown and she was three weeks behind *Parramatta* in construction. *Yarra*'s commanding officer designate was Commander 'Red' Merson who had also just left Navy Office, and there were all the portents for these two new frigates to become 'chummy' ships. In a piece of historical symmetry, the first two ships constructed for the new Commonwealth Naval Force (renamed the Royal Australian Navy in 1911) were *Parramatta* and *Yarra* and the new frigates would be commissioned in time for the RAN's 50th anniversary naming celebrations.

The process of completing a ship and then running acceptance trials before commissioning into the Navy is invariably extremely busy and not without its pressures. This was exacerbated in the case of *Parramatta* by being the first of the class. The Rivers had significant design changes to better suit operations in the Pacific. Much of this was not apparent externally except for the large Dutch LW-02 long-range air-search radar atop the mast. All the living quarters were air-conditioned and *Parramatta* was the first RAN frigate built with bunks and not hammocks. These modifications, combined with delays in obtaining some overseas sourced equipment, put pressure on the schedule. Other delays were caused by the faulty workmanship of some new equipment, an overtime ban by the militant Painters and Dockers Union and a change of program to allow *Parramatta* to be part of the 50th Anniversary Fleet Entry. Through all this Guy had to work with the dockyard and naval technical staff, to hold fast on some matters and compromise on others. This was symbolised by *Parramatta* taking part in the Fleet Entry on 15 June 1961 while still on acceptance trials and flying the merchant navy red ensign. The full-speed trial for the ship took place on one of those perfect days at sea, flat calm with a deep-blue ocean. One of the dockyard apprentice draughtsmen, John Jeremy,* went forward to lean over the bow of the ship to watch the

---

*   John Jeremy went on to become the General Manager of Cockatoo Island Dockyard.

spectacle of the ship cutting through the sea at 30 knots with dolphins playing in front. After a few minutes Jeremy was met by a Chief Petty Officer who said, 'Captain's compliments son – only fools and stokers lean on guard rails!' The conditions were not always perfect and Jeremy recalled,

> On a rather rough day during trials Guy Griffiths was standing at one of the bridge windows which could be opened. It was closed, but not adequately sealed, and when the ship took a green one there was a great wall of water over the bridge. Guy was soaked, but without a word turned and disappeared below to change returning a few minutes later as immaculate as ever.[2]

On 4 July, somewhat unusually, *Parramatta* was to be handed over into the Navy and the White Ensign raised while at sea off Sydney Heads. The transition was done in a short ceremony in the presence of the Minister for the Navy, Senator John Gorton, the Attorney General, Sir Garfield Barwick, the Chairman of Cockatoo Docks, Mr Aubrey Wiltshire, the Flag Officer Commanding East Australian Area (FOCEA) Rear Admiral George Oldham and the Mayor of Parramatta, Alderman Alfred Thomas. On returning alongside a commissioning service was conducted. The day was noted by the ship's company as their 'independence day' from the ministrations of the dockyard. To add to the pressure, Guy's Executive Officer* had a mental collapse on the morning before sailing and had to be taken to the Balmoral Naval Hospital later that day.

The ship's gunnery officer was Lieutenant Commander Geoffrey 'Snow' Gafford, who had served with Guy in *Anzac*. Guy appointed him the Executive Officer. Out of these inauspicious circumstances was to come a very good working relationship between Captain and Executive

---

* The Executive Officer was also known as the 'First Lieutenant' in destroyers and frigates.

Officer. Initially, 'Snow' continued as the gunnery officer where his excellent specialist knowledge shone through. By nature a reserved man, 'Snow' soon knew both ship and men and, by virtue of his extensive sea service, had great credibility in the eyes of the ship's company. Under his broad supervision, Lieutenant Ian Bartlett, who had recently completed a 'Little G' course at *Cerberus,* took over the day-to-day running of the Gunnery department.

It is often said that one of the best preparations for sea command is being Executive Officer, or second in command of a ship. This experience gives an understanding of the underlying administration of the ship and is the normal progression in the contemporary RAN. Guy had not been an Executive Officer of a ship before and indeed neither had about half the commanding officers when he joined the Fleet. He had, however, like these men, extensive sea experience.

When assuming command of a ship, an officer brings to the position, good and bad experiences of serving under captains during his or her career. These influence an individual's approach to command, and in Guy's case his shining examples were Tennant, Nichols and Harries. There were other very effective captains such as Collins and Gatacre. There is also one's own leadership experience in various positions of authority and one's own temperament. Whatever style of command a naval officer decides to implement, it has to be true to their personality and suited to the situation in which the ship finds itself. Guy's approach was orthodox, in which he would strictly adhere to rules, regulations and naval customs to maintain good order and discipline. He set a high a standard for himself, his ship and those ashore whose duty it was to support the Fleet. In the words of one admiral Guy ran a 'taut ship', but one that was clearly cheerful and already showing esprit de corps.[3]

Among *Parramatta's* Officers of the Watch was Lieutenant Sam Bateman who had the previous year been the Executive Officer of the armament stores carrier *Woomera* when she caught fire and sank off Sydney with the loss of two sailors. *Woomera* was disposing of time-expired ammunition and it was thought a parachute flare, which contained a friction igniter, may have been triggered, starting the blaze. Bateman and his captain were each acquitted at their court martial. His posting to *Parramatta* was to give him the opportunity to get his career back on track. Initially, Bateman found Guy to be an intimidating presence on the bridge but one who was fair and equally demanding on everyone. Bateman's time in the frigate resurrected his career with Guy recommending him for a sea command.*

After commissioning, *Parramatta* still needed to complete a range of trials before she could be fully accepted. Some equipment such as the sonars and radio sets still had to be set to work, while a range of tools for maintenance had yet to be provided. In his first *Report of Proceedings*, Guy laid out in a detailed and unvarnished way the deficiencies in the ship and the shortfalls in support from the dockyard and the naval engineering and stores areas. His report created a stir both in Fleet Headquarters and Navy Office. The Third Naval Member, Rear Admiral Ken Urquhart, responsible for naval engineering, wrote a minute to Vice Admiral Sir Henry Burrell giving reasons for the deficiencies.[4] Burrell was, however, unconvinced by Urquhart's explanations and his deputy Rear Admiral Alan McNicol wrote 'I wonder if all the congratulatory signals were justified.'[5]

By sticking his neck out and making himself unpopular in some circles, Guy was able to get the attention of the hierarchy to help get *Parramatta* fully functioning. Steadily, the necessary parts were provided, with dockyard technicians being sent to sea when necessary to get equipment operational. *Parramatta* undertook her 'work-up' off the south east coast, occasionally in company with other ships. During this intense period Guy was delighted to learn that Carla was pregnant with their first child. All things being equal, she would give birth before *Parramatta* deployed the following year.

---

* Later Commodore W.S.G. Bateman AM, RAN (1938–2020). He would command four ships in his naval career.

At this time there was no formal assessment by an independent Fleet staff that a ship working up was operationally ready to join the Fleet. Rather, it was up to the Captain to make that assessment. *Parramatta* formally joined the Fleet in November, whereupon the tempo of activity increased and she started taking part in Fleet exercises. Also now operational was her sister-ship *Yarra*, who was invariably be in company with her. Both *Parramatta* and *Yarra* joined as the Second Division of the 1st Frigate Squadron, while the old Q class frigates, still in commission comprised the First Division.

The new *Parramatta* was the third ship to bear the famous name in the RAN. The second *Parramatta* was a participant in the 'Tobruk Ferry Run' that supplied the troops of that beleaguered garrison port during World War II. After five months running the gauntlet, *Parramatta* was sunk with only 24 survivors from her 160 crew. In recognition of her deeds, members of the Rats of Tobruk Association came aboard the new *Parramatta* and presented a chart of the Ferry Run's route. The mood of the short ceremony was summed up by one of the 'Rats' who simply said, 'We will never forget what they did for us.'[6] A grateful Guy said that the new ship's company knew they had a lot to live up to, but that he knew 'the present *Parramatta* would fulfil whatever role they were called upon with dignity and courage'.[7]

II

On 29 August 1961 Carla gave birth to a son, also named Guy. The following April, in a time-honoured tradition, the baby was christened onboard *Parramatta* with the inverted ship's bell acting as the font. His engraved name was the first to be inscribed on the inside of the bell for posterity. On Good Friday, 20 April 1962, *Parramatta* and *Yarra* sailed from Sydney for a six-month South East Asian deployment. Their sailing date was advanced ahead of Easter in view of the Indonesian invasion of West New Guinea and the possible need for Australia to show a naval presence in the area. They would form part of the Strategic Reserve. Although 'Red' Merson of the *Yarra* had joined the Naval College a year ahead of Guy, he had been promoted later to the rank of Commander. Guy was thus senior to 'Red' Merson and *Parramatta* would be in charge whenever the ships were together, as well as taking the lead for administrative matters. Guy thought this situation could be awkward for 'Red' but it was not so. 'Red' was by nature very sociable and easy going and was to prove a great asset and support to Guy.

Their first port call was in Cairns for fuel and the Anzac Day commemorations. They made their mark with 200 men from the frigates taking part in the Anzac Day March. The next fuelling stop was at *Tarangau* naval base on Manus Island. For Guy this visit brought back memories of *Shropshire* and Manus as a base for the US 7th Fleet in 1944 and 1945. The ships fielded Combined Frigates' teams in seven sports but only won in rugby and cricket. During their time at sea, the ships undertook a range of trials and training so as to be well placed when they joined the other Commonwealth ships. The frigates, as 'Red' Merson was later to remark, soon became 'Siamese twins'.

Through his sea service to date, Guy had observed the propensity for most captains to confine themselves to their cabins in harbour as well as the bridge and operations room at sea. As such they could be remote from most of their sailors. Guy was increasingly uncomfortable with this in the contemporary navy. He recalled, 'I decided that really the only way of meeting the ship's company because they were in various places throughout the ship when I was on the bridge or something is to take a walk.'[8] As such he became a familiar figure walking through *Parramatta* including the hot machinery spaces at different times of the day or night. Through these walks Guy had the chance to check the material state of the ship, get to know his men through conversation on an individual basis and get 'a feel of the ship'.

The two frigates initially joined the Strategic Reserve not in its base in Singapore, but in Manila. In port were the RN aircraft carrier *Ark Royal*, wearing the flag of Rear Admiral John Frewen,* and her three frigates, as well as *Melbourne* and the destroyers *Vendetta* and *Voyager*. After just two days in port the five Australian ships were due to sail for Japan under the command of FOCAF, Rear Admiral Alan McNicol. In Manila, both RAN frigates embarked several Hong Kong Chinese laundrymen for the duration of the Asian part of their deployments. This long-established practice was inherited from the RN. The laundrymen, for a modest price, would wash, starch and iron officers' and sailors' tropical uniforms as well as tailor and repair clothing. At night they did a brisk trade in cups of noodles to those still hungry on watch. Sailors generally struggled with the names of the laundrymen and nicknames were quickly assigned with 'Scorcher' a favourite. The laundrymen were invariably well-experienced in the ways of sailors and were very welcome additions to a warship. It was a lucrative concession and many a laundryman's child had their education through to university paid by this work. Their embarkation came to signify that an RAN ship was properly 'Up Top'.†

In May 1962 the RAN Task Group visited three ports in Japan in the largest Australian naval visit to the country since the war. In harking back to days past, the host ship for the *Parramatta*'s visit to Nagasaki was the new Japanese Maritime Self Defence Force frigate *Mogami*. Guy well remembered the previous ship of this name from the Battle of Surigao Strait. For the men of task group, and especially the commanding officers, it was an almost ceaseless round of receptions, tours and other events. In between these activities there was still room for sport and Guy had the satisfaction of seeing *Parramatta* inflict a rare defeat on *Melbourne* in rugby.

The Task Group visit to Japan was at a time when formalised trade between the two countries had been resumed for only five years and already the symbiotic relationship between Japan's revitalised manufacturing and

---

*   Later Admiral Sir John Frewen, GCB. (1911–75).

†   The term 'Up-Top' is used by RAN officers and sailors to refer to Asia. It is in contrast to the RN use of the term 'Far East'.

Australia's resource and agriculture sectors was plain to see. For Guy the improvements in Japan's prosperity since the Korean War years were striking. After the very successful Japan visit the Task Group split with *Melbourne* and the two destroyers bound for Australia.

Parramatta and *Yarra* proceeded together to Hong Kong. Already these new frigates were proving themselves to be operationally much more capable and versatile than the older frigates they replaced. It led one Navy Office staff officer, who had read Guy's *Report of Proceedings* to remark 'This report reads more like that of a fleet destroyer, rather than that of an anti-submarine frigate.'[9] It was a perceptive remark about the nature of the 'New Navy'.

In Hong Kong the Australian frigates joined the Strategic Reserve task group of *Ark Royal*, the cruiser *Tiger*, five RN destroyers and frigates and New Zealand's new frigate *Taranaki*. The RAN frigates spent two weeks alongside for maintenance and recreation. During their stay a young sailor from the British maintenance ship *Hartland Point*, then alongside, was lost overboard. *Parramatta*'s divers helped recover his body. Guy was President of the subsequent Board of Inquiry which found that Able Seaman James Elleston fell when working on one of the *Hartland Point*'s boats then swung outboard. Tragically, he hit his head on the jetty and then fell unconscious into the water.[10]

The Strategic Reserve ships sailed for SEATO Exercise Pot Luck with the US aircraft carrier *Hancock* and her consorts. This was the most demanding exercise to date for *Parramatta* and *Yarra*. As one of the few Commonwealth frigates with a doctor, *Parramatta* was chosen by *Ark Royal* as the default rescue destroyer. This involved being stationed about 1,000 yards on the port quarter* of the carrier during launch and recovery of aircraft when a helicopter was not undertaking the duty. After the flying cycle *Parramatta* would then quickly resume her sector in the screen. This tasking was demanding on both captain and the bridge team, and excellent training. The purpose of Pot Luck was to test the air

---

* The 'quarter' is a position 45° on either side of a ship's stern.

147

defences of Okinawa. After a short visit to the island for an exercise wash-up, the eleven Commonwealth ships departed for Singapore, conducting Exercise Homerun en route. Both frigates were in Singapore on 4 July, *Parramatta*'s first birthday. Indicative of the goodwill between the two frigates, *Yarra* sent over a birthday cake with a map of *Parramatta*'s extensive travels iced on top. In that time *Parramatta* had steamed over 31,000 nautical miles whilst her 250 men had consumed 30 tons of meat, 30 tons of potatoes, nearly 6,000 eggs and over 20,000 litres of milk.

The next major exercise of the deployment was the three-week-long Far East Fleet Tactical Exercise (Fotex 62*)* in the South China Sea, which involved *Ark Royal*, the commando carrier *Bulwark,** *Tiger*, eight escorts and the submarine *Andrew*. The Commander-in-Chief, Far East Fleet commanded the force in *Ark Royal*. He was Admiral Sir David Luce whom Guy last encountered on Staff Course when Luce was the Director. Luce spent a day in *Parramatta* to observe the new ship and speak to her men. During Fotex 62 the Fleet spent the weekends anchored off Pulau Tioman, where there were rowing and sailing races and other sporting activities onshore. *Parramatta* had embarked one of the Navy's 14 ft sailing dinghies for the deployment to compete in the events. Guy, a keen sailor, competed in one of the races with Lieutenant Bateman as his forward hand. Conditions were quite fresh and Guy had the misfortune of capsizing not far off the flagship's quarterdeck. Sam Bateman expected some embarrassment on Guy's behalf but instead he took the incident in good humour.[11]

After a short visit to Singapore both ships were involved in another exercise, this time Battery, which had a focus on an amphibious assault along the Malay east coast in the face of a submarine threat. Both frigates practised bombarding shore positions in support of the operation. After *Battery*, *Parramatta* and *Yarra* proceeded to Hong Kong once more in company with *Bulwark*, arriving on 23 August 1962.

---

* HMS *Bulwark* was commanded by Guy's former gunnery instructor Captain J.S. 'Fish' Dalglish CVO, CBE, RN (1913–95).

One week into the port the powerful typhoon Wanda approached the colony from the east. Guy's experience in *Sydney* in riding out typhoon Ruth had shown that remaining in harbour was unwise. As Wanda got closer, Guy called on the Commodore-in-Charge Hong Kong, Commodore Adrian Butler, and told him that he wished to take *Parramatta* and *Yarra* to sea and evade Wanda. After lunch on 31 August the ships sailed and proceeded southwards towards the Paracel Islands with the two LW-02 radars providing a clear outline of the southern rim of the typhoon. Whilst riding out the storm they were tasked to search for the tug *Kowloon Docks* which was towing SS *Sletholm* from Shanghai. The search proved fruitless and later one survivor from the tug reached the shore of mainland China. On the frigates' return three days later here were widespread signs of Wanda's destructive power. The destroyer HMS *Caesar*, which left later to take over the search, had sustained substantial damage to her upper deck and boats whilst in harbour.

The six-month deployment was nearing an end. There was just one other significant activity to undertake. On 15 September both frigates arrived at Malaya's western gateway seaport of Port Swettenham (now Port Klang).* Since the 1948 federation of Malaya, Australia had engaged in a range of initiatives to support the young nation. In the naval realm, a RAN officer had, since 1960, commanded the Royal Malayan Navy (RNM). The current chief was Commodore Tony Synnot.† The port visit was an opportunity to strengthen the ties between the two countries. It began auspiciously when Commodore Synnot, Guy and 'Red' Merson called on the Prime Minister Tunku Abul Rahman. The Prime Minister, who was seven years into his fifteen-year tenure greatly impressed Guy. Through his discussion it was clear to Guy that Tunku Abul Rahman understood his people and their aspirations and was 'one of the wise men'.[12]

Among the busy round of engagements was the reception held on

---

*   Port Swettenham is now known as Port Klang.

†   Later Admiral Sir Anthony Synnot KBE, AO, RAN (1922–2001). He was the brother of Commander Tim Synnot.

both frigates. The well-attended event was graced with the presence of the charming Sultan of Selangor who Guy and 'Red' Merson had called on earlier in the day at his palace.* Guy was left with a positive impression of the young country, its leaders and fledgling military.

After four hectic and successful days the ships sailed for a brief port visit to the Singapore naval base and then passage to Darwin. A week into the passage, the frigates had an early morning rendezvous with their Strategic Reserve reliefs *Queenborough* and *Quiberon*. The other three commanding officers joined Guy onboard for breakfast and a handover. There was, however, a melancholy conclusion to the rendezvous. The ensigns of the four ships were lowered to half-mast and a memorial service was held onboard *Queenborough* for Able Seaman Brian Pelgrave, who had been lost overboard two days before.

Parramatta and *Yarra* returned to Sydney on 10 October. This first deployment by the new River class frigates, in which they had steamed about 30,000 nautical miles, had been most successful. In various exercises they had been able to practice their skills against submarines, their primary mission. They had also demonstrated that, unlike their RN counterparts of the time, their long-range radar made them useful radar pickets to provide early detection of aircraft approaching a task group. What impressed Guy about the deployment was the calibre of his officers and sailors and the great enthusiasm with which they approached their myriad activities. From a professional perspective Guy had not only commanded a ship on a long deployment for the first time but had the additional responsibility of being a Divisional Commander. This was in the context of a difficult start to the commission as a new first of class frigate with a plethora of technical issues. It was a significant achievement. Rear Admiral McNicol observed that Guy had been uncompromising with the dockyard and had shown himself to be a 'driver' 'who expects from others the standard he sets himself'.[13]

---

* The Sultan of Selangor was His Royal Highness (*Duli Yang Maha Mulia*) Sultan Salahuddin Abdul Aziz Shah ibn Almarhum Sultan Hisamuddin Alam Shah Al-Haj, (1926–2001).

Parramatta went into refit on 22 October and Guy's period in command came to an end on 9 January 1963 with the ship about to emerge from dockyard hands. He was relieved by Captain Brian Murray with *Parramatta* now sporting a black band at the top of her funnel as Leader of the Frigate Squadron.

III

After his experiences with the newest warship class in the Fleet, Guy returned to Navy Office. By this time Vice Admiral 'Arch' Harrington was CNS. Guy was to head the Tactics, Trials and Staff Requirement Division.* There were five other divisions in the Naval Staff dealing with matters such as intelligence, plans and operations. The former was led by David Hamer who was the first of Guy's class to be promoted to Captain. The Naval Staff reported to the Deputy CNS who was Rear Admiral Tom Morrison, another veteran of Leyte Gulf.

Guy arrived in post at a time of great change for the Navy as it entered the missile age. In the first instance the need was to acquire ships armed with 'surface to air guided weapons' or SAGW, in the jargon of the day, to counter the threat of jet aircraft. The other weapon being developed was a torpedo-carrying missile to engage hostile submarines at long range from a task group. The RAN's first two missile systems were to enter service in 1964. They were the short-range anti-aircraft Seacat missile in *Derwent* and long-range anti-submarine Ikara in *Stuart*.

Even more significantly, in 1961 the government, with strong impetus from its energetic Navy Minister, Senator John Gorton, had selected the American Charles F. Adams class guided missile destroyer to provide area air defence of the Fleet.[†] For a Navy previously having British-derived ships and systems this was a radical decision viewed with

---

* The Directorate of Tactics & Staff Requirement was later renamed the Directorate of Tactics & Weapons Policy.

† At this time it was assessed that there was not a viable replacement for the Sea Venom fighter and *Melbourne* would become a helicopter carrier. In the end the US Skyhawk fighter-bomber replaced the Sea Venom.

misgivings by many traditionalists. Technically, however, the US design with its Tartar missile system and associated radars was much more advanced than the British County class destroyers. The initial plan was for two Charles F. Adams class destroyers to be built in the US, with the first commissioning in 1965. A third ship was ordered in January 1963.[*] To have half the fleet armed with SAGWs, the second aspect to the plan was for *Voyager* to be retrofitted in 1966 with the Tartar missile.[14]

There was therefore much supporting work needed to realise this vision. One of the useful early documents Guy produced was a comprehensive technical and operational analysis of the strengths and weaknesses of first two River class frigates. He hoped that this would be of value in the later builds in the class and indeed for specifying any future frigate design.

Within a month of Guy joining Navy Office the Government also announced that the RAN would once again have a submarine arm. In recent years, the RN had based the 4th Submarine Squadron in Sydney but that advantageous arrangement was coming to an end. Four Oberon class submarines would arrive in Australia between 1967 and 1970. Guy led his staff in developing the naval staff requirement for a destroyer and submarine tender that could support the new Fleet in prolonged operations into the region. To be named *Stalwart*, she was locally designed and built, commissioning in 1968. *Stalwart* was well conceived and proved a great success.

In August 1963 Carla received the unexpected news that her father, who was still working as a general practitioner in *Nürnberg*, had died after contracting hepatitis from a patient. Carla, who was newly pregnant, flew to Germany with son Guy to support her mother. However, because of the poor pressurisation of the aircraft at the time, Carla then thought it best to await the birth of the child in Germany. Erica was born on 16 November 1963.

---

[*]   The Navy proposed the names of *Brisbane, Adelaide* & *Perth*, but the final names were *Perth, Hobart* & *Brisbane*. See Naval Board Minutes 8 March 1963 (NAA).

The nature of Guy's work and much of Navy Office changed dramatically as a result of the tragic collision between *Melbourne* and *Voyager* on the evening of 10 February 1964. Sixty-eight men were lost in *Voyager*. In the words of Sam Landau, the Navy Secretary, it was a 'national calamity'.[15] Guy thought the accident 'shattered' the Navy, which found itself ill-placed to deal with the tragedy and its fallout. Vice Admiral Harrington planned to hold a Board of Inquiry, but Prime Minister Robert Menzies sensed that the size of the tragedy and the need for transparency demanded a different approach. He decided on the day following the collision to hold a Royal Commission. This reflected a lack of confidence in the Navy to deal with the matter without the urge to protect the Navy from criticism. Menzies' sense of the insular nature of the Navy at the time was valid. The Spicer Royal Commission had significant deficiencies and was to be followed by an unprecedented second Royal Commission.* For his part Guy supported the need for an external review. The tragedy affected his Navy Office duties in two ways. The first was his involvement in developing options for government to provide *Voyager*'s replacement. The second was dealing with some of the issues arising from the first Royal Commission.

In regard to *Voyager*'s replacement, Australia was offered the loan of a destroyer from Britain, the *Duchess,* and another from the US, the *Twining*. Australia accepted the offer of *Duchess* as she was a sister-ship of *Voyager* and so easier to support. In the space of a week the longer-term options were developed in Guy's division. They were either purchase of a fourth Charles F. Adams destroyer, a smaller US destroyer escort or one, or possibly two, additional Type 12 frigates. Eventually, the government agreed with the Navy's recommendation for an additional two frigates. Cabinet initially directed that these ships be 'repeats' of the last Type 12 – *Derwent*. Once the news was received, Guy directed his small staff to quickly dust off his paper on *Parramatta* and develop the cogent

---

* The details of the *Melbourne–Voyager* collision and the two Royal Commissions are well described in Professor Tom Frame's definitive *Where Fate Calls*.

arguments why the new ships should incorporate lessons from the first four ships as well as incorporating newer technology. After the success of the Dutch LW-02 radar in the existing River class, Guy was very receptive to the suggestion by one of his staff officers, Lieutenant Commander John Smith, that Dutch 'digital' technology gunnery and missile fire control systems should be evaluated for the new ships. The result was the incorporation of these systems, as well as some of the enhancements from the new RN Leander class, into the two new frigates, *Swan* and *Torrens*.[16] As with *Stalwart* they were very successful in service and indeed some of their new systems were retrofitted into the four earlier frigates.

The other major contribution Guy made in Navy Office at this time was in trying to get a benefit for the Navy from the evidence arising in the first Royal Commission. As the proceedings were underway, Guy had arranged for the daily transcripts to be sent to his staff officers for examination of the material, procedural or training deficiencies that had been identified and determination of remediation action. This required a good liaison with Fleet Headquarters as well as the supporting areas of the Navy. This initiative, in part, led Rear Admiral Morrison to write that Guy was 'always looking for ways of getting more efficiency in our Fleet and he has shown the ability to pick out the important matters that require attention'.[17]

Through his efforts with his division Guy had gained a formidable reputation for his well-researched and argued staff work, as well as the long hours he put into his labours. He was rewarded by promotion to Captain in June 1964. Guy's advocacy in some matters could face equally strong contrary opinions as well as conservative resistance to change. Admiral Harrington, well known for his own strong views, remarked that while Guy was 'a good and determined officer – he must learn to take no for an answer and to do so gracefully'.[18]

In early 1965, towards the end of his tenure in Navy Office, Guy was called in to see Admiral Harrington. As always 'Arch' was straight to the point. He asked what Guy thought of becoming the next Australian

Naval Advisor in New Delhi. Guy, who was very keen to return to sea, chanced his arm and said, 'not much.' Harrington then said, 'I thought so, so you had better go to the US and command the second of the Charles F. Adams destroyers *Hobart*.'[19] Needless to say, Guy was 'on cloud nine'.[20] 'Arch' then reminded him that he could not take his family as he would not be away longer than twelve months. Guy's appointment as the next 'missile ship captain' was reported in the major newpapers around the country as well as in the US in *The Bay City Times*.[21]

Domestically, Guy and Carla had seen Canberra grow as a city since they had last lived there. Indeed, when Carla returned to Canberra with the two children, the city had changed dramatically with the gradual filling of the long-planned Lake Burley Griffin. As happened with so many couples, the appeal of the city grew with the presence of a young family. A popular outing was visiting Guy's old *Shropshire* shipmate, James Osborne, at his farm near Gundaroo, particularly in mulberry season. Although knowing *Hobart* would eventually be based in Sydney, it was decided that Carla, having the friendship of other naval wives, as well as her colleagues at the West German Embassy, would remain in Canberra with the children while Guy was in the US.

7
Wartime Sea Command
HMAS *Hobart*

The elegant and intrepid Aussie DDG.
Quartermaster Antonio Robles, USS Edson[1]

I

On 15 July 1965, for the first time in his naval career, Guy flew rather than sailed to a new overseas appointment. Instead of taking a direct route he took the opportunity to travel via West Germany and visit his widowed mother-in-law Dr Hilda Mengert. She lived in Nuremberg and Guy spent an enjoyable few days really getting to know her for the first time. After this interlude Guy took a transatlantic flight and then made his way to Bay City, Michigan, where *Hobart* was being built by the Defoe Ship Building Company.

On the day after Guy arrived in Bay City, the lead ship, *Perth*, was commissioned into the RAN in a ceremony over in Boston. Bay City is located on the shores of Saginaw Bay on Lake Huron and at the time had a population of just 50,000. In a *Navy News* article for sailors destined to join *Hobart*, Bay City was described as 'a particularly friendly and hospitable place: its single main street, old houses and hotels give it the atmosphere of an Australian country town'.[2] The shipyard was the main employer. The President of the shipyard was Mr Thomas Defoe, grandson of its 1905 founder Harry J. Defoe. Originally the Defoe

Boat and Motor Works, the yard got its first Navy contract in 1917 to build torpedo chasers. During World War II the company scaled up to build more complex destroyer escorts and unusually, constructed their hulls upside down and then turned them over, to save time and improve the welding quality. One of the Australian sailors described Defoe as a 'shipyard in a cornfield'. By the time Guy arrived in the city, Defoe had built over 130 warships but their three USN and three RAN Charles F. Adams class destroyers were far and away the most complex ships they had built. Guy marvelled at how Defoe could build such advanced ships in such a modest yard.* Notably, the Defoe ships came to be regarded as the best built of the Charles F. Adams class.[3]

As in the case of *Parramatta*, Guy joined *Hobart* after she had been launched and was fitting out. There were few of the ship's company at the yard during this phase of construction. Two larger contingents arrived in the US on Qantas flights, at the end of October and in mid-November. They went straight to the Fleet Training Center at Rhode Island for their necessary Pre-Commissioning Training.

Perth had paved the way with Australian modifications to the baseline design. Most substantial was the provision for the Australian Ikara missile system that would eventually be fitted amidships in Australia. Less complex, but no less significant, was the fitting of separate petty officers' accommodation and the enlargement of the officers' wardroom to provide for a bar. In all these matters 'Old Man' Defoe and his team were most accommodating to the RAN: indeed, it was said that this was at the expense of their profitability. To the Australians there were also some unique American amenities that attracted considerable attention. The first was a laundry able to wash all the ship's company's uniforms and even return officers' shirts neatly pressed in plastic bags with small black-paper bow ties with the message 'Your shirt, Sir.'[4] Second, was an ice-cream making machine and finally there were the soda fountains or soft drink dispensers which the sailors soon called 'wowser bowsers'.

---

*   Defoe did not receive further Navy contracts and went out of business in 1976.

Guy's Executive Officer was Commander Richard Nunn, who was a Direction specialist.* There were some familiar faces and Guy's Marine Engineering Officer, Commander Bill Money, had served with him in *Parramatta*. As an indication of the complexity of the ship, the wardroom consisted of 20 officers, which was a lot for a destroyer. The Heads of Department were all Commanders, which was a rank higher than in the USN ships. The selection of this very senior group by the RAN was in the words of one of *Perth*'s officers, Lieutenant David Shackleton,† 'a very sensible hedge against the unknown of acquiring, for the first time, a completely foreign designed and built very advanced warship. This expertise provided a very powerful basis on which to draw and build.'[5]

To the junior officers, Guy came with 'a formidable reputation – a gunnery officer and a man who was clearly admiral material.'[6] One of them captured their feelings by remarking, 'Well, if it's off to war, thank heavens that it's with Guy Griffiths.'[7] Guy viewed it as important for the officers to set an example with their standard of dress. He soon told the assembled officers that they were a thoroughly scruffy lot! He said that the inherited (American) habit of wearing soft collar shirts was to cease – back to a stiff collar and studs from now on. Lieutenant Ian Holmes thought to himself 'Captain, there isn't a laundry to starch collars for miles.' Guy then turned to the Supply Officer, Commander Dick Brown, and said 'Go to the boot of my car and you will find boxes of paper collars.' Guy had thought it all out and brought them from Australia.[8] In a short time, however, Guy would have a change of view on the subject of uniforms.

The sailors varied in experience from a few with World War II experience to others straight from recruit school. Their number, 312, was the largest for any RAN destroyer to date. The complexity of the new

---

* Direction Officers specialise in fighter direction and the interaction with supporting aircraft more generally. They are also responsible for the management of the Operations Room and Radar Plot sailors.

† Later Vice Admiral D.J. Shackleton, AO, RAN (1948–). He was Chief of Navy 1999–2002.

systems required a much higher level of technical training for officers and sailors.

The selection of the Charles F. Adams class destroyers heralded some of the biggest changes experienced in the RAN. The three ships were the first major surface warships that were not of British or Australian origin.[*] They were advanced in almost every aspect, from their high-pressure steam plants that could propel the ships up to 35 knots, to their array of sophisticated radars, high-powered sonar, modern 5-inch guns and the Tartar missile which could shoot down an aircraft at a range of 25 kilometres.

Perhaps the most profound challenge was the absorption of an array of new technologies, procedures, supporting logistics systems and new jargon. Even compartment and damage-control markings were completely different. While foreign to the Australian sailors at first, it all made sense once understood. As one British admiral wrote, it was 'an eminently practical but novel system' of doing business.[9] In the USN, the ships were referred to by the nomenclature DDG and this term quickly passed into the RAN lexicon.[†] Compared to *Parramatta*, *Hobart* was twenty metres longer, nearly double the displacement and had eighty more men. Perhaps even more telling was their logistical complexity. The RAN's Daring class destroyers had 7,000 different line items of spare parts, while *Hobart* had 39,000.[10]

One of the distinctive features of the USN at the time was its very comprehensive and well-resourced shore and at sea training regime. It was far and away the leader in this facet among world navies. As the sophistication of these arrangements became more fully apparent it was a revelation to both Guy and his ship's company, exemplified in the diverse technical courses the men attended on their specialist equipment. For his part, Guy undertook a range of warfare focused-courses to prepare

---

[*]   Initially the Australian Government ordered two ships (*Perth* & *Hobart*) with a third (*Brisbane*) being ordered in 1963.

[†]   The classification 'DDG' is a combination of 'DD' for destroyer and 'G' for guided missile.

him for his sea command. One of the features of the individual training was the number of USN specialist courses in which *Hobart's* officers and sailors came either first or second in the final assessments. In part this was due to their seniority and the selection of *Hobart* personnel, but also the innate quality of the ship's company.[11]

Another striking feature of the USN approach was the comprehensive suite of Bureau of Ships' publications on the ship's systems. Importantly, in the face of the unfamiliar, there was a very positive approach by the ship's company and Guy later remarked, 'All hands seemed to be well aware of the challenges of this new ship, with new design characteristics, new conditions of habitability, new weapon systems, and new capabilities.'[12] Sport has always been a means of bonding a new ship's company and *Hobart* was no different. On the wintery but picturesque sporting fields at Newport, Rhode Island *Hobart* played exhibition matches of rugby and Australian Rules football for their American hosts.

Hobart with a crew of contractors and some RAN and USN personnel, conducted builder's trials running out of Bay City. For the final three days there was an assessment by the USN Board of Inspection headed by Rear Admiral Harry Reiter. The Board found the ship to be 'in a fine state' and recommended its acceptance by the US government. Australia was acquiring the ship from the US government, not from Defoe.[13] The commissioning of *Hobart* to the RAN was to take place in Boston and the ship left Defoe for the unfamiliar passage through the Great Lakes and the lock system to the sea. As *Hobart* sailed by Buffalo, at the entrance to the Niagara River, Guy was greeted on the shore by his old friend Fred Hip and his family. Guy and Fred had maintained their friendship since 1944 when *Nashville* and *Shropshire* first operated together.

On 1 December *Hobart* entered a floating dock at the Bethlehem Steel Works, East Boston for minor hull work, painting and cleaning. A week later she was refloated and moved to the Boston Navy Yard where on 9 December she was handed over by Defoe to the USN. The following week the ship's company moved onboard in preparation for the commissioning. As the day neared Guy was very conscious of the weather. For the preceding week the temperature got no higher than 5°C and there was the prospect of snow on the big day.

The Commissioning Ceremony on 18 December 1965 was attended by 500 Australian and American officials, new-found friends, as well as the small number of families of the ship's company that had moved to the US at their own expense. The ship and the dockyard were dusted with snow. The senior attendees were the Australian Ambassador, Mr Keith Waller and the Australian Naval Attaché, Captain Eric Peel, to whom *Hobart* would report on commissioning. The senior US representative was Vice Admiral Charles Melson, President of the US Naval War College and the Commander of the Newport Naval Base. Two Australian clergymen undertaking post-graduate study at Harvard University officiated at the ceremony.*

Among the guests arriving for the commissioning was retired Captain Harry Howden, who had commissioned the cruiser *Hobart* just before World War II. Under his brilliant command *Hobart* had survived service in the Red Sea, the Mediterranean and numerous Japanese air attacks in the dire days before and after the fall of Singapore. With the RAN losing so many ships in the face of the Japanese onslaught, this idiosyncratic captain was seen by *Hobart*'s sailors as both their saviour and the ship's talisman. To Guy and some of the older hands who knew of the 'Howden aura' his presence at the commissioning was a good omen for the new ship. Howden had arrived in Boston at his own expense, but his baggage had been lost on one of the connecting flights. Always the dapper dresser, Howden had gone to one of Boston's leading tailors and had them promptly make a suit and two shirts. Reflecting on the successful commissioning day, Guy only wished he had made more of Howden's attendance which meant so much to him.

---

* The clergymen were Reverend C.W. Peck of the Baptist Church and Father Greg Dening of the Society of Jesus. Dening later went on to become the Max Crawford Professor of History at the University of Melbourne and a noted historian of the Pacific.

The new RAN destroyers were allocated eight weeks for post commissioning training before passage to Australia. After completing further trials off Boston, *Hobart* would sail to Long Beach, California to undertake some form of work-up. In early January with *Hobart* alongside at the Boston Naval Yard continuing her fit-out, Guy flew to Long Beach to visit Captain Ian Cartwright and his team in *Perth* to discuss their experiences. Needing to truncate their shakedown program for their return to Australia, *Perth* had undertaken a shortened hybrid RAN–USN work-up training program.[14] It became clear to Guy that while the details of the USN's work-up regime were unclear it was immeasurably more thorough than the contemporary RAN practice. Guy called on the Fleet Training Group organisation in San Diego. To his delight he found the Commander of the Sea Training Group was none other than his other old *Nashville* friend Ira Bonnett, now a Captain. Guy asked Ira for 'no niceties for the Australians' but to treat them exactly as if they were a USN ship.[15]

Returning to Boston, Guy and *Hobart* commenced a demanding set of at sea weapons trials. A challenge was that these daytime trials had to occur well offshore and with daylight only between 0700–1630 all the passages in and out of Boston were at night. Indeed, the only daytime passage in or out of Boston was when *Hobart* finally left for the US west coast on 25 January 1966. By then those *Hobart* families who were in the US had returned to Australia.

Hobart's next phase was the conduct of further trials and practices in the Virginia Capes exercises areas off the US Atlantic Fleet's homeport of Norfolk. It normally boasts 'one of the most favoured climatic regions in the world',[16] but *Hobart* entered port in a snowstorm with gale force winds. On 1 February *Hobart* took onboard her missile and gun ammunition outfit for the first time and then commenced a busy two weeks of alongside equipment calibration and at sea exercises. On the weekend, to provide some relief, *Hobart* chartered three Greyhound buses to take officers and sailors on a tour of Washington, DC. *Hobart*'s sea program was continually hampered by poor weather, but Guy was struck by the flexibility the USN applied to rescheduling events to achieve *Hobart*'s milestones. In the process, the personal interactions at all levels with the men of the USN provided a valuable foundation for future dealings. Among the ships operating in the same area as *Hobart* was the imposing nuclear-powered guided missile cruiser *Long Beach*. *Hobart* would have more to do with her in the future. Fittingly, *Hobart*'s departure from Norfolk was marked by fog, passing showers and an enthusiastic but damp brass band on the wharf. Even during a subsequent week off Florida's Jacksonville exercise area, the poor weather followed the ship.

On 1 March fortunes changed as *Hobart* sailed close by Miami Beach in by now unfamiliar dazzling sunshine. The passage to California took *Hobart* through the Panama Canal. Guy had of course passed through the canal in the opposite direction 24 years earlier in the *Karamea*. Such had been the advances in naval technology that the shape and capabilities of the modern guided missile destroyer would have been inconceivable to Midshipman Griffiths and his shipmates. Passage through the Panama Canal is a rare occurrence for Australian sailors and in his *Report of Proceedings*, Guy wrote 'Cameras were in evidence at all points to record the passage through this great engineering achievement.'[17]

Hobart arrived at Long Beach Naval Shipyard on Sunday 13 March. From the lowering of the freshly painted white gangway it was clear this was a smart and efficient shipyard. For the first time in nearly two months the boilers could be shut down and shore steam provided. The following day shipyard staff descended on the ship and work began on a comprehensive maintenance period to prepare the ship for her 'shakedown'. This was a sea period to test all systems and evaluate the ship's operational performance. After a week of intensive shipyard work, the shakedown began in various West Coast exercise areas. A major milestone was *Hobart*'s first successful Tartar missile firings on aerial drone targets on the Pacific Missile Range. The ship conducted her torpedo firings in the beautiful waters of Puget

Sound off Washington State. This allowed *Hobart* to visit Vancouver; the first RAN visit since the cruiser *Adelaide* in 1924. During the port call a contingent of *Hobart*'s men marched to the city cenotaph on Anzac Day. On the return passage to the southern exercise areas *Hobart* had an enjoyable visit to San Francisco.

Hobart then sailed to San Diego for intensified training, both in shore simulators and at sea. One of the features of the sea training was the presence of over thirty officers and sailors from the Sea Training Group to coach and assess the *Hobart* team. While in San Diego, Guy made the acquaintance of a senior official in the Mexican Customs Service. This remarkably generous individual invited Guy and the entire ship's company to a Saturday lunch at his country club. With just a reduced duty watch left onboard *Hobart*, nearly 300 officers and sailors climbed into buses and took off for Mexico. It was a hot day and the first Margarita was most welcome. After that straight tequila was served. The host had a couple of goats brought onto a far hillside and tethered. He took up his rifle and shot them. They were then butchered and the meat dropped into vast vats of bubbling hot oil, as were the cleaned intestines and pretty much everything else. Lunch consisted of goat and avocado mash on flat bread with salad and, of course, more tequila. Two mariachi bands played and the sun beat down. Lieutenant Ian Holmes recalled,

> I was talking to one Chief Petty Officer and in mid-sentence he fell flat on his face. He was amongst the first. By the close of proceedings just enough people remained to carry the others to the buses, allowing us to return to the ship. The duty watch didn't know what had hit them and getting everybody to their bunks took a long time. Sunday was very quiet.[18]

It was during *Hobart*'s period in San Diego that Guy saw the benefit of the American khaki working uniform for officers and senior sailors, rather than the RAN's impractical white summer equivalents. So Guy allowed his officers and senior sailors to wear khaki uniforms with RAN rank insignias as a 'trial' but without telling the authorities back home, whom he suspected would say 'No'.[19] It proved popular and became accepted uniform onboard and his suspicion of there being a lack of acceptance by senior officers in Australia was well founded.

During the sea training *Hobart* had her first man overboard. Fortunately for Able Seaman Gary Hughes the sea was calm and he was recovered in just over four minutes. This busy training period culminated in the Final Battle Problem conducted at sea on 28 May in which *Hobart* obtained high marks. At the debrief, Captain Ira Bonnett, concluded his remarks on their performance by saying 'Glad you're on our side.'[20] This very structured training was, in Guy's assessment, 'an invaluable one and much information was obtained on the operation of a DDG which otherwise may not have been gained'.[21] Guy also now knew he had an outstanding ship's company.

The following day the ship held a reception on the Ikara deck for the USN sea training staff and on 30 May sailed from San Diego for the last time. *Hobart* was not to return to Australia just yet, however. The ship sailed to San Francisco for further shore training, system testing and additional missile firings on the Pacific Missile Range. The extended periods alongside allowed the men to see the many sights California boasted. About a third of the ship's company attended the Los Angeles International Games and became a vocal cheer squad for the Australian team. The ship finally sailed for Australia on 3 August. Rather than steam to her designated home port of Sydney, the ship was first to sail to her name port of Hobart.

Hobart had made a fine start to her service in the RAN. It was in no small measure due to her captain and this was appreciated by her ship's company on whom Guy had made a positive impact. As a second-time captain he no longer had to prove to himself that he could fulfil the role. To his men he had come with a fine war record, was immaculately

165

turned out and looked every inch a destroyer captain. Guy kept himself very fit, did not smoke and only drank in moderation. Importantly, he set high professional standards which he demanded of himself and was scrupulously fair. Through his experienced officers and senior sailors, the ship's routines and practices were well organised and strictly in accordance with the naval practice of the day. Guy's approach was to respect the competence of the officers and senior sailors and not to micro-manage them in their duties. He later remarked of the time,

> You let them get on with their job. They gain confidence and so it seeps through. If you interfere unnecessarily, you're sort of nagging and picking and that doesn't put anybody right at all. Your authority is there by virtue of your position and your rank. You don't need to be nasty or something or picky to establish that authority. I don't think Captain Nicholls in *Shropshire* raised his voice almost the whole time he was aboard when I was there with him for just about a year, but everybody respected his authority.[22]

With this approach to command, the ship's company was confident and individually knew where they stood and what was expected of them. Guy continued the practice, that he first used in *Parramatta*, of being a familiar figure, frequently walking through the ship and getting to know his men. He would make a point of going to a different part of the ship each day. If he was down in the engine room where the temperature could easily be over 45°C, he would be invariably offered a coffee to go with the chat. Through that deep interest in people and informal interaction which minimised their differences in rank, Guy learnt much about the complexity of the ship, his men and their concerns. He later considered that his walk-arounds were one of the highlights of his time at sea.

The delivery voyage to Australia involved a further week's training in the Pearl Harbor area and then a refuelling stop in Nadi. Off the

New South Wales coast *Hobart* rendezvoused with the RAN's flagship *Melbourne* and six other ships of the Fleet. In the words of Captain David Wells in *Melbourne*, 'the newest and latest arrival to the Australian Fleet was warmly welcomed by all ships present'.[23] *Hobart* immediately took fuel from the oiler *Supply* before sailing on to Hobart.* As the ship steamed up the Derwent River to her berth, *Hobart* was loudly welcomed by ships' sirens and car horns. Over 1000 people lined the wharf and gave the ship a 'boisterous' Tasmanian welcome. *The Mercury* reported that Guy 'docked the $45 million vessel like a new-born babe. Not an inch of paint was scratched.'[24] The destroyer was variously described in the local media as 'sleek but so lethal' and a 'Real Tartar'.[25] The six Tasmanian crew members were particularly fêted. Carla and several the wives of crew members flew down for the visit. *Hobart* was given the Freedom of Entry to the city, with Guy and the ship's company marching through the city with a large and appreciative crowd lining the streets. The official entertainment was extensive and ranged from a formal dinner at Government House to complimentary tickets to the cinema and to an Australian Rules semi-final match. Among the numerous tours of the ship was one by group of old *Hobart* and *Shropshire* men. In another, sailors donned pirate costumes for a tour by Legacy children who were given 'a slap-up day they will never forget'.[26] For its part the Navy used the port visit as a recruiting opportunity and an advertisement appeared saying that 'as a sailor of the RAN you'll be a true 'missile age' man.'[27]

After four very full days *Hobart* sailed for her much-anticipated arrival in her homeport of Sydney. A large crowd of family and friends awaited the ship at Garden Island Dockyard on 7 September. For some of the crew it had been a separation from family of eighteen months and for many, for over twelve months.† Even during the one month's leave and maintenance period alongside there were many visits to the

---

* It was the largest amount of fuel *Hobart* took from a replenishment ship during Guy's command.

† Fortunately, the new Chief of Naval Staff Vice Admiral Alan McNicoll allowed HMAS *Brisbane's* families to accompany the ship's company to the USA.

ship by ex-service groups and the general public. *Perth* and *Hobart* were of considerable interest to the broader Navy, with formal and informal tours taking place for officers and sailors alike wanting to see what the 'new navy' looked like as well as trying to appreciate the challenges of supporting such complex ships.

On 16 October, barely five weeks after returning to Sydney, *Hobart* sailed for her first major exercise. It was Swordhilt in the Coral Sea involving twenty-eight Australian, British, New Zealand and US warships. This was the largest naval exercise off Australia to that time. The strong RN presence included the aircraft carrier *Victorious*, two County class destroyers and 15 other ships. Swordhilt provided an interesting comparison between the RN County, which was originally the preferred RAN destroyer solution to the eventually selected USN Charles F. Adams class. In contrast to *Kent* and *Hampshire*, which both experienced teething issues with their engineering plants, *Hobart*'s speed and reliability were evident. One occasion exemplified that difference at the time. *Hobart* was on the port quarter of *Victorious*, wearing the flag of Flag Officer Second-in-Command, Far East Fleet, Vice Admiral Charles Mills*. The Admiral ordered *Hobart* to take station on her starboard bow. Normally, *Hobart* would pass astern of the aircraft carrier and then proceed up her starboard side. As *Hobart* had all four boilers connected, Guy rang on 30 knots and steamed up *Victorious*'s port side, and then Guy requested permission to cross the bow. *Hobart* then crossed the bow a good mile ahead and neatly took station. She would have looked very business-like from *Victorious*' flag bridge.

Guy was convinced, 'of the superior capability, flexibility, reliability and maintainability of the DDG'.[28] Guy and some of his officers attended the post-exercise reception onboard *Melbourne* and to Guy's surprise Admiral Mills told him that 'he could not understand why the RAN had bought that American rubbish'.[29] Mills was not alone in this view and it reflected a somewhat insular perspective by some RN senior

---

* Vice Admiral Sir Charles Mills, KCB, CBE, DSC (1914–2006).

officers about their systems and practices and a lack of appreciation of the sophistication of those of the USN.[*]

II

Australia's military commitment to the Vietnam War began in 1962 with a small army training team. Three years later, in May 1965 an infantry battalion was despatched with a second battalion one year later. From the outset *Sydney*, now converted to a fast troop transport, was undertaking supply trips to the conflict zone that would earn her the nickname of the *Vung Tau Ferry*. As the Australian Government looked to make an even more substantial contribution, the Navy initially considered some minesweepers, but the logistic problems combined with their limited potential impact made this unattractive. The new American built DDGs were ideal both for their potential contribution and their supportability through the US 7th Fleet. Following its emphatic win in the November 1966 election, Harold Holt's Government approved the deployment of a DDG, a third infantry battalion, a squadron of RAAF bombers and a Navy diving team. With *Perth* having been fitted with the Ikara anti-submarine missile system and due to conduct trials, *Hobart* was selected to be the first DDG to deploy to the war. The decision was publicly announced by the Prime Minister on 23 December 1966. *Hobart* would deploy in March 1967.[30]

After the extended period in the US, the Christmas leave period was particularly welcome for Guy and the ship's company. While the Navy wanted to retain as much expertise as possible in *Hobart*, there were competing individual demands such as sailors coming to the end of their sea time or the need to undertake career progression training. As a result, around one third of the ship's company changed over and this included a new Executive Officer, Lieutenant Commander Ian James. Guy soon

---

[*]   See also Grove, E. (ed.), *The Battle and the Breeze: The Naval Reminiscences of Admiral of the Fleet Sir Edward Ashmore*, Royal Naval Museums Publications, Stroud, 1997, 238.

came to appreciate his support and strong organisational skills.

Towards the end of the leave break the South Vietnamese Prime Minister Air Vice Marshal Nguyen Kỳ and Madame Kỳ visited the ship. The visit emphasised to the ship's company the importance of their assignment and Guy found Kỳ to be appreciative of Australia's support. In mid-February *Hobart* commenced a pre-deployment shakedown. Importantly, the new men onboard, who had not had the benefit of the period in the US, had to adjust to the new systems and be made to feel part of the team. There were various faults with the radars and missile systems that required the persistent efforts of the weapons' electrical sailors to be rectified before departure. Their cheerfulness and pride in their systems in the face of all these frustrations greatly impressed Guy.

On the morning of 1 March while *Hobart* was at sea off Jervis Bay she, along with the rest of the RAN Fleet, lowered the White Ensign with the Cross of St George and raised the new Australian White Ensign with its blue Southern Cross and Federation Star. It was a most popular change and Guy wrote that 'the significance of this act was appreciated by all onboard'.[31] *Hobart* was destined to be the first RAN ship to fly it in action. During the work-up, Army intelligence officers were embarked and gave the men well-received briefings on Vietnam and the war.

As the day of departure approached the preparations gathered pace. Such were the materiel shortages associated with the new DDGs that 5-inch gun ammunition was transferred from *Perth* to *Hobart*, to ensure she had a full outfit. Besides the sailors from the two destroyers being involved in the evolution, men from *Melbourne* and *Sydney* willingly gave a hand. On 7 March over a thousand people gathered at Garden Island for *Hobart*'s sailing. *The Sydney Morning Herald* reported, 'Sailors with brawny, tattooed arms gently held bawling babies.'[32] Families threw coloured streamers to the sailors who tied them to the guardrails. With memories of *Anzac*'s extended deployment to Korea and the already prolonged separation his crew had from their families, Guy hoped that *Hobart*'s deployment would keep to its planned six-month duration.

This was a sensitive issue, made more so by a newspaper report that the deployment was for nine months. It took some time, after prompting by Guy, for Navy Office to refute the report.[33]

Hobart's initial destination was the US 7th Fleet's base in Subic Bay in the Philippines. Whilst steaming north off the Australian coast the RAAF continued to provide aircraft for training *Hobart's* air defence teams. This became a template for future deployments. *Supply* was prepositioned off Manus island to give *Hobart* a top-up of fuel and the ship had a very short port visit to the island base for other provisions. In order to have as much time in Subic Bay for briefings and final preparations, Guy decided on a fast passage of 23 knots. For the majority of his ship's company who had not experienced operational service, this was unusual. Lieutenant Rob Walls* later remarked that the fast passage had a psychological impact on the crew because it showed that *Hobart* was going into a war zone.[34] Guy assessed the mood of the ship thus, 'They knew they were serving in a ship which had commendable capabilities and were confident of meeting the challenges ahead.'[35]

On 15 March *Hobart* arrived in Subic Bay and was hosted by another DDG, *Henry B. Wilson*. To welcome them to the 7th Fleet was none other than its Commander, the distinguished naval aviator Vice Admiral John Hyland Jr, who had flown from Japan especially to meet *Hobart*. The week's briefings were invaluable, as was the chance to rectify small defects at a base replete with all the spare parts and expertise necessary. The meetings allowed Guy and his officers to forge personal relationships with some of the key officers and senior sailors who would help support *Hobart*. The judicious use of the senior sailors and wardroom bars as well as a well-attended cocktail party onboard greatly helped in that socialising effort.

Guy's overriding impressions of Subic Bay were its high tempo and impressive logistics capabilities. Indeed, *Hobart* had arrived around Subic

---

*   Later Vice Admiral R.A.K. Walls AO, RAN (1941–). He was Vice Chief of Defence Force 1995–97.

Bay's peak with over 200 ship visits a month. Adjacent to the naval base was the Cubi Point Naval Air Station which was the largest in Asia and a major hub for the US war effort. These facilities abutted the small city of Olongapo, home to the over 15,000 local shipyard and air-station workers, not to mention the hundreds of bars with attendant women, mostly from rural areas to entertain the sailors. To many *Hobart* sailors, used to the haunts of Hong Kong and Singapore, Olongapo had much heightened sense of danger and vice. Guy thought Olongapo was 'a dreadful place' and 'uniquely unattractive'.[36]

For the remainder of the month *Hobart* conducted training with USN ships and aircraft. On one occasion, when leaving Subic, *Hobart* passed *Kent* with Vice Admiral Mills embarked. With *Kent* just on a goodwill port call, the contrast in operational purpose and capability between the two destroyers was stark.

III

The naval war in Vietnam had many parallels with that of Korea. By the time of *Hobart*, deployment, up to four aircraft carriers were on task to wage a campaign of attacking infrastructure, interdicting enemy supply routes as well as supporting troops on the ground in an operation known ominously as 'Rolling Thunder'. The duties of the destroyers were to escort the aircraft carriers, interdict North Vietnamese inshore infiltration and supply craft, and bombard shore targets. The last task was now termed Naval Gunfire Support, or NGS for short. The interdiction work off the South Vietnamese coast largely fell under Operation 'Market Time', whilst the missions further north in the Gulf of Tonkin were part of Operation 'Sea Dragon'.

One difference between the two wars was the greater complexity of air operations. The number of aircraft, particularly jets and helicopters, called for more sophisticated arrangements to track and control air movements. To facilitate this, the USN had one of its guided missile cruisers or larger destroyers fitted with the computer-based Naval Tactical Data System (NTDS)* to coordinate a Positive Identification Radar Advisory Zone, known as PIRAZ.† The PIRAZ ship would be stationed about 30 miles off the North Vietnamese coast to provide early detection of any Northern Vietnamese aircraft. She was also to ensure sufficient height and horizontal separation of US aircraft and reduce the chances of friendly forces firing on their own forces. The advanced control measures were new to the RAN and represented another facet of naval operations that involved a steep learning curve in *Hobart*.

On the morning of 28 March, *Hobart* finally sailed for the Vietnamese coast to take part in Operation Market Time. With the benefit of the extensive briefings, Guy and his leadership team decided to modify the watch-keeping arrangements. This was to ensure the ship would be able to conduct NGS against shore targets around the clock if necessary, while sustaining sufficient air defence and damage control capabilities. To achieve this, 40% of the men would be in a two watch Defence watch, whilst the engineers with their arduous engine room duties would be in shorter three watches. The remainder of the crew would be 'day men' and on call. This was a far cry from the long periods of Action Stations in *Shropshire* which had been difficult to sustain.

Hobart joined the 7ᵗʰ Fleet Cruiser–Destroyer Force commanded by Rear Admiral Mark Woods.‡ *Hobart* was assigned the callsign 'Purple Royal'. In his welcoming signal Woods wrote 'Fighting is easy, it's the

---

* Naval Tactical Data System was a computerised information processing system developed by the USN. It was first deployed in the early 1960s. It took data from radars and other sensors and then displayed video symbology on radar screens to provide a more accurate tactical picture from which decisions and optimal weapon assignment could be made. Improvements in computers and radars incrementally improved NTDS performance. *Hobart* was not NTDS fitted and radar operators had to manually detect and track radar contacts. In 1974 *Perth* was the first RAN DDG to be retrofitted with the Australian variant of NTDS, the Naval Combat Data System (NCDS).

† PIRAZ duties also included air control, vectoring air tankers to returning strike aircraft, hostile air warnings, warning aircraft if approaching Chinese airspace, control barrier combat air patrols and coordinating search & rescue.

‡ Rear Admiral M.W. Woods, USN (1918–99).

paperwork which is the problem.'[37] The humour had more than an element of truth to it for the paperwork took many forms. The orders, local procedures and publications received in Subic Bay were voluminous. From the time of being attached to 7th Fleet *Hobart* was receiving 1,000 signals a day. It required an experienced eye to ensure nothing significant was missed among this message traffic. Usefully, a 7th Fleet officer was embarked in the ship for the duration of her attachment. Importantly, and what had proved difficult for the US intelligence organisation to accept, *Hobart* had been given a security dispensation, and was receiving relevant sensitive US intelligence that was marked NOFORN or No Foreign Eyes. For all intents and purposes, *Hobart* was to be treated as a USN ship.

At 0600 on 31 March, *Hobart* joined the US destroyer *Fechteler* near Yankee Station, where the on-task attack aircraft carrier was stationed. This Station was roughly at a mid-point between Da Nang and the Paracel Islands.* Three *Fechteler* officers came onboard *Hobart* and conducted the handover. Once complete, *Hobart* steamed inshore to her assigned bombardment sector. It lay off Duc Phuo in Quang Ngai province, which was garrisoned by both a battalion of US Marines as well as one from the Army of the Republic of Vietnam (ARVN). It did not take long for *Hobart* to enter the war. At 1145 *Hobart* engaged a concentration of Viet Cong (VC)† with forty-seven 5-inch rounds at a range of 23,500 yards, with an air spotter giving corrections. The DDGs possessed the new 5'/54 calibre gun which had a substantial advantage over the older destroyers' 5'/38 calibre with a maximum range of just 17,300 yards.‡ *Hobart* was accurately firing at ranges that *Shropshire* had rarely attempted.

During the evening of the first night on station, a second fire mission

---

* Yankee Station was at 17°30'N 108°30'E.

† The Viet Cong was the National Liberation Front of South Vietnam and Cambodia. It had a military wing formally known as the People's Liberation Armed Forces of South Vietnam.

‡ The 5-inch/54 gun had a maximum operational range of 24,900 yards. The calibre of a gun reflects the ratio between the length of the gun barrel from the breech to the muzzle in relation to the diameter of the shell. Therefore with 5-inch/54 mount the gun barrel was 54 times the 5 inches. A longer barrel length normally increases range and accuracy.

against the VC was conducted and then the ship was tasked to undertake Harassment and Interdiction (H&I) engagements against a variety of targets. The latter tasking often involved just single rounds without a spotter observing fall of shot. It was reminiscent of the discredited night-time harassing fire finally dispensed with in the Korean War. Guy took an equally dim view of its tactical value.

Hobart soon settled into a pattern of being ready to provide NGS to the Marines during the day and conducting H&I to hamper the VC's night-time movements. A visiting *Sydney Morning Herald* correspondent wrote 'the sailors of the *Hobart* appear at the moment to have only one complaint – they can get no daily beer ration while the ship is on the gunline'.[38]

Every day or so *Hobart* would rendezvous with a replenishment ship to take on fuel, food, stores or ammunition. These evolutions required *Hobart* to come up at speed and take station on the beam of the replenishment ship at a distance of about 35 metres. Caution had to be exercised not to puncture the replenishment ship's unseen underwater bow pressure wave which could result in *Hobart* being sucked alongside, or even worse pushed in front of the larger ship. Once in station, and depending on the sea conditions, the interval apart could be slowly closed to as little as 20 metres to expedite the passing of the replenishment spanwire, before opening back out to about 35 metres. Simultaneously, a team of sailors on the fo'c'sle tended a line with small, coloured flags attached, indicating the changing distance between the ships. Constant vigilance was required in station keeping. Typically, the Captain or Navigating Officer would con (i.e. manoeuvre) the ship throughout the evolution. Likewise, on the bridge, the Chief Coxswain or another very experienced helmsman would be on the wheel. In benign conditions more junior officers would be given the opportunity to con once the ship was settled in the replenishment position. This gave them the opportunity to feel the subtle forces of interaction. Once the resupply was complete and the spanwire and other gear was returned, *Hobart* would accelerate and gently steer out from the replenishment ship.

Once proficient, ships could undertake more complex replenishments. Some supply ships could provide more than one commodity and *Hobart* could simultaneously receive fuel, stores or ammunition from two different stations either forward, amidships or aft. These evolutions could be undertaken at night with both ships darkened except for a variety of dimmed lights to indicate different replenishment positions and lines between the ships. In addition, some of the USN's newer replenishment ships, such as the Mars class, possessed helicopters which allowed the simultaneous stores resupply by vertical replenishment or VERTREP.

The USN's sophisticated logistics system was unrivalled and these replenishments at sea were initially very demanding. *Hobart*'s seamanship and teamwork grew immeasurably, Guy had always consciously placed great store in the ability of *Hobart*'s men to complete replenishments to a high standard. Over time Guy gave more officers the ship-handling experience of these evolutions. Such was the proficiency attained that if Guy were needed in the Operations Room* at the time of replenishment, he would allow his Navigating Officer to supervise the bridge and officers of the watch to conduct the ship-handling.

Guy received an early close glimpse of the war when he accepted an invitation to call on the newly arrived Lieutenant General Foster Lihue commanding the 1st Marine Division, based at Chu Lai. Leaving his Executive Officer in command, Guy flew by a Marine helicopter inshore and then low along the coast to Chu Lai, 110 kilometres south of Da Nang. The base was garrisoned by 34,000 troops and in addition to its supporting helicopters had six squadrons of Phantom and Skyhawk fighter bombers. The scale of the American enterprise in just this part of the country was astounding. The Operations Centre briefings to Guy not only emphasised the importance of NGS but highlighted that the Marines thought about 60% of all enemy supplies came via small inshore

---

* In the USN the Operations Room was known as the Combat Information Centre (CIC). Over time the term CIC was used in some RAN DDGs and later FFGs.

vessels. Clearly any assistance *Hobart* could provide the Marines and US Coast Guard units attempting to interdict this flow would be very worthwhile.

The following day *Hobart* called a passing patrol craft alongside and Guy exchanged some sailors for the day to help better understand each other's operations. Guy also put in place informal arrangements whereby *Hobart* would resupply these craft whenever possible. Some of the NGS missions provided urgent support. On the night of 9–10 April, an ARVN observation post came under heavy VC attack. *Hobart's* supporting fire helped repel the VC and resulted in 15 of them being killed.

In the middle of the month *Hobart* ranged further along the coast and also supported US Army forces ashore. Around midday on 11 April, as *Hobart* completed a fire mission in the Duc Phuo area, a report came over the communications net that a patrol boat had embarked an 8-year-old boy badly injured by his junk's engine flywheel. Guy ordered *Hobart* to close the patrol boat and embarked the boy for treatment in the sickbay. Once treated the boy was sent by boat to the landing ship USS *Washtenaw County* and then airlifted ashore by helicopter.

The tempo and wear on Guy and *Hobart's* ship's company can be gauged by the activities of 14 April. During the early hours *Hobart* conducted H&I firings until 0600. From 0715 to 0830 she replenished ammunition from *Haleakala*, then undertook a fire mission on the gun line from 1120 to 1154. In the afternoon *Hobart* refuelled from *Kennebec* then conducted a further bombardment until 1655 before resuming the H&I firings from 2130 until 0400 when *Hobart* had to provide an immediate call for fire to save an ARVN detachment being overrun by VC.

These initial days on the gunline had, in Guy's view, provided *Hobart* and her team with a sound grounding before dealing with even more complex and demanding operations to the north. This came soon enough on 16 April when *Hobart* entered the Operation Sea Dragon Area of Operations which ran from the Demilitarised Zone (DMZ) northward along the North Vietnamese coast.* This meant the enemy would not be the VC but the People's Army of Vietnam (PAVN).

Once in the Sea Dragon area *Hobart* joined Task Unit 77.1.1. This consisted of the four destroyers. The Commodore was Captain Harry Johnson in *Duncan.*† Guy and some of his specialist officers called on him for a briefing. It was explained that the overall objective of Sea Dragon was to prevent the transfer of enemy supplies south along the coast via coastal and inland waterways using barges, junks and sampans. Naval operations off Vietnam were replete with many acronyms and these vessels were known as waterborne logistic craft or WBLC. Reflecting on the new mission, Guy expected that, while the tempo would be greater, the absence of nightly H&I firings would allow *Hobart*'s men to get more sleep. Operations were in fact to prove busier, and the crew would spend many hours closed up at Action Stations.

In Sea Dragon operations *Hobart* could expect to come under fire from PAVN shore artillery. The concept was that most fire missions would be undertaken by the more modern ships with their longer ranged 5-inch/54 guns, while the older destroyers would have their 5-inch/38 guns ready to engage any enemy shore batteries. In the first instance Johnson in the older *Duncan* teamed up with *Hobart* for the deliberate bombardments.

No sooner had Guy returned to *Hobart* than the guided missile cruiser *Boston* joined the formation. *Boston* flew the flag of Rear Admiral Woods. *Hobart* soon took station alongside the flagship and Guy was transferred to her by high-line to formally call on the Admiral. He found

---

* The Vietnamese Demilitarised Zone marked the border between North and South Vietnam. It was up to 40 kilometres wide and ran from east-west about a 100 kilometres north of the city of Hue. Although it was nominally described as being at the 17th parallel, almost all of the DMZ was to the south of the parallel.

† In the USN a 'Commodore' is the honorific title given to an officer of Captain rank who commands a group of ships or submarines. During *Hobart*'s time off Vietnam the Commodores commanded either Destroyer Squadrons or smaller Destroyer Divisions. The other destroyers were commanded by officers of Commander rank. Commodore had been a substantive rank in the USN only in the periods 1943–47 & 1982–83.

Woods very experienced in Sea Dragon operations. Although newly promoted, Woods had served on the gunline in his last command, the guided missile cruiser *Canberra*.

The first action took place on the following day, 17 April. *Hobart* engaged shore targets with 51 rounds while *Duncan* opened fire on suspected artillery sites. The next day Johnson handed over commodore duties to Captain Ardwin Franch in *Collett*. Once again, when conducting bombardments, *Hobart* would team up with the commodore's ship.

When not conducting NGS or replenishing from the impressive array of logistic support ships, *Hobart* would sweep inshore looking for WBLCs. On the morning of 21 April the spotting aircraft alerted *Hobart* to some barges. *Hobart* and *Collett* closed the coast at speed while the spotter duly directed their fire. One barge was sunk and four others badly damaged. In the process *Hobart* had attracted the attention of a battery of PAVN artillery which opened fire. She was immediately straddled, with eight 85mm and 100mm shells landing around her and two exploding before hitting the water. Guy immediately stepped in on the bridge and increased speed and manoeuvred his ship clear of the danger. His calm and decisive intervention left an indelible impression on those present on the bridge. *Collett* opened fire to suppress the artillery. As *Hobart* cleared out to sea she took with her some shrapnel scars on the superstructure as souvenirs of the first encounter where she traded blows.[39] It was now clear to the crew that being shot at had to be expected.

The following morning *Hobart* and *Collett* continued sweeping for WBLCs before being assigned to engage two targets not far inland. In a reversal of roles *Collett* steamed inshore for the bombardment and *Hobart* stood ready to engage any shore batteries. The enemy reaction to *Collett*'s presence was quick. Two shells exploded in the air near *Collett* and *Hobart* immediately opened fire on the shore flashes. Both ships withdrew without any damage. On *Hobart*'s bridge the men became more prepared for the enemy fire. One Officer of the Watch, Lieutenant Harry Daish later wrote, as 'I had a grandstand view of proceedings. The drill on spotting enemy fire was to alert the Operations Room, order full speed ahead and put the wheel hard over to clear the scene as quickly as possible.'[40] Guy was keen, however, for those men who normally worked below decks to come to the bridge during lulls in the action, to see the North Vietnamese coast and be briefed on what was going on. He was particularly pleased when one day the Chief Stoker Alf Skinner wandered up. Guy held the seasoned engineer in high regard and enjoyed his laconic observations, on the Navy and life in general.[41]

In an unexpected turn of events, *Hobart*'s first patrol entered a third phase. In recent weeks within 7th Fleet there had been explosions in some 5-inch/54 gun mountings. It was finally decided to suspend their use and x-ray suspect ammunition lots for any flaws. This necessitated 'musical destroyers' whereby only older destroyers were assigned to NGS duties and the newer ships were given other tasks. In the case of *Hobart* she was assigned on 23 April to escort the Yankee Station aircraft carrier *Kitty Hawk*.

The 6-year-old *Kitty Hawk* was the last word in US aircraft carriers before the shift to nuclear propulsion. She displaced over 76,000 tons and had an array of ninety aircraft for a variety of missions. Guy was invited onboard to call on Captain Paul Pugh and the embarked Commander 7th Fleet Attack Carrier Strike Force, Rear Admiral David Richardson.* The admiral had been an aviator in the Pacific Campaign and had coincidentally been Executive Officer in *Badoeng Strait* off Korea when Guy was in *Sydney*. Richardson was in overall charge of naval forces off Vietnam and was working to better integrate intelligence reporting into operational planning. Guy found *Kitty Hawk* to be a hive of activity as strike packages were regularly launched during his visit. In a tour of the ship Guy viewed the capabilities of her NTDS system in operation, as well as the earliest version of a satellite navigational system. This intriguing positioning system was produced by Johns Hopkins University and had an accuracy of about 200 metres at sea and four metres when alongside.

---

* Later Vice Admiral D.C. Richardson, USN (1914–2015).

The Naval Campaign in the Vietnam War

To Guy the potential of the system was enormous and he reported its use back to Australia.[42]

Hobart spent a week with *Kitty Hawk*. During that time the destroyer was either acting as rescue destroyer, stationed astern of *Kitty Hawk*, or forming part of the protective screen. Whilst *Hobart* was in company, *Kitty Hawk* conducted the first carrier strike on a North Vietnamese air base, which was the MIG fighter field at Kep. For those strikes *Hobart* was stationed closer to the coast in case there was a retaliatory strike on the carrier. While not experiencing the activity of Sea Dragon, it was a stimulating environment and provided the opportunity for some *Hobart* sailors to spend a day in *Kitty Hawk*.

On 29 April, *Hobart* detached from *Kitty Hawk* and joined *Carpenter* and *Fechteler* for passage to Subic Bay, arriving the following day. After thirty-two days of constant operations, *Hobart's* first patrol came to an end. Guy later wrote 'April 1967 had undoubtably been the most rewarding month since commissioning'.[43] In that time the ship had steamed 8,792 miles, conducted 69 fire missions in the course of which she had expended 2,319 5-inch rounds that were directed at enemy troop concentrations, bunkers, barges and sampans; killing or wounding about 100 enemy soldiers. To sustain herself at sea, *Hobart* had conducted twenty-six underway replenishments in the month.[44] For Guy the patrol had validated the high priority placed on training and maintenance and he was proud of his men's efforts. *Hobart* had experienced a wide variety of tasking that well prepared her for the remainder of her tour.

During the week alongside, *Hobart* was resupplied for the next patrol and her men availed themselves of the amenities both on the base and at Olongapo. The ship also received a visit from the South Vietnamese Ambassador, His Excellency Bhan Dang Lam, who gave a heartfelt address to the officers in the wardroom on the value of *Hobart's* contribution to war effort. For Guy this period allowed him to catch up on much needed rest. Lack of sleep was a constant state of affairs when at sea. When off the Vietnamese coast Guy was invariably awake for up to twenty hours a day, relying on naps to keep going.

As quite often happens, ships form particular bonds with other ships through frequent chance meetings and associations, both at sea and in port. In *Hobart*'s short life she had formed two of them, one with the tanker *Passumpsic* when they first met in Boston, then in Long Beach before meeting again off the gunline. The other ship was the cruiser *Long Beach*. They first met in *Hobart*'s work-up on the US west coast and now *Hobart* was nested in Subic Bay with her and *Boston*. Following a reception with *Long Beach* and *Hobart* officers, the two captains decided that the cruiser would embark rotations of two of *Hobart*'s air-intercept controllers (AICs) on her PIRAZ duties. Lieutenant Walls and Leading Seaman Corrie Halliwell were initially embarked. For AICs, this was the big league and was the first time any RAN personnel had been exposed to PIRAZ and to NTDS.

On 6 May, *Hobart* sailed for her second patrol as part of *Kitty Hawk*'s screen along with *Carpenter* and *Fechteler*. Once *Kitty Hawk* reached Yankee Station, *Hobart*, with the 5-inch/54 ammunition issues resolved, steamed to join the Sea Dragon force. On the morning of 8 May, as had become the practice, *Hobart* teamed up with the commodore's ship. In this case she was *Allen M. Sumner* commanded by Captain Bruce Althoff.* *Hobart*'s arrival coincided with Althoff receiving the handover brief with the out-going commodore, Captain Richard Johnson in *Samuel N. Moore*. Guy also attended and they found the focus of operations was interdicting enemy coastal traffic along the coast near the (Song) Kien Giang River. In addition, there would be the regular NGS missions identified from intelligence reporting and aerial reconnaissance. After lunch that day *Hobart* and *Allen M. Summer* combined to engage barges

---

* Captain W.B. Althoff (1925–2009) was two years younger than Guy, but because of the older entry age in the USN had not entered the US Naval Academy until 1946. He had, however, subsequently gained a degree from Yale as well as a post-graduate degree from George Washington University. He was representative of a new cohort of USN officers in command with tertiary qualifications. It was a development that would not be seen in the RAN for a generation.

on the Kien Giang as well as some adjacent warehouses. In the evening they engaged four targets before hitting the Quang Khe ferry complex. The following day the destroyers similarly bombarded the Huu Hung ferry complex further down the coast.

The pattern developed of *Allen M. Sumner* and *Hobart* either conducting bombardment of pre-determined shore targets or engaging WBLCs attempting to steal down the coast at night. In one such bombardment of an enemy supply post at My Trung, a very large explosion was observed indicating an ammunition cache had been destroyed. Later that morning the ships closed the Kien Giang River to engage some WLBCs. In the course of the engagement both ships came under concerted shore battery fire. Fifty rounds landed around *Hobart* with the closest about twenty yards from the ship. As both ships cleared the area at speed *Hobart* fired sixty rounds at the shore batteries. At least one battery was destroyed.

Becoming more attuned to Sea Dragon operations, yet still having fresh eyes, Guy and his team could see that the less-than-optimal coordination between 7th Tactical Air Force and the 7th Fleet meant that opportunities to strike at the PAVN being missed. Guy gained approval for his Operations Officer, Lieutenant Commander Don Weil, to fly to Da Nang to talk to USAF operational planners to improve matters.

The destroyers closed the Kien Giang River the following day to strike at WBLCs once again. This time the ships steamed towards the coast at 25 knots in the hope of avoiding fire from shore batteries. There was no return fire and three vessels were sunk and six damaged. They returned twice in the night to engage more WBLCs. This daily pattern continued, interrupted only by replenishment of fuel, ammunition and food from the now familiar array of logistic ships. During that week the two destroyers damaged or sank 89 WBLCs as well as damaging 19 buildings. On the morning of 16 May, while *Allen M. Sumner* was bombarding a road bridge, an enemy road convoy appeared and *Hobart* quickly engaged it destroying ten trucks.

The following morning, *Hobart* continued the campaign against ferry terminals, this time destroying one at Truc Li. These important facilities were increasingly defended and 15 PAVN shore batteries returned fire with *Hobart*. Of the 130 rounds fired at her one fell within 10 feet while 35 landed within 50 yards. Once again *Hobart*'s luck held and there was no damage to the ship. *Hobart* and *Allen M. Sumner* engaged the shore batteries as they withdrew at high speed. Three were silenced. Later that morning, more WBLC were attacked by *Allen M. Sumner* while *Hobart* destroyed another shore battery.

IV

The Vietnam War was to be the first conflict that Guy had been involved in where there was not overwhelming public support for Australia's participation. On sailing from Australia, however, the correctness of *Hobart*'s deployment, as well as the increased Army commitment, were not widely questioned in Australian society. Anti-war feeling was slowly growing, partly in opposition to the use of conscripted troops, but more generally to Australia's involvement in a long-running conflict in a country with few historic links to Australia.* This questioning of national policy specifically touched on *Hobart*'s involvement when Labor MP Gordon Bryant spoke in Parliament and likened *Hobart*'s shelling of coastal targets to when 'German ships shelled villages during the Spanish Civil War, and called on the Government to ensure that Australian forces did not attack civilian targets'.[45] The Prime Minister, Harold Holt said in reply an 'unhappy accompaniment of war was that civilian casualties occurred despite the best precautions'. Guy and his men in *Hobart* were generally unaware of this political discourse. As in the Korean War, some targets were used for both military and civilian purposes. *Hobart*'s recent attacks on ferry terminals were a case in point. They were used by both

---

* An August 1969 Gallup Poll indicated 55% favoured bringing Australian troops home, and only 40% favoured them staying. The large Vietnam Moratorium demonstrations would begin in Australia in 1970.

civilian ferries and PAVN watercraft. As such, civilian casualties were almost certainly an inevitable consequence of their targeting.[46]

In the conduct of the overall war, the US Commander, General William Westmoreland,[*] had pursued an attrition strategy to reduce the manpower and supplies of the enemy. An impediment to this strategy, at the time of *Hobart*'s deployment, was the PAVN's use of the DMZ as a sanctuary for operations south of the zone. Operation 'Hickory', which began on 18 May, was the first US incursion into the DMZ to engage PAVN in their safe haven. Seven battalions of the US Marines would be deployed across the DMZ, supported by ARVN elements. As part of Hickory a subordinate operation, 'Beau Charger', would involve an amphibious landing of Marines to enter the DMZ in the Ben Hai River area. On 17 May *Hobart* and *Allen M. Sumner* joined a force of two cruisers, *Boston* and *St Paul,* along with the destroyers *Fechteler, Edson* and *Joseph Strauss.* They were to support an Amphibious Ready Group of the amphibious helicopter carrier *Okinawa* and three other amphibious ships. The hospital ship *Sanctuary* would stand offshore. At 0400 on the following morning the cruisers commenced their bombardment, with *Hobart* and the other destroyers opening fire on shore targets two hours later. There was a spirited duel between ships and shore batteries, with at one stage ten enemy rounds bracketing the troop-laden amphibious ship *Point Defiance.* For nearly two hours the ships engaged PAVN positions before the 0800 landing by Marines. Beau Charger was also supported by carrier-based aircraft, as well as bombers from the 7th Air Force. The destroyers each fired between 500–1000 rounds at shore targets. For a period, the spotting of their fall of shot was hampered by one of the Marine spotters ashore being killed.

Hobart's targets were enemy mortar and artillery positions. After her expenditure in recent days Guy had to economise on rounds per target. Even so *Hobart* expended 525 rounds and at the end of the first day had

---

[*]   General William Westmoreland's title was the Commander Military Assistance Command, Vietnam.

only seven powder cartridges[*] left onboard and had to rendezvous with *Joseph Strauss* for an impromptu and unusual destroyer-to-destroyer top up. The hectic day's events led Guy to signal, 'The barrels are smooth, the barrels droop, we're out of powder, what's the scoop !!!'[47] *Hobart* soon returned to the gunline, but no further missions were required of her.

The landing was a success although fourteen Marines were killed while the PAVN lost about 44 dead on the first day.[48] More broadly, Operation Hickory broke up the PAVN sanctuary but also led to the civilian depopulation of much of the DMZ. For their part *Hobart* and *Allen M. Sumner* returned to Sea Dragon duties on 19 May. Operation Beau Charger was, for both the USN and the RAN, their first amphibious operation since the Korean War.

On passage to the Sea Dragon operating area, both ships replenished fuel from *Tappanhannock* and ammunition from *Rainer*. Returning onboard were Lieutenant Walls and Leading Seaman Halliwell who had gained invaluable experience controlling fighters and strike aircraft in *Long Beach*. It was one of the highlights of their careers.

A difficulty for the USN in integrating a foreign warship into their formations was that it was rarely done and such ships were generally a completely unknown quantity. *Hobart* was different in that she was a US-built ship and had passed through the USN training system. Nevertheless, her integration was complicated by *Hobart*'s commanding officer being of captain rank and therefore senior to all but the commodore. She would in the normal course of events take charge of 'junior' ships, hence the reason for *Hobart* being paired with the commodore's ship. By the end of May Rear Admiral Woods and successive commodores had seen enough of Guy to give him greater responsibility. Accordingly, on 19 May Guy was directed to detach from *Allen M. Sumner* and take *Fechteler* under his command and Guy immediately understood the significance of the event. On departure Althoff signalled he would 'sorely miss' *Hobart*. Guy

---

[*] A powder cartridge is a brass or steel canister filled with propellent placed behind the shell projectile in the gun breech to propel the shell to its target.

thought that of all the commodores he had served with, Althoff best understood and exploited *Hobart's* capabilities. The *Hobart* and *Allen M. Sumner* had an eventful 10 days together in which they had most notably sunk or damaged 34 WBCCs and destroyed or damaged eleven coastal batteries, expending nearly 2,000 5-inch rounds. While *Hobart* demonstrated the capabilities of the latest generation of destroyer, Guy reflected on the prowess and efficiency of *Allen M. Sumner*, a World War II veteran, and opined to Althoff that he hoped that 'DDGs age as effectively'.[49]

The tasks for *Hobart* and *Fechteler* were to interdict WBLCs and engage shore targets in the Bay of Brandon area. The area, colloquially known as 'the Slot', had a high concentration of both fishing vessels and shore artillery. Guy's strategy was initially to conduct fast sweeps inshore to better understand the vessel patterns, assisted where possible by aerial surveillance. Only in this way could they identify the PAVN supply craft. In terms of the NGS task, Guy was conscious that *Hobart* had previously been fired upon in this area. NGS would invariably be at night and Guy elected to engage the targets at long range and at speed. The first such fire mission was on 21 May and went well, but on the next evening the bombardment was cancelled because the moon presented a clear silhouette of the destroyers to the shore artillery in that part of the coast. In the early hours of 24 May the two destroyers closed the coast at speed and engaged three shore targets and, as they were engaging the last position, shore batteries opened up with inaccurate fire on *Hobart*. Later that morning Guy transferred another two Air Intercept Controllers, Lieutenant Robert Howland and Leading Seaman Gary Barnes, to get experience in *Long Beach*. Just after lunch, 20-year-old Able Seaman Wayne Godenzie on watch in the Operations Room heard a faint aircraft beeper on the Air Distress Net and then saw an Emergency IFF on his radar display.* These indicated a downed aircraft. It was one of *Hancock's*

---

* Identification, friend or foe (IFF) is a radar-based identification system. It uses a transponder that provides a response to an interrogating signal or coded number to identify ships and aircraft.

A-4E Skyhawks which had taken ground fire into its engine after a bombing raid on Hinh Binh. *Hobart* successfully vectored a helicopter to rescue the young pilot.[50] In the late afternoon the destroyers again closed the coast for a fire mission and were engaged again by shore batteries with some inaccurate gunfire.

In the early morning of 25 May the ships were undertaking another fire mission, supported by two A-1H Skyraiders ground-attack aircraft from *Bonhomme Richard*. Guy regarded the slower Skyraiders above all other aircraft for their spotting abilities.* In this case these aircraft, as well as providing spotting information, were undertaking armed reconnaissance, in the course of which they attacked in turn a cluster of WBLCs with rockets. The second aircraft took anti-aircraft fire from shore and crashed into the sea. *Hobart* directed a helicopter to the scene but there was no sign of the pilot, 23-year-old Ensign Richard Graves.[51]

After lunch Rear Admiral Woods arrived on the scene in *Boston* and proceeded with the destroyers to bombard a large concentration of WBLCs off Cua Can River. The normally active shore batteries seemed intimidated by *Boston*'s large shell detonations. Woods was conscious that ships were running the gauntlet of the shore batteries but, as he signalled to his Task Group, 'By risking your lives to get the boats and trucks, you surely saved many more down south.'[52] This was the last mission for *Hobart* in her second patrol and she handed over to *Benjamin Stoddert*. During the patrol *Hobart* had destroyed or damaged 9 coastal batteries, 33 WLBCs, 10 trucks and an ammunition dump. After fuelling and storing from *Castor* and *Sacramento* both destroyers sailed for Subic Bay, arriving on 28 May.

As with *Hobart*'s earlier experiences with the US work-up regime, operating with the USN for extended periods allowed Guy to better identify some of their procedures which would be useful innovations for the RAN. These he selectively proposed both while still on deployment

---

* Compared to jet aircraft, Guy felt the propeller-driven Skyraider flew at an optimal speed and height for observing the fall of shot and were well-practised in the duty.

and after he returned to Australia. One was the US Casualty Report (CASREP) system in which a ship would report her equipment defect to other ships and up the command chain. If local knowledge or spares were available the defect could be repaired quickly. Initially, Guy was a lone voice advocating such innovations and, to some in the Navy hierarchy, a zealot, but as other RAN ships deployed and more people became exposed to the DDGs, these and various other ideas were adopted.

IV

During her maintenance period in Subic, *Hobart*'s gun barrels were once again replaced. The arduous nature of the patrols combined with the need for essential maintenance squeezed the opportunities for *Hobart*'s men to get adequate rest and recreation (R&R). After just nine days alongside in Subic Bay *Hobart* again set sail. She was not immediately to return to patrol, but instead to pay the RAN's first visit to Taiwan. On 7 June *Hobart* arrived in the very busy and congested port of Keelung on the northern tip of the island, to a very warm welcome from the Taiwanese. Part diplomatic and part recreational the visit was a great success. With an annual rainfall is nearly three metres, Keelung has the distinction of being the rainiest major port in the world with rain expected on every second day. Not unexpectedly the ship's reception was held in a downpour with guests good-naturedly moving between the bridge, the wardroom and Guy's day cabin. Of the visit Guy wrote that 'as a change from Subic Bay, the Ship's Company found Keelung distinctly refreshing and made the most of their opportunities for R&R in the island country'.[53]

In drizzling rain *Hobart* sailed from Keelung on 11 June. Instead of immediately rejoining the Sea Dragon ships, she was ordered back to Subic Bay to fit additional equipment. The timing was fortuitous as it coincided with the handover ceremony of Rear Admiral Woods to Rear Admiral Walter Combs Jr* onboard the new flagship *St Paul*. Guy had

---

*   Rear Admiral Walter V. Combs Jr, USN (1914–2001).

enjoyed serving under Woods, who had shown the confidence to let him take US destroyers under his command. In combat Guy had impressed Woods with his 'imagination and resourcefulness coupled with his courage (which) were directly responsible for the success of a number of engagements with enemy shore batteries'.[54]

Rear Admiral Combs was a 'destroyer man' of some distinction who had earned the Silver Star commanding the destroyer *Harrison* which had beaten off kamikazes in the Okinawan campaign in the final phase of World War II.[55] Combs was later to remark that at this phase of Sea Dragon the North Vietnamese were doubling their dispositions of shore batteries to counter the ever more effective work of the Sea Dragon ships. He assessed that 'the communist batteries are highly mobile, sometimes radar controlled and manned by dedicated and accurate gunners'. He reasoned it was only a matter of time before one of his ships would be hit.[56] The additional equipment *Hobart* installed included electronic warfare sensors to detect the PAVN fire-control radars and a mortar to fire 'chaff' rounds to decoy these radars from the ship. This was the first time such a system had been fitted to a RAN ship. It was into this heightened threat environment that *Hobart* sailed for her third patrol.

Embarked for the initial part of the patrol was *Daily Telegraph* correspondent Reg McDonald. While the Vietnam War has often been described as a 'television war', technical limitations still meant that naval operations off the coast were invariably covered more traditionally, with a resultant time lag in stories. McDonald reported on how active *Hobart* has been and that she 'has probably seen more action than most Australian ships which took part in the Korean War'.[57] In particular, he noted how many times *Hobart* traded fire with the enemy. One of *Hobart*'s young sailors told him, 'The sight of water bursts as enemy shells straddle your ship and the rattle of shrapnel against the ship's superstructure from air bursts quickly make you realise that you are in a real shooting war.'[58]

Initially, *Hobart* sailed not for Sea Dragon, but for operations with Task Group 76.5, the Amphibious Ready Group or 'the ARG' as it was commonly referred to.* The intent for this formation was to undertake Operation Beacon Torch which was a series of amphibious landings by elements of the US Marine 1st Division with the intent of searching for and destroying PAVN and VC supplies in the area south of Da Nang, below the DMZ. The other destroyer assigned to provide NGS was *Harry E. Hubbard,* while air support would be provided by the Marines. There were complementary operations with Marines operating from inland; Operations Brown from the north west and Adair from the south. Guy and some of his officers and senior sailors went onboard the flagship *Tripoli* for briefings on the operations which would take place between 18–22 June. In another 'first' for the RAN, Guy would command the protective screen of the ARG as well as the naval bombardment.

At 0500 on Sunday 18 June *Hobart* was on station waiting for a call for fire. At about 0545 the first waves of helicopters flew from the ARG with Marines, while others went ashore in landing craft. These initial insertions were unopposed and *Hobart* did not get her first fire mission on a VC position until 1400. This was well inshore and at 24,100 yards distant was only 800 yards inside *Hobart*'s maximum range. Anti-climatically this was the only mission for the day, while during the night there were only occasional calls for harassing fire on the VC. The lack of activity was in part due to the need by the 7th Fleet at the time to economise on 5-inch/54 ammunition and to use the older 5-inch/38-gun ships wherever possible. Because *Hobart* was operating further south than normal, on 21 June Guy organised for seven Australian Army officers to come onboard to observe her operations. That afternoon the ship bombarded a further seven VC positions and continued H&I firings through the night. After the experience of Sea Dragon patrols, to Guy the war in the south had aspects of strange and 'notable unreality'. He wrote at the time,

---

* The Amphibious Ready Group consisted of *Tripoli* (LPH), *Ogden* (LPD), *Monticello* (LSD), *Tom Green County* (LST) & hospital ship *Sanctuary.*

The sea of lights from the nearby city of Da Nang and surrounding villages twinkled apparently undisturbed by the battle in progress a few miles to the south. Brightly lit merchant ships lay at anchor within a few miles while *Hobart*'s guns fired H&I throughout the night, with the ship steaming through dozens of surprisingly unconcerned fishing craft a few thousand yards from the beach. In fact life appears to go on as normal despite the shore bombardment, air attacks and artillery firings that disturb what were otherwise 'peaceful' tropical nights.[59]

On the morning of the last day of Beacon Torch, *Hobart* cleared the amphibious lodgement area to close *Manatee* to refuel. She then steamed towards Da Nang and rendezvoused with HMAS *Derwent* near the port. The frigate with FOCAF, Rear Admiral Richard Peek embarked, had detached from the RAN Task Group of *Melbourne*, *Vampire* and *Supply* then undertaking the RAN's annual Asian deployment. It was an oddity for *Hobart* to come into contact with another RAN warship operating in a peacetime mode and, no doubt, conversely so for *Derwent*.

Peek wanted to observe operations and *Hobart*'s part in them. The Admiral had commanded *Tobruk* off Korea in 1952 and so had a sense of the style of operations, if not their increased complexity. Once onboard Peek was briefed on operations and after lunch Guy brought *Hobart* alongside the anchored *Tripoli* where the soon to be confirmed Under Secretary of the Navy, Charles Baird, and Admiral Hyland came onboard *Hobart* for discussions. Baird, a former Marine, would later write to Guy to say that 'from every quarter I heard that *Hobart* is doing a superb job'.[60]

Fortuitously, *Hobart* was called back to the Beacon Torch area and Peek was onboard whilst *Hobart* engaged another VC position. The admiral returned to *Derwent* before sunset. Peek assessed *Hobart* to be smart and efficient and that Guy had 'excellent knowledge of her operational capabilities'.[61] He was somewhat surprised though to learn the extent to which Guy allowed officers of the watch to conduct replenishments at sea, even at times with Guy not on the bridge. This was something Peek had not experienced. It was, however, a reflection of how well worked up *Hobart* was and that she was at a competency level well above the rest of the Fleet. *Hobart* would go on to complete over 150 replenishments, which was an unprecedented figure thus far for a deployed RAN warship.

As *Hobart* steamed north into the night towards the DMZ, 'gun flashes lit up the sky and the rumbling of heavy artillery fire was indicative of current operations'.[62] In the early morning light *Hobart* joined six warships awaiting their turn to obtain fuel and ammunition from two replenishment ships. It was back to the now familiar Sea Dragon 'gang' of *St Paul, Benjamin Stoddert, Allen M. Sumner, Samuel N. Moore, Theodore E. Chandler* and *Edson. Hobart* had returned in time for another change of commodore with Captain Robert McClure replacing Althoff. With a new commander, *Hobart* reverted to being consort to the commodore's ship, this time *Edson*. The two destroyers steamed towards the stretch of coastline between Cape Lay and Cape Mui Ron. They promptly made their presence felt by sinking two and damaging four WLBCs later the afternoon. That evening they engaged bridges and causeways near the mouth of the Song Kien Giang.

The next day, 24 June, *Hobart* received by helicopter another Australian visitor, the Commander of the Australian Forces, Vietnam, Major General 'Tim' Vincent,* accompanied by the new Commander of Task Force 77, Rear Admiral Roger Mehle,† who had replaced Rear Admiral Richardson. Mehle was a World War II fighter 'ace' who in 1944 earned the Silver Star in the 'Great Marianas Turkey Shoot'. After a short tour and lunch, the visitors departed by helicopter leaving the destroyers to engage another group of WBLCs, destroying six of them. The opportunity was also taken to engage shore artillery sites in the

---

*   Major General D. (Tim) Vincent, CB, AM, OBE (1916–95).
†   Rear Admiral R.W. Mehle, USN (1915–97).

vicinity. For the next week *Edson* and *Hobart* patrolled the northern part of the Sea Dragon area but found or were assigned few targets. Their reassignment to the southern Sea Dragon area on 2 July was timely. The following day the destroyers engaged the Vinh Son military area and a nearby truck park. Quartermaster Tony Robles, one of *Edson's* sailors later recalled of *Hobart*, 'This intrepid warship was one of our Captain Vermilya's preferred associated gunship(s) while I was onboard, with high respect for her captain.'[63]

Guy once again took command of the task unit when the *Edson* swapped with *Preston* to act as rescue destroyer to the Yankee Station aircraft carrier. *Preston* was particularly keen for some action after a couple of weeks of 'chasing bird-farms' as the aircraft carriers were colloquially known. She was not disappointed and later that day *Hobart* and *Preston* were called upon to bombard the My Duyet Thong Highway Bridge which they partially destroyed. This was followed by engaging WLBCs along the nearby coastline. The following morning two more WLBCs were sunk and in the afternoon a Skyraider reported a further clutch. The problem was the aircraft was running low on fuel and had little time on task. Guy responded by having the destroyers close at 25 knots to engage the targets. Three WLBCs were heavily damaged.

A couple of days of occasional NGS missions, H&I firings and replenishments were interrupted on the afternoon of 8 July when one of *Hobart's* sailors heard on a communications circuit the 7th Air Force Control Centre calling for any aircraft airborne with Variable Time (VT) fuzed bombs. There was no reply so *Hobart* replied she had VT shells available. *Hobart's* offer was readily accepted and she closed to within range of an enemy artillery site in wooded country northwest of Cape Lay. Two USAF spotting aircraft provided the direction. The result was all rounds hitting the site and a large resulting explosion. The earlier visit to the 7th Air Force at Da Nang might have paid dividends. During this part of the patrol Guy used his consort to suppress the shore artillery sites whilst *Hobart* conducted fire missions on targets further inland. *Preston* was his most willing partner in these enterprises. In one engagement, the old *Preston* fired 282 rounds at the artillery sites on the nearby coast with Guy remarking that 'needless to say there was no aggressive action' from the sites.

On 9 July Guy handed over his duties to Captain Keith Johnson in *Hollister*. After de-briefing Rear Admiral Combs onboard *St Paul* on the state of inshore operations, *Hobart* detached for a much-anticipated port visit to Hong Kong. During the week alongside many men stayed ashore in hotels and all the crew used the time to decompress. Also in port was *Edson*. Four of her sailors ventured into the unfamiliar surroundings of the China Fleet Club. A large group of *Hobart* sailors insisted they join them and then shouting them drinks to 'celebrate' their time together. Quartermaster Robles said they appreciated their *Hobart* hosts' 'rough and ready courtesy' which reinforced his father's tales as an American sailor in Brisbane during World War II. On 17 July just before leaving, Guy was told by the Commodore, Hong Kong that his ship was the first for some time to have no Shore Patrol Report raised about them.

Before returning to Vietnamese waters *Hobart* spent four days in Subic Bay to effect system repairs and otherwise prepare for the next patrol. Guy was informed that *Hobart* would be assigned to Attack Carrier Striking Group 77.6 commanded by Rear Admiral Harvey Lanham* in *Forrestal*. The aircraft carrier was still in port and would be the first Atlantic Fleet carrier to take part in the war. Guy called on Admiral Lanham and was told that of the destroyer screen, two would be kept with the carrier and remainder rotated through *Sea Dragon* to bolster that operation. It promised to be an interesting patrol. Before sailing Lieutenant Commander Weill, with Admiral Coombs' blessing, flew once more to Da Nang to continue work to improve co-ordination between Air Force and Navy.

In keeping with Lanham's scheme, *Hobart* and *Chandler* were initially lent to the Sea Dragon operations and patrolled off the Song

---

*   Rear Admiral H.P. Lanham, USN (1913–69).

Kien Giang. For the next few days some of the firing opportunities were hampered or curtailed by USAF air activity in the area, which underscored Guy's attempts to improve co-ordination. On 27 July *Hobart* damaged a highway ferry, truck park, storage area, an artillery site and four WLBCs. The following day yielded similar results.

Just after 1100 on Saturday 29 July *Hobart* was on patrol ninety-five miles to the south of *Forrestal* when a signal reported a major fire onboard the aircraft carrier, just five days into her first patrol. By chance one of *Forrestal's* utility helicopters was hovering above the nearby *Chandler*, taking on fuel. Guy ordered the aircraft to close *Hobart* and embark her doctor, 27-year-old Surgeon Lieutenant Leo Barnett, for transfer to *Forrestal*. For Barnett, *Hobart* was his first ship having only joined the Navy three years earlier. Previously, he had been the Senior Surgical Registrar at Brisbane General Hospital. What awaited him was on an altogether different scale. Meanwhile Guy took *Hobart* and *Chandler* at speed towards the carrier.

As *Forrestal* prepared for her second strike of the day, electrical interference had ignited the motor of a Zuni rocket carried by a Phantom fighter bomber on the starboard quarter of the flight deck. It shot across the deck striking the external fuel tank of a fully armed Skyhawk fighter bomber on the port side. At least one of the Skyhawk's 1,000-lb. bombs fell to the deck, cracked open and caught fire soon setting off other bombs and rockets and fuel. The stern of the ship was soon an inferno.

By the time *Hobart* and *Chandler* arrived on the scene *Forrestal's* two escorts were rendering assistance. *George K. Mackenzie* had picked up some of *Forrestal's* men from the water whilst *Rupertus* in an impressive piece of seamanship had closed to twenty feet from the carrier's stern to play her fire hoses into the intense fire. Through the day and evening helicopters transferred fire-fighting equipment from the other ships, including *Hobart*. For those on *Hobart's* upper deck viewing the burning *Forrestal*, a powerful image was aircraft being pushed overboard to prevent them also being engulfed in the inferno. In all 134 men were killed and another 161 injured.

Once the fires started to be brought under control *Forrestal* steamed slowly towards Subic Bay. It would be over fourteen hours before all the fires were extinguished. That evening the hospital ship *Repose* arrived to take onboard the injured. *Hobart* and *Chandler* stayed in company until just after midnight. Less than four hours later the two destroyers conducted NGS on enemy positions which continued on and off until 0500. Part of the forenoon was then taken up with refuelling from *Mispillion*. Whilst alongside two USN official war artists, including the noted Salvatore Indiviglia, came onboard to record the activities onboard *Hobart.** During the afternoon and evening more shore and waterborne targets were engaged until 2130. Action stations were called once more at 0450 to engage the Vung Chau storage area. It was a gruelling tempo on the crew and on Guy in particular.

Surgeon Lieutenant Barnett finally rejoined *Hobart* by helicopter via *Intrepid* on 31 July. He returned tired and subdued. He, like the other medical staff in *Forrestal,* had made many difficult clinical decisions in a compressed time-frame guided by the maxim of 'maximum good for the maximum number'. When asked in *Hobart*'s sickbay how it went Leo Barnett could only remark, 'I did my best, but for some there was nothing to be done other than make them comfortable and ease their pain.'[64] Soon Guy received a signal from Admiral Lanham which said Barnett's assistance 'had directly contributed to the saving of many lives'.[65]

On 1 August Guy handed over Task Unit duties to Captain Merlin Schwittters in *Rupertus,* to rejoin Sea Dragon operations with *St Paul.* They proceeded to the Bay of Brandon where an air spotter soon identified WLBC traffic. Because the aircraft was low on fuel they engaged the watercraft at long range with *Hobart* sinking one and damaging five others. In a night-time engagement *St Paul* fired on two inland targets whilst *Hobart* put down suppression fire on shore artillery positions. The following day the ships were joined by *Blue* and the two destroyers

---

*   A Salvatore Indiviglia sketch of *Hobart* is held in the Special Collection of Hofstra University Library, New York State.

continued fire suppression whilst *St Paul* engaged enemy positions inland. Their presence finally led to a reaction and shore artillery batteries engaged the ships. *St Paul* was bracketed by about 100 shells and received shrapnel inboard whilst the destroyers were each straddled by a dozen rounds. *Hobart* fired 44 rounds at the batteries and laid smoke to cover the withdrawal of the ships. Once out of enemy gun range *St Paul*, with the aid of the air spotter, concentrated on the batteries and destroyed one of them. For the next six days the three ships engaged enemy positions or infrastructure.

In a glimpse into the future of naval operations, *Blue* had embarked a modified DASH* drone helicopter as part of the Snoopy Trial. The DASH had been equipped with a camera to allow the ship to conduct its own air surveillance and spotting. Both destroyers undertook two successful NGS missions until on 7 August the DASH crashed into the sea due to either a mechanical fault or small arms fire. *Hobart* laid smoke and covered *Blue* while she salvaged her DASH. For the remainder of the day and into the night *Hobart* supported *St Paul* in fire suppression and engaged a highway ferry and military installations.

On 8 August after a major replenishment *St Paul* handed over to *Boston*. As the newly arrived cruiser and *Hobart* closed the coast at speed to intercept WLBCs they came under heavy fire from shore batteries. About 200 rounds, mostly directed at *Boston*, landed around the ships which caused them to open from the coast at speed. The ships came under fire once more on 11 August when six shore batteries engaged them with between 150–200 rounds. The closest came within 150 yards of *Hobart*. The ships fired over 300 rounds in response and *Hobart* fired off chaff to distract the enemy 'Crosslot' fire-control radars associated with the shore batteries. Over the following two days the ships had more success when they sank nearly forty WLBCs.

In the early hours of 16 August, *Hobart* undertook her last Sea

---

* The Drone Anti-Submarine Helicopter (DASH) could be armed with two lightweight torpedoes for use against submarines. It had a range of about 22 miles (35 km) from the ship.

Dragon fire mission in company with *Boston*. It was against the Tien Dien and Phu Lap highway bridges. On completion, *Hobart* transferred some personnel and documents across to the flagship in a high-line transfer. As *Hobart* broke away *Boston* graciously fired a 21-gun salute to Australia in recognition of *Hobart*'s Sea Dragon service. As *Hobart* sailed toward Subic Bay, Admiral Coombs in *Boston* signalled, 'As a fellow destroyer sailor may I say that I have not seen one more smartly handled than *Hobart*.'[66]

From 18 August *Hobart* spent a productive ten days in Subic on maintenance before sailing for her final port visit to Hong Kong. In a rough passage the ship steamed a circuitous route to avoid Typhoon Madge, which also seemed hellbent on a Hong Kong landfall. Ultimately, *Hobart* arrived half a day late on 30 August in the Crown colony, where the sailors could finally relax. After four days *Hobart* sailed for her final patrol which would once more be off the coastline around Cape Lay.

On 6 September, *Hobart* rendezvoused with the destroyer *Du Pont* with the commodore, Captain Ernest Cornwall Jr embarked. *Hobart* soon took on another official war artist, this time an Australian Army officer, Lieutenant Ken McFayden, who joined for a week.* He had arrived at a busy time in the patrol. *Hobart*'s new consort was in a sorry state. Eight days earlier her after gun turret knocked out by a direct hit from a shore battery which killed a sailor. In addition, her remaining over-worn gun barrels had reduced her effective range. Despite this the two destroyers quickly settled in as a team and on the first day had six NGS missions.

The situation on the ground was challenging with large numbers of PAVN in the area. The Marines estimated they were outnumbered three to one. To add to the difficulties there was a shortage of air spotters, while those spotters on the ground were hampered by enemy movements. Despite this, over coming days the destroyers engaged bridges and troop laden sampans. At dusk on 8 August *Hobart* undertook her last and

---

* Some of Lieutenant Ken McFayden's *Hobart* artwork is held in the Australian War Memorial collection.

largest ammunition resupply from the inauspiciously named *Pyro*. In an example of how worked up *Hobart* had become, in just over an hour the ship embarked 1,349 shells and cartridges. No sooner was this completed then she came alongside *Cimarron* for stores and the largest refuelling she had undertaken off the Vietnamese coast. After completing the refuelling at midnight *Hobart* closed the coast for H&I firings through the night on PAVN positions.

For the next two days *Hobart* supported the Marines by engaging fifty-seven targets which were typically PAVN troop concentrations, or their storage areas. In doing so she expended over 500 rounds. *Hobart*'s last day on station, 11 September, involved early morning H&I firings before a top-up of fuel from *Chemung* and then passage to Subic Bay. *Hobart* arrived on 14 September and berthed alongside her relief *Perth*. Later that morning Admiral Hyland came onboard *Hobart* and addressed the ship's company. The Admiral had earlier sent a signal to Guy which in part read,

> Your performance in Westpac (the Western Pacific), as the
> first RAN unit in support of the war in Vietnam has been
> absolutely superb. There has been no operation in which
> you were involved that you and your men did not perform
> in a truly outstanding manner.[67]

The rest of the day was consumed with the officers and sailors providing handovers to their *Perth* counterparts. *Perth*'s commanding officer was Guy's former shipmate Captain Peter Doyle.[*] On 15 September *Hobart* sailed for Sydney with just a refuelling stop at Manus Island. Embarked for the passage was Guy's relief, Captain Ken Shands, whom Guy had known since Naval College days. The ship's company enjoyed the luxury of cruising watches and attended to maintenance and the appearance of the ship prior to her arrival home.

---

[*]   Later Rear Admiral P.H. Doyle, AO, OBE, RAN (1925–2007).

Hobart had been at sea for 160 days of her 204-day deployment. While off the Vietnamese coast *Hobart* had fired over 10,000 rounds at 1,050 targets. In response the North Vietnamese had fired on *Hobart* nine times, with the ship sustaining only minor shrapnel damage. For Guy the success of the deployment was testament to efforts of the ship's company. In particular, he found that the professional competence of his crew and the confidence that it engendered within the ship was a significant factor. This was in part due to the high standards he set, his desire not to micro-manage and his willingness to extend opportunities to junior officers and sailors. Examples of this included the ship-handling opportunities given his junior officers and allowing sailors the opportunity to be air intercept controllers, normally the preserve of officers. These initiatives were unheard of in the rest of the Fleet at the time. Nearly 40 years later Guy reflected,

> Our achievements rested upon various factors. The ship, its weapon systems and their capabilities ... Mail arrived regularly. Food was either good or very good. Quarters were cramped for the 330 men onboard, but air-conditioned living quarters provided a reasonable quality of rest off watch. Most importantly, I had an outstanding ship's company.[68]

For Guy personally being conscious of the high performing team he led also reduced the stress that he was under in command. He would later remark,

> I was confident in what the ship could do and the more we operated in Vietnam the more we convinced ourselves that we could do it well. It is not boasting or anything like that. It's a case of a warm feeling of confidence and that stuck with us right throughout. So yes, there were stresses on the captain, for instance when the shore targets or shore guns

shot at the ship about ten times. You don't sort of hang around and wait for something to hit you, you avoid it. That's a tense period but the rest of the time when we were shooting, when we were carrying out our assigned tasks I was confident that the shells would fall in the right place because the team was good and the equipment was first class.[69]

Hobart returned to Sydney on 27 September after nearly seven months away. Some 1,200 family and friends awaited them on the wharf at Garden Island. Two days later Guy handed over his command. Guy had much to offer the Navy with his recent experiences. Guy was surprised, however, that he was not asked to call in on Navy Office to debrief on his ship's deployment. In terms of his next posting, the two areas in which he could logically contribute were either Fleet Headquarters or Navy Office. But Guy had learnt while deployed that his next appointment was to be neither of these options. Instead, he was to be temporarily promoted to Commodore on 23 December 1967 and proceed to Malaysia.* Guy was told that he would replace Commodore Allen Dollard, who was the out-going CNS of the Royal Malaysian Navy. He would not be the CNS but an advisor.

V

In recognition for his and *Hobart*'s performance, Guy would later be appointed to the Distinguished Service Order.† Twenty-seven of *Hobart*'s

---

* At that time in the RAN the rank of Commodore was temporary and only applied whilst the officer was in a particular post. On completion the officer either was promoted to Rear Admiral, reverted to the rank of Captain, or left the service. Of note, Captains over six years seniority were on the same pay scale as a Brigadier. In the RAN the rank system changed in 1975 to align with the Army and RAAF when the rank of Commodore became a substantive rank.

† The Distinguished Service Order (DSO) is awarded for meritorious or distinguished service by officers of the armed forces during wartime, typically in actual combat. The DSO is part of the Imperial honours and awards system. In 1991 the Australian System of honours and awards was instituted. The

officers and sailors would also receive medals, a Mention in Dispatches or a Naval Board Commendation.

Part of Guy's success in *Hobart* and *Hobart*'s success in Vietnam was in no small measure due to the easy manner he had with the men of the USN. Rear Admiral Combs wrote that Guy, 'made many friends for himself and his ship in the US 7th Fleet, where he is both liked and admired'. He went on to say that 'He obviously commands the full support of his officers and men; the outstanding performance of his ship attests to this and it is immediately obvious even to the casual visitor.'[70]

But perhaps the most important element of Guy's performance in command of *Hobart* was his role as a wartime commander. Combs, who with 44 destroyers under his command, wrote that Guy and *Hobart* were equal to the very best. In particular, when engaging North Vietnamese positions Guy and his team had gained a reputation for their thoroughness, the originality of their planning and their high standards in execution. During Sea Dragon Guy impressed Combs with his ability to 'grasp the essentials of complex situations and to act promptly and precisely, and a deft and sure hand in handling his ship'.[71] Deservedly, *Hobart* was received a United States Navy Unit Commendation and Guy was awarded the US Legion of Merit.

At the time and in later life Guy considered his command of *Hobart* during the Vietnam War the high point of his career. He told Rear Admiral Peek that for him personally it had been 'an exhilarating and rewarding experience'.[72] *Hobart* had performed admirably and paved the way for the subsequent RAN deployments. Lieutenant Murray Forrest* said at the end of the deployment the pride felt by everyone onboard in what they had achieved was extraordinary.[73]

Captain Peter Doyle remarked that a hallmark of Guy's sea commands was his 'ability to get the best out of a team'.[74] Guy's previous

---

comparable award in this system is the Distinguished Service Cross. Guy was the only DDG commanding officer awarded the DSO.

* Later Rear Admiral M.B. Forrest, AM, RAN (1942–).

seagoing experiences in *Repulse*, *Shropshire*, *Anzac* and *Parramatta* had prepared him for his wartime command. His approach to command and his temperament suited the ship and the occasion. To many of *Hobart*'s officers and sailors, Guy was the finest Captain they had served under. Petty Officer John Rae, who was in charge of the sickbay, best summed up that sentiment when he wrote of Guy,

> Certain breeds of men come upon the earth preordained as to what they will be and why. Guy Griffiths was a sea Captain from the top of his head to the tip of his toes. A distinguished good-looking man with the leathery skin of an outdoor life, his eyes were a deep blue in colour which could twinkle with amusement on occasions but turn agate ice blue when annoyed. He was not a big man in stature, but possessed 'presence' that made others automatically drawn to him in a respectful way. A ship's Captain especially of a warship, has an awesome responsibility – his voice, his thoughts, have absolute power over the lives of his crew and the destiny of his ship. A warship has the ability to destroy other ships, shore emplacements, support troops ashore, and other myriad tasks for which it was built. A Captain is prepared to die for his ship, and a ship's crew is responsible to its Captain, and if he is truly a good Captain then the crew will be prepared to die for him. Guy Griffiths was such a man. I have never met anyone like him, before or since.[75]

As a postscript to *Hobart*'s service, there lay a quirk of naval history. The first *Hobart* under the command of the commissioning captain Harry Howden had miraculously escaped damage or casualties during repeated Japanese air attacks. Her luck ran out thirteen months later when, commanded by her next captain, Harry Showers, *Hobart* was torpedoed, but survived, with the loss of thirteen men. The second *Hobart* under Guy's command survived unscathed nine shellings by North Vietnamese shore gunners. In her next deployment, under the command of Captain Ken Shands, she survived unhurt until hit on the thirteenth attack on her. It was doubly unlucky, as the attack came not from North Vietnamese shore gunners but from a mistaken USAF Phantom fighter-bomber. Two missiles hit the ship and two sailors were killed. After a month's repairs in Subic Bay *Hobart* resolutely returned to the 'gun line'.

8

Flag Officer

Commodore Griffiths is a professional sailor to his fingertips.
Commodore K Thanabalasingham, Royal Malaysian Navy

I

On 7 September 1967, while *Hobart* was still conducting her last patrol off Vietnam, *The Straits Times* of Singapore reported that Captain Guy Griffiths now commanding HMAS *Hobart*, would take up the new position of Adviser to the Royal Malaysian Navy.'[1] The article was based on an announcement the previous day by the Australian Minister of Defence, Mr Allen Fairhall. There were no details on what the position involved. For his part, Guy subsequently did the rounds of the relevant Defence and Navy Office directorates in Canberra seeking guidance on his forthcoming appointment. The information was meagre. To prepare for his forthcoming position, Guy undertook from late October 1967 a 10-day Malay language course at the Defence Language Training School.

The background to the change from an Australian to a Malaysian to head the RMN set the context for Guy's time in Malaysia. Following the Indonesian–Malaysian Confrontation* and then the announcement of the British withdrawal from the region, the Malaysian Prime Minister

---

* Confrontation was an insurgency during 1963–66 that was waged by Indonesia against the newly formed Malaysia. Indonesia opposed the creation of the new state.

Tunku Abdul Rahman decided that all Malaysian armed services were to be commanded by Malaysians. At the time, only the Army was so commanded. Because of the absence of any Malaysians of a suitable rank, it was initially proposed that the Navy and the Air Force would be commanded by Malaysian generals. Both Army candidates demurred on the basis that they knew little of these services and their tenure they reasoned would adversely affect their Army careers. Undeterred, the Prime Minister selected the 31-year-old Lieutenant Commander K. Thanabalasingham* to be promoted to Commodore and become CNS, a jump of three ranks.†

The news of the policy change and Thanabalasingham's selection was received within the RMN, according to the CNS Designate, with 'utter disbelief'.[2] Indeed, when Thanabalasingham first read the signal announcing his appointment he thought it was a practical joke. Only when he received the formal letter a day later did he realise his appointment was genuine.[3]

Thanabalasingham was an intelligent and well-performing officer, who got on well with junior and senior officers alike. Fortuitously, he was also of Tamil descent and thus his selection navigated the sensitive Malay and Chinese racial issue. In short, if there was to be an indigenous CNS then Thanabalasingham was the ideal choice. As such there was much goodwill within the RMN towards him. He took up the post on 1 December 1967, a week after Guy and his family had arrived in country.

The new Adviser arrangement could have been a potentially awkward one for the two Commodores. Guy was thirteen years older than Thanabalasingham with considerably more sea and command experience. This situation was complicated by a communications

---

* Later Rear Admiral Tan Sri Dato Seri K Thanabalasingham PGAT, PSM, SPMS, DPMT, DIMP, JMN, SMJ, AMN, PKB, PPA, PPM, PJM. His name K. is a patronymic, not a family name, and he should be referred to by the given name, Thanabalasingam. To his friends he is known as 'Thana'.

† A similar but less dramatic approach was taken by the Australian Government in 1948 when it selected the young and junior Rear Admiral John Collins to be the RAN's first Australian born CNS.

breakdown where the specifics of the new role were not communicated to Guy. So while the outgoing CNS, Commodore Dollard gave Commodore Thanabalasingham a thorough handover, it was only on arrival and in initial discussions with Thanabalasingham that Guy came to fully understand his duties.

To the immense credit of both 'Thana' and Guy, they appreciated the Prime Minister's intent and the significant challenges that faced the RMN. The Navy now had expanded roles, more complex ships in the offing and a need to have a larger and more highly trained personnel strength. After attending an operations briefing soon after his arrival, Guy decided it best not to attend future meetings. He reasoned that it was of more value to offer his services in areas such as training which would be critical if the RMN was to meet its expanding roles. This approach proved most productive. Guy became Chairman of the Training Review Team and developed policy papers on manpower, training and other issues. One practical outcome was the increase in specialist training in Australia and elsewhere, but the bulk had to be undertaken in Malaysia. The local training capacity had to be expanded accordingly. Guy's advice was also sought on a range of other matters. What did not go unnoticed was that because of the shortage of staff officers, Guy 'often carried out work well below his rank but always voluntarily and with great good-will and cheerfulness.'[4]

Importantly, both men soon came to like and respect each other and were keenly aware of the others' position. Thanabalasingham valued Guy's well considered advice and enjoyed his pleasantly direct and sensitive approach, that was laced with good humour. Besides having a close working relationship, Guy and 'Thana', who was a bachelor, regularly played golf and socialised together.

After the rigours and separation associated with command of *Hobart*, Guy and Carla revelled in the opportunity to experience family life in Kuala Lumpur. Carla, having spent nine years in the then Dutch East Indies, ten years in Shanghai and then six in Hong Kong, felt very much at home in Malaysia. They lived in an area where mostly expatriates resided and was known locally as 'UK Heights'. Young Erica thought it a blissful period and later recalled,

> So trips to the market feature strongly in my memory, with my brother and I rescuing a duckling and taking him home as a pet and my mother paying 'protection money' to the boys in the market carpark to protect our car ... We lived life as expats in the Far East in the late 60s – there were many parties and many holidays – to the Cameron Highlands to go walking through the jungle and to the coast.[5]

Socially, Carla and Guy were popular members of the Defence, diplomatic and business social scene. Their next-door neighbours were the Smurthwaites, with Dick Smurthwaite heading up the Colgate-Palmolive company in Malaysia. In an early conversation Guy learnt from Dick that he had been a pilot onboard the escort carrier *Ommaney Bay* which Guy had watched ablaze en route to Lingayen Gulf.

During Guy's tenure racial tensions between the Malay and Chinese populations simmered. There was a perception held by some Malays, that the minority Chinese, who lived mainly in the cities and towns, controlled too much of the economy. On 13 May 1969 violent sectarian riots took place following the general elections. Anywhere between 200–600, mainly Chinese, were killed. During the period of unrest Guy was assigned a soldier when moving through the city. He sat in the front passenger seat of Guy's car with his .303 rifle poking out the window. The racial prejudices were brought home to Guy and Carla when their Chinese housekeeper sought sanctuary for her mother and six children in the grounds of their residence. This was strongly opposed by their Malay cook. However, the family was taken in for their safety.

After the riots the national mood had changed to one of a more Malay nationalist nature. In late 1969, Thanabalasingham told Guy 'in the prevailing conditions in the country that perhaps his Adviser's role should come to an end.'[6] It was a view Guy shared, and was subsequently endorsed in Canberra. So, in October 1969 Guy, Carla and the family returned to Australia. Prior to his departure, Commodore Thanabalasingham, wrote of Guy,

> He has borne a curiously difficult role as Naval Adviser to me with cheerful and friendly resignation. The job has not taxed him in any way as the duties are light, but for an officer of such obvious ability and experience he has shown enormous restraint in rendering advice of the highest order only when necessary.[7]

There was mutual respect with Guy greatly impressed by Commodore Thanabalasingham's considerable achievements.[8] Indeed Thanabalasingham went on to command the RMN until 1976 and retired as a Rear Admiral at just 40 years of age. In that time he oversaw its development into a highly regarded regional navy. Tan Sri Thanabalasingham is rightly regarded as the 'Father of the Royal Malaysian Navy'. For his part, Guy had assisted the RMN in many unsung ways along its early path of development. The friendship of the two men, thrust together as they were in unusual circumstances, has at the time of writing been maintained for over five decades.

II

The family did not have long in Australia, as Guy had been selected to attend the Imperial Defence College in London. After just a month in country Guy and the family flew to London on 11 December 1969, first to find a house before Guy started his studies the following month. Instead of London lodgings, Guy recalled his time at the Lygon Arms Hotel and the beauty of the surrounding countryside. With the assistance of Douglas Barrington, Guy and Carla found a suitable house in Broadway.

The children went to the local village school and soon all the Griffiths family came under the Cotswolds' spell.

The course Guy was about to embark upon was held in the stately Seaford House on Belgrave Square. The institution, headed by Air Chief Marshal Sir Donald Evans,* boasted three two star officers on the directing staff.[†] There were sixty-five course members: forty from the UK Armed Forces and the Civil Service, with the remainder from the Commonwealth and the US. Guy was one of six Australians on the course and by this stage Guy had reverted to his substantive rank of Captain. Guy found his class colleagues 'a great bunch of fellows.' In particular, he developed a firm friendship with a gregarious Scot, Brigadier Bob Lyon. He was an experienced artillery officer who had served in World War II and most recently in Borneo.[‡] Lyon was destined to go into a similar staff job as Guy after the course.

For many attendees this was the first such staff course which was joint and not single service. The objective was to prepare senior officers and officials of the UK and other countries for senior positions in command or in strategic headquarters. The emphasis was on developing their analytical powers, knowledge of defence and international security, and their strategic vision. The College itself was embarking on a major transition, with its name soon to change from the Imperial Defence College to the Royal College of Defence Studies. The new title reflected the loss of Empire and the changed strategic circumstance of Britain in the world. The Cold War, in all its manifestations was the dominant theme.

While many of the officers had World War II or Korean War service, Guy was one of the few officers with recent wartime experience. This was

---

* Air Chief Marshal Sir Donald Evans KBE, CB, DFC (1912–75).

† Star Ranks are: One Star – Commodore, Brigadier & Air Commodore; Two Star – Rear Admiral, Major General, Air Vice Marshal; Three Star – Vice Admiral, Lieutenant-General, Air Marshal; Four Star – Admiral, General & Air Chief Marshal.

‡ Later Major General Robert Lyon CB, OBE (1923-2019).

underscored when he attended the investiture of his DSO by the Queen at Buckingham Palace on 17 February 1970. It was a rare occasion for the Sovereign, whereby she was awarding a decoration for distinguished operational service in a conflict in which the UK was not a participant. For Guy and the family, it was a memorable occasion.

One of the strengths of the staff course was the manner in which it mixed lectures, tours and social activities to not only allow the students to be prepared for the next phase of their career but also to recharge their batteries and establish professional networks. In this regard Guy was a well-liked member of the course to which he brought 'a broad and sensible approach to problems.'[9] Studies completed in December 1970 and Guy learnt he would return once more to Canberra to the Operations and Plans section of Navy Office. It was a belated, and to Guy a perplexing appointment. Guy's experience would have been much more useful in Canberra, fresh from the first destroyer deployment with the 7th Fleet in the Vietnam War, not three years later.

III

When Guy returned to Canberra in early 1971 the new CNS was Vice Admiral Richard Peek, who had been FOCAF when Guy was in *Hobart*. Guy replaced his classmate Jim Willis as the Director General Naval Operations and Plans (DGNOP) reporting to the Deputy CNS, Rear Admiral David Wells. Guy had Captain David Leach running his Plans area, whilst Commander Michael Ward looked after the Operations side. Guy and his team provided the necessary papers to present the Navy's position on a full range of policy, force structure and operational issues. Whilst the Imperial Defence College course was Cold War focused, its ability to encourage students to think in strategic terms and be able to express their thoughts on paper at that level had prepared Guy well for his new position.

The early 1970s was an inflection point for Australia's strategic outlook and for the RAN. With respect to the Vietnam War, the DDGs were in their final year of operations on the 'Gunline' and in March 1972 *Sydney* would return from her last logistics trip to Vung Tau. More broadly, the US was seeking to reset its foreign policy in the region. Elsewhere, India and Pakistan just had a short sharp war, while Britain, burdened by debt, had decided to accelerate withdrawal of its military forces from east of Suez. These changes and uncertainties were reflected in the *1972 Strategic Basis Paper* which was produced by Defence and taken by the Minister for Defence, James Killen, to Cabinet for endorsement. From the foundation of this strategic assessment would come a revised force structure for Government consideration. To complicate matters for Defence, however, there was a change of Government, with Gough Whitlam's Labor Party taking power in December 1972.

Guy and his team were involved in providing comment on and analysis of, the *Strategic Basis Paper*. For his part, Guy was concerned the Paper was too South East Asian centric. In particular, it was largely silent on the Indian Ocean and the Middle East from where much of Australia's trade and oil supplies emanated or passed through. In addition, Guy would later lament,

> There appeared to be no forward thinking of the relationships between foreign affairs, international relationships, strategies for Australia and its interests, coming down to what should we do for defence or deterrence.[10]

An important piece of work, which impressed both Peek and Synnot, was a paper Guy wrote on the future Fleet composition in the context of the *Strategic Basis Paper*. It called for the maintenance of a balanced fleet with a range of capabilities which included two small aircraft carriers, eight submarines, seventeen destroyers, a pair of replenishment ships and two amphibious ships. This would enable sustained operations in the region.[11] This paper was in part underpinned by operational research undertaken by the RAN's Research Laboratory. Guy was conscious, however, that the central Defence bureaucracy was also undertaking important operational analysis on the future force, yet the Navy was not paying sufficient attention to it. He was also aware that the Air Force would increasingly oppose *Melbourne*'s replacement, as it would compete for scarce Defence funds needed to replace its fighter force. In the public arena, while the Navy's performance in the Vietnam War demonstrated professional competence, it was by now an unpopular conflict. Guy felt also that the public image of the Navy was more coloured by *Melbourne*'s collisions with the destroyers *Voyager* and *Frank E. Evans*[*] than its Vietnam achievements.

For Guy there were major problems that were to occupy him during his tenure in Navy Office. By the nature of warship construction, with all the preliminary design work required, it could often take over ten years from the first decisions to a ship entering the water. As such, few matters that Guy and his team dealt with reached a conclusion during his three years in post. Naval programs, if for no other reason than their inherent expense, made them an area of particular attention within both Defence and Government. The three important issues that Guy dealt with were the aircraft carrier replacement, the upgrade to the DDGs and the replacement of the first batch of Type 12 frigates.

No project attracted more attention than the replacement of *Melbourne*. The ship had been reprieved from being reduced to a helicopter carrier by the 1967 acquisition of US-sourced aircraft to replace the Sea Venoms and Gannets. This gave the ship a new lease of life and capability. It was to be further enhanced with the 1972 decision to replace the Wessex with the more capable Sea King helicopters. The ship's eventual replacement, however, remained a vexed issue.

In contrast to the aircraft carrier machinations, there was not discussion so much on whether the frigates needed to be replaced, as on

---

[*] The first collision with HMAS *Voyager* in 1964 resulted in the loss of 82 lives and the second with the destroyer USS *Frank E Evans* in 1969 with the deaths of 74 US sailors.

what with. The Navy's recent experiences in Confrontation and in the Vietnam War informed its requirements. In terms of capabilities the design had to include a 5-inch gun suitable for shore bombardment, one to two helicopters for anti-submarine warfare, a surface-to-air missile system, such as Tartar, and provision to for an anti-ship missile of the type starting to be fitted in warships at the time. Whilst generally uncontroversial, the sticking point was the size and cost of the ship. In Guy's earlier time in Navy Office there had been a desire to get these ships down below 2,000 tons and he had made himself unpopular by pointing out that it was impractical to fit all the required systems into such a hull. Guy had argued that the Navy had to be better at explaining the issues within Defence and Government. He found that little had changed.

The proposed new ships, called the Light Destroyer or DDL, would be in the region of 4,000 tons (a DDG was 4,500 tons). In 1972 the MacMahon Government endorsed the DDL concept but the new Whitlam Government was concerned about the growing cost and schedule delays with the indigenous design. In part these costs appeared higher than than possible overseas costs, because all the design and set-up overheads were allocated to the first batch of three ships. As a result, Defence was directed to look for an overseas existing design. The outcome was the selection of the US Oliver Hazard Perry class guided missile frigate, which possessed most of the desired DDL capabilities, with the exception of having a 3-inch and not a 5-inch gun. Not unsurprisingly at 4,100 tons she was DDL in size. Eventually, four ships would be built in the US and another pair later in Melbourne. A fifteen-year hiatus in major warship construction in Australia.

While Guy thought the DDL cancellation a short-sighted one, there was more satisfaction with seeing the Government approve the fitting of a naval combat data system into the DDGs. Having seen the power of the improved decision making and weapon assignment of NTDS fitted US ships off Vietnam, Guy was a strong advocate of this game-changing program.

The other major development in Defence, in which Guy was more observer than participant was the reorganisation of the Defence Group of Departments. A review was announced in December 1972 by Defence Minister Lance Barnard and completed in November the following year.[12] The review was led by the Secretary of the Defence Department, the formidable Sir Arthur Tange, who was regarded as one of the last great mandarins of the Commonwealth bureaucracy. It resulted in the biggest change to the Defence organisation since Federation. Among the major developments were the abolition of the single service departments with their ministers and a concentration of authority in the central, predominantly civilian, bureaucracy. To a large extent Guy thought that the changes were inevitable, but that the influence of the bureaucracy over the military leadership had gone too far. In the Navy's case, Guy was concerned it was less well prepared for the new arrangements. It had benefited from the advocacy of a Navy Minister and, as previously mentioned, relied more than either the Army or the Air Force on the expertise and corporate memory of public servants.

As Guy left Navy Office at the end of 1973, he remained most concerned that the use of airpower at sea was not fully understood and that the Navy continued to be poor in explaining naval strategy to Government. In part he reasoned that there were too few naval officers with sufficient grasp of strategy beyond the tactical use of forces at sea. More was needed to educate them so they were able to explain to the public, Government and Defence what occurs beyond the view from the beach.

IV

For Guy there was one more sea command that beckoned, the aircraft carrier *Melbourne*. He assumed command on 18 December 1973. The flagship had by this time been in commission for 18 years and had steamed over 610,000 miles or around the world nearly 25 times. Although not having had war service, *Melbourne* had been the centrepiece of the 'Cold War' RAN. She had an eventful career and while both her collisions were not necessarily *Melbourne*'s fault, they had ended the careers of her captains. There were also periodic aircraft losses off her modest-sized flight deck. Yet when Guy assumed command she had lost just five aircraft in launching or recovery operations. It was an enviable safety record for any aircraft carrier. *Melbourne* was therefore a high-profile command, but one not without professional risk. Guy relished the prospect.

Guy took over *Melbourne* from his classmate John Goble, who was just the second aviator to command her. Another classmate, Jim Willis had earlier commanded the ship. For his part Guy was no stranger to her or aircraft carriers, having previously served in *Sydney* twice and *Melbourne* thrice. The ship had just returned from another Asian deployment but as events were to unfold, Guy's tenure was to be atypical, because it did not involve such a deployment. It was, however, to prove one of the most memorable periods in the ship's long career.

Guy's reputation of being a hard but fair captain, backed by an impressive war record preceded him. The ship's company soon found substance to this reputation. One of the sailors, Jim McGeachie vividly recalled an early address by Guy which included the statement, 'I don't want to hear anyone telling me that they are *just* about to do something, I want to hear that you are *actually* doing something!'[13] Guy was to prove to be a popular and greatly respected captain.

Early on in his command a young sailor appeared before Guy at his disciplinary table, for being absent without leave. On questioning the sailor Guy learnt he had been told how big *Melbourne* was and how difficult the living conditions were and he soon 'shoved off for a few days to think it over'.[14] The sailor's dilemma revealed a flaw in the joining routine. Unlike Guy's experience in *Repulse*, new joiners were not welcomed onboard, shown around the ship and helped find their feet. Guy quickly fixed this management deficiency.

Since Guy had last been in *Melbourne* the ship had changed

significantly. In 1969 the carrier received a new air group which consisted of A-4 Skyhawk fighter bombers, S-2 Trackers anti-submarine aircraft and Wessex helicopters. This was an all-together much more capable air wing but needed an upgrade to the ship's single catapult. The margin for error at take-off was finer than before and immense effort was required to keep the catapult serviceable. To under-score that point a Skyhawk had been lost three weeks earlier, when the catapult failed.[*]

Besides providing the platform for these aircraft, *Melbourne* was normally the fleet flagship. Whilst *Melbourne* prepared for her shakedown the new FOCAF, Rear Admiral David Wells, assumed command on 4 February. Guy had first met Wells when he was on the staff of Commodore John Collins in the Philippines Campaign and Guy was in *Shropshire*. Guy was confident that they would work well together. But this was not to be just yet, because *Melbourne* was first to sail to San Francisco, to embark the RAAF's twelve new Chinook heavy-lift and five additional Iroquois helicopters and transport them to Brisbane.

Melbourne sailed on 11 February without her air group to allow space for the new helicopters and their substantial stores outfit. Unusually the ship had embarked soldiers from A company 2/4th Battalion, Royal Australian Regiment who would take part in Exercise Pacific Bond II in Hawaii where the ship would make a two-day refuelling stop. It also had in its hangar a large number of crated exhibits and other material destined for the Australian pavilion at EXPO 74 in Spokane. There was even a proposal to bring back the newly acquired and controversial abstract impressionist painting *Blue Poles* on her return voyage.[15] The prospect of safely transporting the expensive artwork was not one Guy relished and so he was not disappointed when the proposal went no further. The passage in fine weather and without aircraft provided the ideal conditions for sailors and soldiers to attack the rust spots around the ship. It also gave Guy with an opportunity to reacquaint himself with the ship prior

---

[*] The Skyhawk fell over the bow when the catapult failed with the pilot being recovered. Larger aircraft carriers in USN and RN service at the time had two catapults.

to the return of the air group.

During a pleasant port visit in Pearl Harbor, Guy caught up with Captain Bruce Althoff, who had been commodore in *Allen M. Sumner* off Vietnam. As a goodwill gesture, *Melbourne* embarked war relics destined for the Nimitz Gallery of the new National Museum of the Pacific War in Fredericksburg, Texas. They would be disembarked in Long Beach. On the evening prior to *Melbourne*'s 23 February sailing, the US 3ʳᵈ Fleet Headquarters received advice of a distress call from the Italian tanker *Giovanna Lolli Ghetti* some 700 miles north-east of Hawaii. The unladen tanker had been bound for Indonesia to take on another load of crude oil when an explosion occurred in one of her tanks. The ship sank three hours later with the loss of seven men. Fortunately, first the Norwegian *Tamerlane* rescued the 31 survivors and then the US Coast Guard Cutter *Mellon* and the Russian fishing vessel *Novikov Priboy* converged on scene to render medical assistance to the burn victims. It was soon clear that if some of the badly burnt seamen were to survive they had to be flown ashore. Guy readily agreed to assist in the operation and *Melbourne* embarked a Coast Guard HH-52 Seaguard helicopter with a doctor. While *Mellon*, with all the survivors onboard, steamed towards Pearl Harbor, *Melbourne* sailed towards her at best speed. When within range the Seaguard flew to *Mellon* and recovered two of the worst burns cases and flew them safely ashore.

Although the visit to continental US was essentially a logistic voyage, RAN visits were infrequent and Guy was keen to maximise its impact. This commenced with a gun salute at the entrance to Long Beach harbour on the morning of 1 March followed by a press conference, official reception and tours. For their part, the ship's company took full advantage of the nearby attractions such as Disneyland and Universal Studios. Four days later, *Melbourne* arrived in San Francisco. Her host ship was the aircraft carrier *Coral Sea*, which had modified a launch by adding a 'flight deck' and renamed her *Coral Sea II,* to escort *Melbourne* into harbour. On arrival the ship offloaded the EXPO material and embarked the helicopters and stores. Once again Guy tried to maximise presence of the ship to raise the Australian profile. Offers of local hospitality, particularly through a 'Dial-a-Sailor' promotion proved very popular.

Melbourne left San Francisco on 9 March and after retrieving the troops from Pearl Harbor the ship arrived in Brisbane to offload the helicopters on 28 March. The music from the welcoming band was momentarily drowned out by a bang as *Melbourne* was pushed hard against the wharf by the tugs. The status of the ship and the conventions of the time were such that Guy still formally conducted courtesy calls on the Premier as well as the Governor and the Chief Justice.

At the end of April 1974 *Melbourne* returned to her normal operations by embarking her air group once more and worked up. Very poor weather led to much of the flight training being conducted inside Jervis Bay. This placed a heavy load on Guy's skilled Navigating Officer, Lieutenant Commander Rod Taylor.* For an aircraft carrier this is both a very busy period and one more prone to incidents as aircrew refresh or even gain their deck landing skills. In this and later phases a close working relationship is required between the captain and Commander Air, who was Ken Douglas. One of the features of *Melbourne* was the depth of experience and expertise in particular areas of the ship such as on the flight deck. Key personnel would spend a significant portion of their naval careers in the ship. There were some onboard that Guy had served with on a number of occasions such as Lieutenant Commander Bill Ritchie, now the ship's Direction Officer, who had been a Petty Officer with him in *Sydney*.

The work-up was in preparation for *Melbourne* to take part in a new major exercise called Kangaroo One to be held at Shoalwater Bay and the adjacent Coral Sea. The purpose of the new series was to exercise all three services in the defence of Australia. It would be the nation's largest peacetime exercise to that time involving 15,000 personnel, 100 aircraft

---

* Later Vice Admiral R.G. Taylor AO, RAN (1940–2002). He was Chief of Navy 1994-97.

and thirty-nine ships from Australia, New Zealand, the UK and the US. *Melbourne* embarked FOCAF for the exercise, and she and the task group sailed on 3 June. For part of the exercise *Melbourne* was the flagship of the 'Orange' or enemy ten-ship naval force. It then was used to support the amphibious landing. For 'Kangaroo One', *Melbourne's* air group was reconfigured to have nine instead of the then usual six Skyhawk fighter-bombers with one used as a tanker to extend their collective range. They had considerable success against the 'Blue' warships and shore targets. When it was announced to the men onboard that their aircraft had got in the first strike before that of the Blue force, a cheer went up through *Melbourne*. The rate of effort of the Air Group was impressive and they flew 385 sorties over the two weeks of the exercise. To Guy, Kangaroo One was 'a great success story' for *Melbourne*, while Admiral Wells later wrote it demonstrated 'that the aircraft carrier is the hardest hitting, most flexible and most versatile of naval units.'[16] One of the experienced naval aviators onboard later remarked he had never seen *Melbourne* operate so well.[17]

On her return to Sydney and whilst awaiting a period in dock, *Melbourne* was struck on her port quarter by the Chandris Line passenger ship *Australis* whilst the liner was manoeuvring in to the berth astern. While adding to the list of incidents in her long life, the little damage done was just added to *Melbourne's* docking work list.

During this period in port one of the more important changes to sailor training started to appear in *Melbourne*. Up to 1973 sailors, who were also known collectively until then as ratings, would first go to sea as Ordinary Seamen. As part of their duties they would undertake communal duties, such as cleaning and basic ship upkeep, before returning to shore for their specialist training. This scheme, called RATSTRUC, provided an opportunity for sailors to get some initial sea experience.* In part due to the growing complexity of newer ships, which also had fewer bunks for

---

* RATSTRUC was the acronym for Ratings Structure, whilst SAILSTRUC stood for Sailors Structure.

trainees, a new system was put in place known as SAILSTRUC. Under this scheme only category trained sailors went to sea. This transition was difficult and emotive, on a number of levels. One by-product was the initial resentment by trained sailors at having to do menial communal tasks, once the preserve of Ordinary Seamen. Unhelpfully, some officers and senior sailors in the engineering departments argued that their more expensively trained sailors should not do communal duties and these should be left to the seaman and supply department sailors. Another complication was that the new SAILSTRUC sailors arrived with competency task books that had to be completed. The early versions were inadequate and the scheme placed an added burden on the fully trained sailors. In response to this disgruntlement, Guy addressed the sailors onboard, explaining the SAILSTRUC's rationale, as well as noting that amongst the benefits of the new system was the new sailors were more mature and the standard of the work on communal tasks was better.

On 1 August Guy was promoted to the substantive rank of Commodore. This was a result of the Navy introducing the permanent rank to conform to the other two services. This rank for a warship's captain was unusual among world navies and the large US aircraft carriers, for instance, were commanded by an officer of captain rank.* The only virtue of the new arrangement was that *Melbourne* was always senior ship in any RAN formation. To Guy, however, the rationale was not compelling and he felt awkward when exercising with the USN.

From the beginning of her docking, *Melbourne* experienced delays largely due to industrial disputes. This was the typical dockyard experience through the period and required a mix of flexibility, resolve and patience on the part of Guy and his men. *Melbourne* eventually emerged in late September to start work-up. The newly joined SAILSTRUC sailors soon impressed Guy with their superior initial training and their enthusiasm for going to sea. It would, nevertheless, take some years before the new

---

*   The Royal Canadian Navy had on occasion a commodore commanding their aircraft carrier HMCS *Magnificent*.

SAILSTRUC scheme realised its conceptual promise.

For the remainder of the year *Melbourne* operated off the east coast conducting training. This included a disaster relief exercise in Jervis Bay where the ship's organisation and communications were tested in assisting a mock-up of a damaged town. This exercise was coordinated by Lieutenant Commander Tim O'Sullivan who had revamped the ship's procedures. At the end of November *Melbourne* flew off her aircraft and berthed in Sydney for maintenance and the commencement of the rotational Christmas leave. It had been a successful year for Guy in which the ship had steamed nearly 32,000 nautical miles. There was the attractive prospect of taking part in the major international Exercise, RIMPAC 75, off Hawaii to contemplate over the summer break.[*]

V

On 20 December 1974 a tropical depression developed about 350 kilometres to the north-east of Darwin. The following day it continued to grow and that night, when about 220 kilometres from the city, it was categorised as a tropical cyclone. By 22 December forecasters expected to pass to the north of Darwin. Cyclones are by their nature unpredictable and on Christmas Eve morning the newly named Cyclone Tracy veered towards Darwin. It struck the city at about 0330. The anemometer at the airport broke with a reading of 217 kilometres an hour and there was a four-metre storm surge. In the port there was substantial damage and the patrol boat *Arrow* sank with the loss of two sailors. In the city another sixty-nine people were killed and about 70% of the buildings were destroyed or badly damaged.

On Christmas morning Guy was at home in Canberra. Like most Australians, he had listened to the emerging story of the devastation

---

[*]   The first Rim of the Pacific or RIMPAC exercise was held in 1971. It involved the navies from Australia, Canada, New Zealand, the UK and the US. Normally based out of Pearl Harbor, RIMPAC became a biennial exercise held in even years.

of the 'Top End' capital. Just as Guy was thinking *Melbourne* would be needed he received a call from his old friend Commodore 'Red' Merson, then Chief of Staff at Fleet Headquarters who said, 'Guy, we've got a bit of a problem, I think. If you can, get up here as soon as you can.'[18] Guy caught the next available flight to Sydney to oversee the preparations onboard *Melbourne*. The first priority was to get the ship ready to sail. One of the duty officers, Lieutenant Commander Bill Ritchie, briefed Guy on his arrival. Ritchie had earlier asked the duty engineer about the state of the engines. His discouraging reply was it would take three weeks, with dockyard assistance, to put them back together. Ritchie opined they would be needed by 0800 the next day. In terms of preparing *Melbourne* for the disaster relief operations, the helicopter squadron now at *Albatross*, was preparing to reembark. This included removing their anti-submarine equipment to provide more space for a utility role. In the absence of a specific list of disaster stores, the ship fell back on its recent exercise in Jervis Bay and Lieutenant Commander O'Sullivan used that as the template to order key stores.[19]

Melbourne sailed in company with *Brisbane* at 1700 on Boxing Day for Operation Navy Help Darwin. She had embarked Rear Admiral Wells, and once at sea, joined by her seven Wessex helicopters. Because many of her men were spread across the country on Christmas leave, the ship departed with 65% of her complement. Yet to reach this number, Guy recalled, 'some incredible tales of assistance given to members of the ship's company, by police cars in remote areas running them into train stations.'[20] One sailor arrived at Taree Station with no ticket but the station master organised him one and he boarded the *Brisbane Limited Express* in time to join the ship. In perhaps a portent of life married to a sailor, in Adelaide one honeymooning bride abruptly bid farewell to her new husband as he flew to Sydney. He was one of seventy men on a Trans Australia Airlines flight that had also brought some sailors across from Perth. Onboard *Melbourne*, as the tracing of the crew was done and gaps identified in key positions, sailors from other ships were ordered to join the flagship.[21]

A second group of ships consisting of *Supply*, *Stalwart*, *Hobart* and *Vendetta* would sail two days later. Once at sea *Melbourne* and *Brisbane* made a fast passage with just a short diversion to Townsville. There they lay off the port to embark more men and stores by helicopter and ferry. This included 200 of *Melbourne*'s ship's company who could not make the sailing from Sydney. By this stage the flagship had also been joined by the frigate *Stuart*.

During the passage, each ship of the two groups had planning sessions and sent ideas for the task ahead to meetings of Admiral Wells, his staff, Guy and Lieutenant Commanders Tim O'Sullivan and Bill Ritchie, who were the Disaster Coordinators. These proposals were then considered for the Admiral's approval. As a result, an array of activities got under way. These ranged from resorting stores into 900-kilogram individual helicopter loads to expedite their delivery on arrival, to the painting of replacement street signs for the city. All personnel were inoculated for cholera and tetanus.

As they approached Darwin, *Brisbane* was detached and arrived on New Year's Eve morning to restore a reliable communications link between the city and Canberra. At first light on New Year's Day, as the ships approached Darwin, a Wessex helicopter took Admiral Wells to the devastated city to scope the task ahead. At midday the two ships anchored in Darwin harbour. Watching their arrival were hundreds of Darwinians who had a less obstructed view of the port due to demolished buildings and the shredding of the trees. One hardened local standing on the balcony of a roofless pub had tears streaming from his face at seeing the arrival of the Navy. Another local said the Fleet's arrival was 'the best New Year's present this town has ever had.'[22] Also awaiting the ships was the larger-than-life Naval Officer Commanding North Australia, Captain Eric Eugene Johnston. His headquarters building had been demolished and had moved his operations to his official residence. Johnston, by virtue of his size and character, was known in the Navy as

'Big E', the same nickname as the US nuclear powered aircraft carrier *Enterprise*. Guy knew Johnston well and considered him a unique and loveable personality who had firm opinions, was wise in his decisions and had an innate ability to charm people. Less obvious, thought Guy, was the fact that Johnston was a deep thinker. Johnston* was to prove an enormous asset to Darwin and the Navy at this time.[23] Looking from his bridge in *Melbourne*, Guy's first impressions of the devastation were,

> ... it was shattering I must say to enter Darwin Harbour and firstly to realise that all the trees on the western side of the entrance to the harbour were basically stripped. It was quite astonishing. All the tops of the houses had been removed.[24]

From a helicopter the scale of the devastation looked even worse, with Captain Peter Sinclair of *Hobart* remarking 'from the air Darwin resembled a huge rubbish dump.'[25] An intense flying program quickly commenced, taking urgently needed disaster relief stores to various parts of the city. Captain Johnston had been joined by Commander 'Toz' Dadswell, who was slated to become *Melbourne*'s Executive Officer from later in the month. He had been sent to run the improvised Headquarters for Johnston and he was joined by Lieutenant Commander O'Sullivan. A pattern developed whereby every morning Johnston and Dadswell would attend the Town Disaster Central Committee. Tasking was then given out to the Fleet. Onboard *Melbourne*, the aircrew briefing room became the disaster relief centre and produced the work schedule for each day's shore parties. Initially, the ships had been asked to concentrate on the three most damaged suburbs in the city's north. The Fleet also provided ideal accommodation for VIPs to inspect the devastation without burdening the city. As such, on the day after her arrival, *Melbourne* accommodated the Governor General, Sir John Kerr and the Acting Prime Minister, Dr

---

* Later Commodore E.E. Johnston, AO, OBE, RAN (1933–97). He was the Administrator of the Northern Territory from 1981–89.

Jim Cairns. Sir John wrote to the Queen that the local morale was high, 'especially with the arrival of the Navy and the use of its personnel in the clean up, the first small beginnings of renewal are appearing.'[26]

In coming days the Fleet was bolstered by the hydrographic ship *Flinders*, which surveyed the harbour for wrecks, then *Stalwart* (with the Fleet Maintenance Unit embarked), *Supply*, *Hobart*, *Vendetta* and *Derwent* and two landing craft *Balikpapan* and *Betano*. The typical work undertaken by the men of the Fleet included repairing air-conditioning units, installing or repairing water tanks, re-roofing buildings and generally cleaning up debris. *Stalwart*'s well-equipped workshops and experienced engineers proved invaluable. Once the urgent work was done, on 5 January all the commanding officers met in the flagship to be briefed on the magnitude of the operation and the systematic work program, with each ship being assigned particular streets. On any one day there were over 1,200 officers and sailors ashore in working parties, with *Melbourne* fielding about 400 of them. Most affecting was the clean-up of the deserted houses. One of the men later wrote,

> ... all their trinkets and everything that were in the house were swept away and blown away over the adjacent property or their property and their lawns and so on. Everything that a person would have had. And so there was this stuff lying around because nobody had touched it and nobody would pick it up and there was timber everywhere and glass all over the place.[27]

The men collected any valuables, recorded their location and took them to *Stalwart* for safe-keeping. One Nightscliff resident asked for help to find her husband's pay packet lost when their house was flattened. Amazingly, the sailors found it. Amongst the revelations were the pre-Navy occupations of many sailors, such as bulldozer driving, fencing, plumbing and vehicle repair, and their ability to put them to good use in Darwin. It was dirty, hot and arduous work, with the beer issue at the end of the day most welcome. Yet even onboard there was discomfort, as *Melbourne's* air-conditioning was not functioning, while her fresh water making capability was also reduced. To support the anchored ships, *Betano* had a busy schedule, which included distributing half a million cans of beer to appreciative ships' companies. Her other notable task was taking over 500 sailors from around the Fleet to a Rolf Harris concert, given onboard *Melbourne* to thank them for their efforts.

In the port precinct the Navy teams undertook immediate repairs to wharves, slipways, some trawlers and the three surviving, but battered Attack Class patrol boats. On 10 January, Guy headed a Board of Inquiry into the loss of *Arrow* and the damage to the other patrol boats. It soon became clear to him that it was very fortunate that no more patrol boats had been lost. Guy heard evidence that on Christmas Eve the late change of direction of Cyclone Tracy had placed the boats in an unenviable position. The path to the open sea would take them through the most dangerous quadrant of the cyclone, while the other exit route, through Clarence Strait, was particularly confined and if Tracy changed course, the prospects would have been bleak. In the end, at 1800 and after discussion with the young commanding officers, Captain Johnston ordered the boats to the cyclone buoys in the harbour. Lieutenant Peter Breeze in *Advance* thought it better to anchor instead.

As Guy knew from experience in *Sydney* and *Parramatta*, staying in harbour was rarely as good as getting to sea, but he could appreciate their quandary and endorsed their actions. By about 0100 on Christmas morning the cyclone buoys started to drag in the growing storm and one by one the patrol boats broke from their buoys. There were nineteen other vessels in the crowded harbour. With varying degrees of success the patrol boats attempted to keep clear of land and other ships. Visibility was at times just one metre. Such was the wind that paint was stripped from their superstructure and they rolled up to 80°, while their pitch was such that at times their propellers were out of the water. The boats' engines were under great strain and in *Arrow* they gave up with the ship subsequently foundering on Stokes Hill Wharf. *Attack* was beached and only *Advance* and *Assail* remained largely undamaged. Subsequent to the Board of Inquiry a number of the patrol boat officers received commendations for their actions in saving their ships and men.

In the city, as the efforts of work parties settled into a routine, Guy like some other ship captains, donned overalls and joined work gangs. On one occasion, as the team of which he was a member awaited the next task on the wharf, one of the warship commanding officers took them to task over their slovenly appearance. He was quickly put to rights by Guy who stepped forward from the team. A sign that the task of the Fleet was nearing an end came was when one of *Melbourne's* teams went to do clean-up work at a hotel, only to find a dozen locals ensconced at the bar enjoying a cold beer.

On 18 January, *Melbourne* and *Hobart* sailed from Darwin, leaving the remainder of the Fleet to continue the work with Rear Admiral Wells shifting his flag to *Supply*. Both ships were to return to Sydney to ready themselves for participation in RIMPAC 75. Darwin's mayor, Harry 'Tiger' Brennan, later said 'We owe the Navy the greatest debt of all.'[28] A major part in the success of the Navy's largest peacetime operation, which involved 3,000 sailors, was that in the words of the Defence Minister, Lance Barnard 'the RAN has the capacity to provide a skilled workforce at Darwin without imposing on the city's limited facilities.'[29] For their part, *Melbourne's* helicopters had made nearly 2,500 landings and transferred 7,800 personnel around the city as part of the effort. Less obvious, but no less arduous, was the work of the marine engineering department which had maintained *Melbourne's* steam plant for power for 35 of the last 38 days. Guy wrote at the time, 'It was a privilege to command such a cheerful, hard-working ship's company.'[30]

VI

After just eleven days alongside in Sydney, *Melbourne* sailed for a shakedown off Jervis Bay to prepare the ship and her air group for RIMPAC 75. After the success of having a larger Skyhawk squadron in Kangaroo One, the ship would once again embark eight fighters. The shakedown was not without incident. At 0325 on 10 February one of her Trackers was lost, when having missed the arrester wires, it flew into the sea. Fortunately, all four aircrew were recovered by *Parramatta*, acting as rescue destroyer. Among the aircrew was Petty Officer Joe Kroeger who eleven years earlier had survived the *Voyager* sinking in the same area.

On 18 February after a hectic couple of days alongside *Melbourne*, *Hobart* and *Parramatta* sailed from Sydney bound for Hawaii. This was a considerable achievement, particularly for the engineering personnel, who would normally have had some weeks to prepare the ships, with dockyard's help, for a major deployment. Some work would still need to be done on passage. In the case of *Melbourne* she was overdue a refit and would have to be carefully managed whilst away. For the first time in one of Guy's *Reports of Proceedings* of his three commands, he noted that three sailors were charged with drug offences. This issue would remain a recurrent but low-level issue for the RAN over coming decades.

Embarked in *Melbourne* once more was Rear Admiral Wells. The relationship between an admiral and his flag captain, who commanded his flagship, is one of critical importance. A poor relationship can flow down not only through the ship but also the Fleet. Guy found Wells to be a tough but fair admiral and importantly 'a leader with a good brain.'[31] They formed a very good working relationship. For his part Wells assessed Guy to be a captain who handled *Melbourne* with 'calculated care and skill' and a 'very competent and firm Commanding Officer,' well respected onboard 'for all his personal and professional qualities.'[32]

In a quirk of history, Guy had been a part of the commissioning crew of all three ships that sailed for RIMPAC 75 and had been commissioning captain of two. The 4,400 nautical mile passage was uneventful with a brief refuelling stop in Suva. Whilst there, Guy renewed his acquaintance with Commander Stan Brown who commanded the Royal Fiji Navy. Stan well remembered Guy's Uncle Harvey and his contribution to Fiji. Guy's grandmother had, as a widow, gone to live with Harvey and Molly and had passed away in Suva. Stan undertook to find her death certificate for Guy. This was the beginning of Guy's interest in his family's past.

Lying in wait as the Task Group steamed towards the Gilbert Islands was the submarine *Otway* which was conducting an anti-shipping exercise en route RIMPAC 75. The Task Group arrived in Pearl Harbor on 3 March with *Otway* arriving two days later. The ships spent the next week preparing for the exercise. *Otway* had recently come out of refit and experienced various defects to both her main engines which jeopardised her full involvement in the exercise. They were resolved with 'the most welcome and ample support from HMAS *Melbourne*.'[33]

One of the important aspects of RIMPACs was relationship building among the participating navies and this was helped by *Melbourne* hosting a reception for 500 civilian and military guests. The RIMPAC exercise series had grown progressively in size and complexity. In 1975 it involved thirty ships, 200 aircraft and 17,000 personnel from Australia, Canada, New Zealand and the US. Besides the tactical phases there was the opportunity to conduct advanced weapon firings on sophisticated instrumented ranges that were unavailable in Australia.

During the tactical phase of the exercise, Rear Admiral Wells commanded the Blue Forces at sea with the opposing Orange Force commanded by Rear Admiral George Kinnear who was Commander Carrier Group One in *Kitty Hawk*. The focus of RIMPACs is less on the tactical outcomes than on practicing complex warfare skills with other navies. *Melbourne*'s operations room was by now obsolete and USN observers onboard found it hard to comprehend how it allowed anybody to know what was going on. During the exercise *Melbourne*'s air group flew over 350 sorties and Guy said at the time that 'RIMPAC 75 presented a tough challenge to *Melbourne* and her squadrons and I am very pleased and proud to say the ship achieved excellent results'.[34]

RIMPAC 75 completed on 21 March and the ships returned to Pearl Harbor for the wash-up and farewells. Tragedy struck an otherwise very successful visit when, on the eve of sailing one of *Melbourne's* sailors, Able Seaman J.P. Armstrong died when he fell from a 19th-floor hotel balcony in Waikiki. The Task Group sailed for Australia on 27 March, with the prospect of a port visits to the Fiji islands en route. Once again in Guy's career, a port visit was interrupted by a cyclone. In this case a tropical depression developed into Cyclone Betty and the three ships sailed early with incomplete complements to weather the storm east of Viti Levu. Fortunately, 'Betty' did not strike the islands. *Hobart* returned into port to recover the rest of her men whilst *Melbourne* used her helicopters for the purpose.

During the deployment sailors walking the passageways late at night in *Melbourne* could be surprised from behind by someone wearing a wolfman costume. It created nervousness for some when doing their solitary rounds in dim spaces at night. It was also a source of general amusement for those not involved. The wolfman prank irritated Guy and 'Toz' Dadswell, for it was fun at someone's expense and did little for team cohesion which was their focus. Needless to say the wolfman saga became part of *Melbourne's* folklore.

The Task Group arrived off Sydney on 11 March and *Melbourne's* aircraft flew off to *Albatross* before entry into port. It was the last time the venerable Wessex squadron would be embarked. After thirteen years service they were to be replaced by the new Sea King helicopters. Also departing in one of the Wessex was the Wolfman, who waved in costume to the bridge as the aircraft flew off. Guy, however, had the last say on the saga. He ordered the Wessex to return onboard for the Wolfman to face the music.

The day was also Guy's last at sea in command. The following week the ship de-stored and de-ammunitioned to prepare her for a year-long refit. It would hopefully allow the ship to remain in service until about 1985. On 30 June Guy handed over to his executive officer 'Toz' Dadswell who was now promoted to Captain.

Guy's only other prospect for returning to sea was to command the Fleet. While that possibility lay in the hands of others, he was informed he was to return to Canberra to become the Director-General Naval Personnel and to lead the Junior Officers Structure Study. Personnel matters had been an abiding interest of Guy and there was potential for him to make a significant contribution.

VII

When Guy returned to Navy Office in June 1975, the Chief of Naval Personnel (CNP) for whom Guy would be directly working was Rear Admiral Alan McFarlane. He had joined the Naval Reserve as a sailor prior to World War II, before being commissioned as a supply officer. McFarlane had a distinguished career in his specialisation and during his tenure as CNP had focussed on improving the pay and conditions. The personnel challenges Guy faced were a mix of enduring and contemporary ones. The inflationary economy had resulted in the Government calling for both financial savings and cuts to the personnel strength. Following the 1973–74 budget the Navy had to cut 1,100 uniformed and 800 public servants. These economies were still being implemented.

The other major area under change was officer career development. In the late 1960s the three Services had in piecemeal fashion introduced tertiary education into their separate naval, military and air colleges in association with different civil universities. For its part the Navy had, with the University of New South Wales established engineering and science degree education, initially at the Naval College, to be completed at the main university campus in Sydney. Arts degrees had followed in 1972. In Guy's view it was a positive and long overdue step in which the RAN had lagged behind not only the other services, but other leading navies. In 1974 the Government decided to create the Australian Defence Force Academy where all career officers would undertake their initial training and tertiary study. There would be much work on the part of the three Services to implement the Government's intent before the first intake arrived in 1986.

The other change that was specific to the Navy, was the creation, by the RN in 1972, of Principal Warfare Officers (PWO) to replace specialist warfare officers in ships. The PWO concept emerged in response to the ever-reducing reaction times required to deal with air, surface and under-water threats in the missile age. PWOs would be more generalists able to employ all above and below water weapons and sensors. As the RAN was still unable to undertake advanced courses in Australia, the replacement of the RN specialist warfare officers with PWOs required the RAN to follow suit. This was a significant development as the old officer structure had largely remained unchanged since the Navy's creation. This led Guy being directed in July 1975 to undertake a fundamental review into officers' training and career progression. Guy's terms of reference were wide-ranging and directed him to also examine the career structure for short engagement (Supplementary List) and career (General List) officers as well as sailors commissioning to become officers. He was assisted by Commander Malcolm Baird,* who had spent some years in naval training appointments. In the first instance, Guy conducted extensive interviews within the Fleet and in the training establishments. He was impressed with the pool of young talent, but felt the existing structure was too rigid and did not sufficiently reward merit. One of the useful changes to encourage this talent was to allow for the early promotion of well reported Lieutenants.

Commander Baird later wrote that as Guy 'addressed what he called 'the officer development process', the list of necessary changes grew. Guy found, however, that there were some who saw no need for change.'[35] In spite of opposition, which waned over time, Guy's review resulted in fundamental change. A key finding of the review was that officers'

---

*   Later Commodore R.M. Baird AM, RAN (1934–).

development was fragmented and divisive. The most dramatic change was a cultural as much as a practical one. All initial officer training was to be concentrated at the Naval College. Up the that point only General List officers attended the hallowed grounds at Jervis Bay. All other officers of the Supplementary List, sailors 'changing over' to become officers as well as chaplain, lawyers, doctors and dentists were trained elsewhere. The other much needed reform was for the training of the Navy's women officers to be integrated with that of their male counterparts. These changes slowly led to a greater cohesion and inclusion within the officer corps.

VIII

On 30 June 1976 Guy was promoted to Rear Admiral and replaced Rear Admiral McFarlane as CNP. On attaining flag rank, Guy had joined a very small group of six Rear Admirals. In addition to the Deputy CNS and the Fleet Commander, there were Rear Admirals responsible for personnel, naval technical services and materiel areas of the Navy. At the time of Guy's appointment there was also one rear admiral in a Defence or Joint position. The numbers of these latter positions would grow significantly over time.

Guy's selection as CNP was a sensible one, for he had not only a keen interest in personnel matters, but had served in the area on two previous occasions. In the normal course of events Guy would have two postings as a Rear Admiral and then either be promoted to Vice Admiral and become the CNS or he would retire. With the recent retirement of Commodore John Goble only Guy and Jim Willis remained from the 1937 Entry. The latter had been promoted to Rear Admiral three years earlier and had already been CNP and was now responsible for Materiel.

When Guy returned to the personnel area as a Commodore it was not with the prospect of becoming CNP. His selection and promotion therefore came with a mix of feelings. He was pleased to be promoted and felt he could make a contribution, but he also calculated this meant he was not going to command the Fleet. Because every CNS since 1948 had commanded the Fleet, it was deduced that he would not, barring any unforeseen development, lead the Navy. This was in part confirmed when in 1978 Guy's classmate Jim Willis was appointed FOCAF and so was almost certain destined to become the next CNS. Jim Willis was in Guy's estimation the most intellectually gifted officer in his class after the now retired David Hamer and would be a worthy selection.*

During his tenure as CNP, Guy wanted to progress the personnel reforms needed to make naval service more attractive as a career. He was particularly concerned that the most sailors did not serve beyond their initial six-year engagement. The significant loss of mid-seniority officers was also a concern.[36] Guy strongly supported the concept of re-engagement bonuses for sailors which was viewed as an unorthodox at the time. To improve officer retention Guy set out three principles to improve their career management. The first was to offer suitable and challenging positions for the individual. The second was that these positions should be consistent with a longer-term career plan and finally they involve where possible the least domestic disruption. While a useful guide, personnel shortages made it not always achievable. The other areas of importance in Guy's tenure were implementing the Junior Officers' review and improving opportunities for officer professional, managerial and academic education.

When one gets into a position of authority it is sometimes possible to put in place long considered initiatives. This was just such a situation when Guy became CNP. Ever since Guy attended the RN Staff College in 1954 he felt that the RAN should have its own. In this way more naval officers could benefit from this type of training. Since that time he had repeatedly seen the Navy suffer from the lack of officers with the strategic analysis and communications skills to formulate and state the Navy's position. Guy therefore set a goal to create a RAN Staff College.

---

* David Hamer left the Navy as a Captain in 1968 and quickly immersed himself in politics. He twice unsuccessfully contested the Federal lower house seat of Issacs for the Liberal Party but became a Senator in 1977.

Left
HMAS *Hobart* on 'Gunline' off the Vietnamese coast. (RAN)

Below
'The elegant and intrepid' HMAS *Hobart*. (RAN)

Commander US 7ᵗʰ Fleet Vice Admiral John Hyland Jr onboard HMAS *Hobart*.
(RAN)

Above Left

Guy Griffiths in his captain's chair onboard HMAS *Hobart*. (Griffiths Collection)

Above Right

Guy is greeted by Carla, Guy Jr and Erica on HMAS *Hobart*'s return to Sydney
from Vietnam. (Griffiths Collection)

Left
HMAS *Melbourne* and
Coral Sea 2. (RAN)

Below
HMAS *Melbourne* with
Skyhawks on deck. (RAN)

Above

Phillip Year's Reunion onboard HMAS *Melbourne* in 1971. *L to R, rear:* David Hamer, Greg Thrum, Jim Willis, John Austin & Harry Bodman. *Front:* Guy Peter Gyllies & John Goble. (Griffiths Collection)

Left

Guy and Rear Admiral Andrew Robertson at the handover of Support Command. (RAN)

Guy with Carla, Erica and Guy Jr. (heidesmith)

Guy and 'Snow' Gafford (Griffiths Collection)

Guy in 2011 with members of the HMS *Prince of Wales* & *Repulse* Survivors' Association. (Griffiths Collection)

Guy and Rear Admiral 'Thana' Thanabalasingham reunited in 2019. (J.Perryman)

Guy and David Mattiske at the Battle of Surigao Strait 75th Anniversary commemorations. (RAN)

Guy opening Griffiths House in 2010 at the Naval College with Chief of Navy Vice Admiral Russ Crane and Captain Jaimie Hatcher. (RAN)

Guy and Carla in 2009. (Griffiths Collection)

In 2017 Guy and the HMAS *Hobart* Association handover models of the first two Hobarts to Captain John Stavridis onboard the new *Hobart*. To Guy's right is the last captain of *Hobart* II, Captain Peter Murray (RAN)

On his second day as CNP he set about realising a College's creation. Fortuitously, his Director of Naval Training was the newly promoted Captain Neil Ralph, who had both completed the RAAF Staff Course and been on the staff of the RN Staff College. Ralph shared Guy's vision and preparatory work began on the initiative. More generally on innovations in naval training, Ralph found that Guy 'gave me confidence that some new ideas being generated would be given a good hearing.'[37]

For Guy, timing was important in realising the RAN Staff College. He was, for example, uncertain of the then CNS, Vice Admiral David Stevenson's view on a RAN Staff College. To ensure he did not get a refusal, he did not raise it with him. Instead, the work steadily progressed to an advanced stage before Guy presented it to Stevenson's relief, Vice Admiral Tony Synnot. Pleasingly, he received strong support. More generally, Guy enjoyed working for Synnot who impressed him with his intellect and his excellent networking ability with the senior echelons in Defence and government. It was something the Navy greatly benefitted from, but rarely experienced, with its Chiefs of Naval Staff.

To ensure the successful establishment of the RAN Staff College, Guy selected Ralph, after his successful command of the frigate *Torrens*, to become the inaugural Director of the Staff College in October 1978. Ralph was in Guy's assessment 'a human dynamo'[38] and had soon identified a building at the Sydney shore establishment, *Penguin* for the college and began assembling the staff. Of note, one of the greatest sources of support for the new RAN Staff College were the long-term public servants working in Navy who could see its value, not only for naval officers, but also for public servants. They helped find the funds from various 'hollow logs' for the fitting out of the College building.

The other important reform during Guy's tenure as the CNP was the institution of an annual Navy fitness test. While Guy had always kept himself very fit through a range of sports and lifestyle, he was not representative of the Navy. Indeed, duty free alcohol and cigarettes onboard ships only contributed to a lack of general fitness. The introduction of an annual fitness test was viewed with horror by many and stories of overweight senior sailors having heart attacks during these exertions spread through the Navy. But to the credit of successive naval leaders, they resisted attempts to abolish it and it can now be seen a most important step in improving the health of the Navy's men and women. Vice Admiral Synnot remarked that Guy had an 'ability to keep up with the changing trends to Society.'[39] Another assessment by one his staff officers was that Guy had 'hewn through the forest of no change.'[40]

During Guy's CNP tenure there were modest improvements in the all-important personnel retention rates, but it was an issue of many strands that would continue to tax future naval leaders. One possible source of additional personnel was the wider employment of women. Guy received varied proposals to post women to sea for specific tasks and for sea-riding experience. Guy was not an advocate of women serving at sea and later wrote of his view at that time,

> I did not consider Australia had reached the stage where it was necessary for women to suffer the indignities of serving in a combat ship at sea – our ships were never designed to provide the privacy which I considered to be essential.[41]

In coming years newer ships designed for mixed-gender ship's companies such as the fourth *Parramatta* and the third *Hobart*, would enter service, and Guy would live to see women officers and sailors serve in the Iraq War and some go on to command warships.

IX

Guy's 37th and final posting in the Navy was in Sydney. In January 1979 he became Flag Officer Commanding East Australia. During his tenure, the title changed to the more descriptive Commander Naval Support Command. As the new name suggested, the Admiral was responsible for much of the logistics, material and training support for the Fleet, including the numerous shore establishments and facilities around Australia. With the FOCAF often at sea in *Melbourne*, 'FONSC,' as he was phonetically referred to, had a heavy social program and this was reflected in having a large official residence. The 1865-era *Tresco* on the Elizabeth Bay waterfront and had a dining room that could seat forty people.

One of the first duties Guy had to undertake was to open the new RAN Staff College on 15 January. In opening the College Guy said that,

> This course should provide students a significant opportunity to reflect and constructively criticise present service doctrine and policy. By gaining some insight into management in industry and its sensitivity to its environment, they should gain the potential to recommend improvements and adjustments in service management.[42]

Guy considered the advent of the RAN Staff College, with its increased output of staff trained naval officers, one of his greatest contribution to the Service. He remained indebted to Neil Ralph for his energy and organisational skills. The Staff College remained in operation until 2000 when it merged with the other single service staff colleges into the Australian Command and Staff College in Canberra. Fittingly, at the new institution the G.R. Griffiths Prize was instituted for excellence in management studies.

As FONSC, a key relationship for Guy was with FOCAF who was in effect his 'customer.' Initially, it was Jim Willis, and in April 1979 the newly promoted David Leach took command. He joined the Naval College five years after Guy, and had been on Guy's staff eight years earlier. Generational change had taken place, as it always would, and it was clear to Guy it was time to retire.

In the 1979 Queen's Birthday Honours List Guy was made an Officer of the Order of Australia 'for service over the period of 42 years and particularly as Chief of Naval Personnel.'[43] Guy retired from the Navy on 17 January 1980, just ten days before the 43rd anniversary of his joining the Naval College. On his departure Guy received messages of goodwill from the Minister for Defence, civic leaders, and old shipmates. These included James Osborne from *Shropshire* and Jim Willis who wrote, reflecting on their time in the Navy together, 'I think we would both do it again if we had the opportunity, but perhaps without that interminable four years at Flinders Naval Depot.'[44]

Perhaps more illuminating about Guy's legacy was the correspondence from two officers who were on course in the US, undertaking the sort of professional education Guy had championed. The first was from a future Chief of Naval Staff, the then Commander Ian MacDougall* who had served in the Personnel Division when Guy was Chief. He wrote that 'even from a distance I always felt that whatever your command or position, only good for the RAN could result.'[45] The other was also from another former subordinate, Lieutenant Commander Hayden Daw who wrote:

> I often wonder whether senior officers quite appreciate the good (and bad) effects they can have on their subordinates. In your case, your appetite for work, your competence and your dress and bearing were a motivation for us all.[46]

Guy left the Navy with the fleet was still centred on the aircraft carrier. It would, however, in a handful of years change significantly. Due to a chain of developments, including the Falklands War, *Melbourne* would be retired without replacement and major cuts would occur in its personnel strength. The month Guy retired coincided with the last 15– and 16-year-old boys entering the Naval College. This was an end of an era, accentuated by the growing number university graduate officers and within a few years the advent of women embarking on sea service. It

---

*   Vice Admiral I.D.G. MacDougall, AC, AFSM, RAN (1938–2020). He was Chief of Naval Staff from 1991–94.

was a Navy continually in transition and one that Guy would watch and continue to contribute to in other ways.

9

Home From the Sea

History is a fascinating subject because it is basically all about people.

Guy Griffiths[1]

I

On his retirement from the RAN, Guy was about to turn fifty-seven and wanted to use his talents both in private industry and in benevolent realms. He was keen after years of dedication to the Navy to strike a better work-life balance. As well as more time with Carla and the family, there was the opportunity to play golf at the Royal Sydney Golf Club and to dig deeper into his family's history. In regard to the latter activity, he aptly wrote that the maxim for amateur genealogists is 'the search continues because it is never completed.'[2]

In an interview with a journalist from *The Australian* newspaper on his retirement, Guy said, 'If someone feels that I can contribute I would only be only too happy to do so. It is too early to pack up.'[3] A corporate opportunity came soon enough when a friend let it be known that the fire security firm of Wormald International was seeking an inaugural Personnel Director. In 1980 Guy joined the firm and set about getting to know its business, structure and people. The company had been founded in 1889 by Joseph and Henry Wormald. Based initially on importing fire doors and sprinklers, it went on to manufacture and import a range of fire safety equipment and cabinets, with eighteen manufacturing plants around Australia and New Zealand. Its size was a product of both growth and acquisition, and, as Guy soon learnt, each section of the business operated as the fiefdom of its head. As such there was little appetite from these men for a consistent personnel policy, let alone central control of personnel matters. Despite this, during his three years with Wormald, Guy laid the foundation for a more modern approach to personnel management, formulating a career development policy and providing advice to line managers on training, counselling and succession planning. Probably the most important contribution Guy made was a performance appraisal system, first in one division and then company-wide so that talent could be better judged and developed. These initiatives gave much greater transparency as to how personnel issues were managed across the company. More changes would follow when Wormald was later acquired by the large US firm of Tyco International.

Guy was also keen to branch out to other areas. In 1981 he accepted an invitation to be a Lay-Member of the Solicitors Statutory Committee of New South Wales. He was one of five new members to join an expanded committee, bringing their number to twenty. Since 1935 the Committee had the task of considering allegations of misconduct by solicitors and clerks. The record of their proceedings was known in legal circles as the 'Doomsday Book'. Guy found his experience in naval administration and the Naval Discipline Act in various capacities had well prepared him for looking at matters in this almost parallel legal system. During Guy's tenure, the Committee became the more accurately named the Legal Profession Disciplinary Tribunal. He would serve on it for seven interesting years.

The reduced work demands following his retirement from the Navy allowed Guy to be more involved in the Freemasons. In 1982 he joined the Lodge Army and Navy. Military Lodges were the first to be formed in Australia and the following year Lodge Army and Navy celebrated its 60th Anniversary. Guy would be the Lodge's Worshipful Master from 1987 to 1988. Although a Military Lodge, by tradition all members were treated as equals and first names were used. At the Lodge Guy was greatly respected for his knowledge of the Craft and his unfailingly courtesy to younger members.

In 1983 Guy established a small consulting business, mainly in educating and assisting private industry in doing business with Defence. In this capacity he also undertook some work for Defence in relation to the Collins class submarines then building in Adelaide. Guy found this rewarding work in which he felt his recent knowledge and long experience were still of value to the Navy. About this time Guy would also regularly speak at Resettlement Seminars for service personnel about to leave Defence. After outlining some of the adjustments they would have to make, Guy encouraged them in their future second careers by remarking that,

> The country needs people with get-up and go who will contribute to its overall development in many ways. The country will sink or swim on its profit account. The real challenge to you is to get out there and contribute to that profit.[4]

As with many retired senior naval officers, Guy was approached to lead various Defence or naval not-for-profit organisations. He had a particular interest in the welfare of veterans and in June 1980 became the National President of the Australian Veterans' and Defence Services' Council (AVADSC) replacing Lieutenant General Sir Mervyn Brogan. In the first instance Guy continued the engagement with the many different veterans' associations to encourage them to become affiliated to the Council. During Guy's time as President, over 40 associations joined the Council, varying from the numerous unit associations to the Partially Blind Soldiers' Association and the War Widows' Guild. All of them saw value in the Council analysing current and planned Government veterans-related policies as well as advocating initiatives to the Government and the Opposition. AVADSC's work involved listening to the concerns of the over 250,000 constituents through their affiliate organisations and then providing advocacy and submissions to the Government.

Many of the affiliated organisations had state-based associations and an important part of Guy's work was engagement with these bodies around the country. In terms of advocacy and engagement, Guy would meet with Government and shadow ministers as well as senior bureaucrats from the Department of Veterans Affairs and the Repatriation Commission. At the monthly Council meetings, where over 30 attendees was common, Guy took the opportunity to have guest speakers from these bodies. He had personal relationships with many of them. Neil Ralph, who had also retired as a Rear Admiral, became Commissioner on the Repatriation Commission while 'Red' Merson led the affiliate Naval Association.

One consistent challenge for Guy was raising the Council's profile with the Ministers and Shadow Ministers of the day. Indeed, the significant churn of Ministers in this portfolio, which was due to factional party politics rather than ministerial performance, led Guy to ask Prime Minister John Howard to retain the very effective Bruce Scott in post because of his 'informed background and rapport with the Australian veterans' movement.'[5] It was to no avail.

Typically, Ministers and Shadow Ministers would engage the Returned Services League (RSL), but much more rarely the Council. Indeed, the relationship between the Council and the RSL was at times fraught, with some in the RSL preferring the Council did not exist. But Guy worked at the relationships at both the Federal and State levels of the RSL. He had a particularly constructive relationship with RSL President Brigadier Alf Garland, who was the only President to attend a Council meeting and engage with its constituent associations. After initial wariness on the part of the Victorian RSL President, the gruff Bruce Ruxton, Guy formed a cordial relationship, with their war service the basis for a common bond. What becomes clear from a review of the Council minutes is that the Council tried to understand the issues and be constructive with the Government. Unlike the RSL, for example, the Council supported the transfer of the Repatriation hospitals to the state health departments, once there were sufficient protections in place to ensure Veterans' services were not compromised. Rear Admiral Ralph later commented that,

> The RSL of course was the larger organisation but was not run as smoothly as AVADSC – there were personalities such as Ruxton leading it who were usually very unreasonable. This gave strength to AVADSC and its advice and counsel were much better developed and reasonable as far as the Repat Commission was concerned. Guy was highly respected as its leader among both members and the Commission. ... I felt absolutely sure that AVADSC was effective because Guy was its leader.[6]

The advocacy required a sustained effort and Guy regularly had to point out to the Government and its bureaucracy the need to provide support to veterans in a timely manner. He often had to remind people of the average age of World War II veterans and that policy change taking four or five years of study and implementation were not responsive enough. Remarkably, Guy served as President for nearly 24 years, finally stepping down in 2004. For most of his tenure he had as his most able Secretary, Wing Commander Peter Alexander. When asked what he would like as a farewell present after his long service, Guy asked for a suitably inscribed *Macquarie Dictionary*.

Another long-term commitment by Guy was as a Director of the Australian Vietnam War Veterans' Trust from 1985 to 2003. The Trust was founded in 1985 as the Vietnam Veterans' Trust with the original purpose of distributing the Australian share of the Agent Orange legal settlement from the US. The funds were allocated to Vietnam veterans in deserving circumstances. The Trust particularly aimed to provide for the growing number of widows who needed assistance for themselves and the education of their children. In Guy's final year with the Trust it established tertiary scholarships for Vietnam Veterans' children.

One of Guy's most rewarding positions in his post-naval career was from 1987, as the inaugural Chief Executive Officer of North Shore Heart Research Foundation. His appointment came through an approach from the irrepressible publicist and philanthropist Sir Asher Joel, who Guy had known for many years. Both men had served in the Navy in the Philippines Campaign, with Joel being on General MacArthur's staff. In the 1970s, Sir Asher had also been an office bearer in the Lodge Army and Navy. Guy, like many before him, found Sir Asher's approaches impossible to refuse.

The new Foundation was created on the instigation of three eminent cardiologists, Professor Stephen Hunyor, Dr Gaston Bauer and Dr John Gunning from the Royal North Shore Hospital. Its aim was to provide seed-funding for research to help reduce the high death rates of heart disease at the time. This would include support to PhD candidates. The cardiologists' concerns were well founded. At around 700 deaths per 100,000 of the population, cardiovascular disease was then the dominant cause of death in Australia. Indeed, its mortality figures had risen steadily since 1916 with only recent signs for any optimism.[7] When Guy joined the fledgling North Shore Heart Research Foundation, he had in the words of its Chairman, John Allison, 'a desk, a chair and a blank piece of paper.'[8] The desk had only three legs and Guy's only employee was initially himself and his primary role was to raise money for deserving research work. Guy's approach was first to talk to the cardiologists and Professor Gregory Nelson recalled Guy's arrival and his admission that he had no knowledge of heart disease or fundraising,

He approached the challenge as would any Commander of

the Fleet. He embedded himself systematically within all the aspects of our Department's activities. He spent time with me in the catheter laboratory. He studied textbooks of the heart's anatomy and he learnt all he could about heart attack management. He then went through every one of our tests from echoes to eps and stress tests. He spent time in the operating theatres and watched coronary bypass and valve surgery. Only then did he come and ask us what we needed. He then went to the community, established corporate visits, and arranged Rotary and Probus meetings. So began the fundraising.[9]

Guy learnt that it was a time of promising developments with the first cardiac stent being implanted just the previous year. This stent research and application, pioneered at the Royal North Shore Hospital, was an early focus of the Foundation's funding; as was the funding of professorial positions at the hospital.

Through his recently acquired knowledge, Guy could discuss the importance of the proposed research with prospective donors in a way they could understand. Guy built up a small and efficient organisation. During Guy's time the Foundation was able to raise around one million dollars. This was done through individual approaches for support, dinners and regular appeals. In his many presentations on the work of the Foundation he would highlight that while the media may report on the daily road toll, which averaged eight deaths, much less coverage was given to heart disease, the silent killer of 150 people each day.

In 1991, with the assistance of the Foundation, the Royal North Shore Hospital established a heart research centre. In Australia this period was one of the most productive periods in the fight against cardiovascular disease, with the halving of the mortality rate. In 2012, North Shore Heart Research Foundation became a nationally focused body and was renamed Heart Research Australia. By its 30th anniversary in 2016 nearly $30 million had been given to research and the mortality rate from heart attack treated at the Royal North Shore Hospital had dropped from 30% to 2%.[10]

II

By virtue of Guy's interest, service and attained rank, he became a member a number of veterans' associations. Guy is a Patron of the HMAS *Canberra-Shropshire* Association and the HMAS *Hobart* Association. He also took over the role of the HMS *Prince of Wales* and HMS *Repulse* Survivors' Association from Vice Admiral Sir Jock Hayes in 1992. With that handover, Guy, wherever possible, kept his former snotties' nurse engaged in the activities of the Association. Hayes described the survivors' bond 'the most cherished among my memories.'[11] As patron of this organization, Guy played a leading role from 2000 to 2005 in the efforts to have the wrecks of both ships protected by an international legal regime and designated as protected maritime war graves. This task, complicated by legal jurisdictional issues, assumed a degree of urgency once it was realized that these and other World War II wrecks in the shallow waters off Malaysia and Indonesia were subject not only to plunder but wholesale removal for scrap. While the Association's efforts raised the issue to relevant Governments this has unfortunately not stopped periodic illegal salvage operations on both wrecks. As President of the Naval Historical Society Guy was an influential advocate for the creation of a national naval museum. This effort was rewarded with the 2005 opening of the RAN Heritage Centre on Garden Island in Sydney.

Even after his tenure at AVADSC President, Guy as a distinguished veteran, has been invited to attend many commemoration services. In 2017 he journeyed to the Prisoner-of-War Memorial in Ballarat for the 75th anniversary commemoration of the fall of Singapore. Among the veterans at that event who Guy met, Ron 'Dixie' Lee who had been a signalman in *Manoora* which steamed close by *Repulse* in the Johore

Strait as Force Z prepared to leave for their fateful sortie. What stuck in Dixie Lee's memory was the general air of smartness about *Repulse* and hearing the music from her band on the quarterdeck. Most memorably at the commemoration was that Guy met once more his class mate David Manning. It was the first time they had seen each other since the Naval College. It was a wonderful and unexpected reunion. David was still in Guy's words, 'the nicest cove'.[12] He sadly passed away twelve months later at the age of 95 years. An amazing achievement for a Burma Railway survivor.

Well into his nineties Guy has been invited to speak to various naval gatherings, historical societies and the media on his war service and experiences. Guy was willing to do so as he felt it important that the sacrifices made by those who did not survive the wars in which he had served were remembered. These events extended to, in his 96th year, giving a paper at a history conference in Malaysia. This invitation provided the delightful opportunity to meet once more 'Thana' Thanabalasingham who had also been asked to speak at the conference. In all these events Guy would prepare himself thoroughly and 'time' his speeches beforehand. Increasingly, for younger members of these audiences Guy may be the first World War II veteran they had seen. What impressed them were Guy's strength of voice and clarity of thought. In his talks Guy tried to communicate not only the details of the events, the deeds and sacrifices of his shipmates, but also to provide some strategic analysis. At the opening of an exhibition at the Shrine of Remembrance, a naval veteran, Ralph Wollmer, recalled that Guy gave his address,

> ... in his inimitable manner he held his audience spellbound. In his address he told of as a young man serving in HMS *Repulse* he 'wet his feet', when the Japanese sank *Repulse*. A member of our group that day was 96-year-old, Doctor V.R. Leonard who is the sole survivor of HMAS *Armidale*. Ray too 'wet his feet' in her sinking and O/D Ray Leonard

subsequently spent nine days in an unseaworthy ship's whaler. We introduced Guy and Ray. Their bonding was instant, intense and with total reverence for each other so much so, that it took esprit de corps to another level.[13]

At this and other events, where the extraordinary heroism of Ordinary Seaman Teddy Sheean* in going down with *Armidale* still firing his 20mm gun at the attacking Japanese aircraft was told, Guy would, if the opportunity presented, highlight the less well-known valour of his friend Robert Davies.

In 1990 Guy attended the Lodge Carringtonia, the oldest Lodge in the central west of New South Wales, on the centenary of his grandfather, Dr Ernest Griffiths being initiated into the Freemasons. Guy spoke of the early hardships of his forebears and those of the district. He also stressed the positive role of the Lodge in the community and the need for it, like the Navy, to adjust to contemporary society without losing its essence. In 2010 Guy was invited to open a new accommodation block named in his honour at the Naval College at Jervis Bay. Accompanying him to the event was his former Commander in *Melbourne* 'Toz' Dadswell. Guy was 'very chuffed' at the honour, for the Naval College years were so formative for him. Griffiths House subsequently received a Royal Australian Institute of Architects award.

The commissioning of the fourth *Parramatta* and the third *Hobart* were also occasions of personal significance. *Hobart* with her war service held a special place in his affections. His command of her was without doubt his career highlight and he had played a critical part in developing a happy and high performing ship's company and enduring culture. The commissioning commanding officer of the new destroyer *Hobart*, Captain John Stavridis invited Guy to speak to his men and women on a number of occasions about his former ship. After a successful commissioning

---

* In 2020 Ordinary Seaman Teddy Sheean was posthumously awarded the Victoria Cross for Australia.

ceremony, Stavridis rued that in the flurry of the day he had not made particular mention of Guy at the event. It was a repeat of history as Guy had the same regret about Captain Howden on his commissioning day. Both Howden and Guy were the talisman for their own ships and their presence and support for the new ships were sincerely appreciated.

Over the years Guy attended a number of HMS *Prince of Wales* and HMS *Repulse* Survivors' Association reunions in the UK. Their special bond remained undiminished over the decades. In 2002 Guy attended the 60th anniversary commemorations of the fall of Singapore and the loss of Force Z. At a service at the immaculately kept Kranji War Cemetery Guy read the Ode to the Fallen to a large gathering of veterans and families. Afterwards Guy visited the grave of Midshipmen James Bremridge. Three years later Guy returned to Singapore for VJ Day 60th anniversary commemorations. On this occasion, he and fellow survivor Ted Matthews unveiled a handsome Force Z memorial plaque at Sembawang dockyard, which those great ships had so briefly visited.

By virtue of the immigration of some *Prince of Wales* and *Repulse* survivors to Australia, there had also been a regular gathering at Gosford. Also invited were the *Vampire* survivors in recognition of the gallant destroyer's efforts in rescuing 225 men from the two ships that fateful December day in 1941. Among the *Vampire* contingent was the larger-than-life Jack Mooney, who had a double association with Guy, because he later served as captain of a 4-inch gun mount in *Shropshire* during the Pacific Campaign. At one of these events Mooney was reunited with one of *Repulse*'s marines, Phil Senior, who Mooney had fished out of the sea. They became firm friends for the rest of their lives. In 1996 Guy delivered Jack Mooney's eulogy.

In 2019, Guy and his daughter Erica journeyed to the UK and attended, with other *Prince of Wales* and *Repulse* survivors, the commissioning of the new aircraft carrier HMS *Prince of Wales*. At this impressive occasion, the survivors were given pride of place. After the formalities, Guy had the opportunity to chat to HRH the Prince of Wales and the commissioning commanding officer. To Guy it was an occasion that opened a new naval chapter in the *Prince of Wales* and *Repulse* story. Later that year, Guy and a handful of veterans attended the 75th anniversary commemorations of the Battle of Surigao Strait in the Philippines. The reception by the Filipino people was warm and generous and the new memorial imposing. Guy had the honour of being the Reviewing Officer for the 'Honouring the Veterans' Parade at Surigao City. During the busy schedule Guy gave a number of media interviews. His old shipmate David Mattiske remarked that Guy spoke with 'a great sagacity which impressed all.'[14]

Guy's interest in naval affairs was not confined to its history. He had written and spoken widely on naval strategy and made submissions to various Defence reviews. Perhaps unsurprisingly, Guy repeatedly highlighted the need for the RAN to once again have an aircraft carrier to provide air power at sea. In 2000 he wrote in a submission to the Government, 'Naval forces deployed further afield in our region are placed in high risk without this capability ... It is high time that this important matter was placed on the agenda for national discussion.'[15]

These many commitments and indeed his willingness, after some initial reluctance, to support the writing of this biography have led Guy to reflect on the Navy, its culture and his career. Guy thought the harsh, and at times brutal, discipline at the Naval College when he was there had lasting effects. This was particularly the case for the cadet midshipmen such as him in leadership positions, who had to administer the discipline. He thought it inculcated a culture of being overly stern with subordinate officers and Guy reflected that it was a surprise when he entered a naval environment different to that. The first experience of this was the more relaxed *Repulse* gunroom under Richard Pool's enlightened leadership. Following the enactment of the 1982 Freedom of Information Act, Guy was able to read for the first time the candid performance reports rendered on him through his career. Hitherto, he had only read the usually very bland 'flimsies' or summaries given to reported upon officers. In the fuller reports there was some criticism of Guy being too stern as a leader. The concept of mentoring and counselling individuals was not one the Navy of Guy's era embraced. It was something Guy felt would have benefited him, his contemporaries and the Navy more generally. On a more optimistic note, Guy was greatly encouraged by the more relaxed, but still professional, approach that exists in the modern Navy. On this subject Guy has remarked,

> I like to believe that the professionalism now if anything is probably better than the professionalism we had in the earlier days. It's no good looking back and saying well the Navy isn't what it used to be when I was a boy, and the only answer to that is thank God it isn't. It's got to change with the times. It's got to get up there and move.[16]

The other reflection Guy has had on the Navy of his time, was its general resistance to new ideas. This he experienced when recommending the adoption of useful practices and procedures from the USN as well as considering acquiring equipment from non-traditional sources. In the realm of personnel matters there was often a reluctance to adjust policy to better align with changes in the Australian society. In part, Guy felt the conservatism of many of the Admirals was due to the absence of continued educational opportunities for naval officers. In Guys' time, the only officers who had any tertiary education were engineers, lawyers, doctors and dentists.* In addition, too few had the benefit of staff training. This state of affairs seemed to inhibit intellectual curiosity and the adoption of new ideas and to engender a corporate small mindedness, particularly at the senior levels. It was a source of disappointment to Guy that, even as he became more senior and hoped to implement greater

---

* The first non-engineer officer to have a degree on the Chief of Navy's Advisory Committee was in 1995.

reforms, he could still sense that irritation among the senior leadership about change.

During his long post-Navy years, Carla and Guy enjoyed other opportunities for overseas travel. This included a number of visits to Europe to attend reunions of the Kaiser Wilhelm School alumni. Guy found this eclectic group of Germans fascinating company. Late in life Carla was diagnosed with Parkinson's Disease and she dealt bravely with its insidious symptoms with Guy's devoted support. Carla passed away on 4 May 2019. Carla's place in Guy's life was enormous and in later years Guy in particular reflected on the wonderful support she had provided in raising the family and running the home during his long absences at sea. Guy wrote 'In earlier generations it may not have been a topic for discussion, and it is possible that some may not have conveyed their appreciation to their ladies.'[17] This was certainly true and Guy himself wished that he had articulated his appreciation more at the time.

Throughout his life Guy maintained his fitness to an impressive level and kept as much independence as his age allowed. At ninety-eight he still took part unaided in the Sydney Anzac Day March.

III

When the Pulitzer Prize-winning historian Barbara Tuchman attempted to describe Fourteenth Century Europe in her bestseller, *A Distant Mirror*, she chose to tell the story largely through the life of the French nobleman Enguerrand VII de Coucy. In his eventful life, de Coucy was present at many of the key events of the age. This allowed Tuchman to illuminate the period, yet 'narrow the focus to a manageable level.'[18] Guy Griffiths is by deed and happenstance the de Coucy of the Twentieth Century RAN. When Guy joined the Navy, bi-planes still operated from its large ships and some of its men had seen action in the Boxer Rebellion. Perhaps he, more than any other man, experienced the Navy's journey from its Depression-era strictures, its darkest days in the face of the Japanese onslaught, its finest hour in the Philippines Campaign and then its reinvention as a capable middle-power Navy, centred on aircraft carriers in the missile age. Importantly, he had personally experienced the realities of war, in all its awfulness, in the three wars of that period – World War II, Korea and Vietnam – in positions of increasing responsibility.

As an individual, Guy grew from an athletic country boy into a highly respected war time destroyer captain. At the end of his naval career, as a Rear Admiral he was, with his spruce comportment and his determination to achieve substantive reforms, the epitome of a Flag Officer to all serving in the Navy. During those forty-two years Guy had also developed as a person and as leader. In his early years he was stern to his subordinate officers and perhaps carried his ambitions for personal advancement too transparently. As he matured, Guy saw his advancement more for the opportunities it presented for the professional challenge to himself and for the reforms he could achieve for the Navy. Since 1959 Guy was greatly supported in his naval career and personal life by Carla, whose strength of character, intellect and charm impressed all who had the privilege of knowing her.

Professionally, Guy's greatest legacy was his outstanding command of *Hobart* in the Vietnam War, which paved the way for subsequent successful deployments by other RAN ships in that theatre. Within the Fleet, Guy's early advocacy of a rigorous sea training regime along USN lines was instrumental in its adoption. This initiative has been a significant factor in the success of all RAN deployments to subsequent conflicts. Within the Navy as a whole, Guy's major contributions were his pivotal role in reforming the structure of the officer corps and in improving its education with the creation of the RAN Staff College.

In realising these achievements, Guy was in the first instance, assisted along the way by officers and sailors who gave of their knowledge of life at sea. This helped him develop into an outstanding naval officer. Perhaps equally important were the examples, both good and bad, that influenced Guy through his career, and the triumvirate of Captains – Tennant,

Nichols and Harries are prime examples of the good. He pursued these great endeavours with the support of teams of dedicated and committed people, be that at sea or ashore. Indeed, it was the accomplishments and camaraderie of collective ships' companies that most left their mark on Guy. He would later remark 'No Admiral or Captain in history achieved his promotion or received his decoration where the major contribution wasn't made by the ships' companies.'[19]

In over four decades following his retirement from the Navy, Guy continued to give his services and his insights to the benefit of Australian society, the Navy and its veterans. His long life and associated mental acuity have enabled sailors born in the Twenty-first Century to benefit from his accumulated wisdom. In so doing, he continues to inspire and serves as a tangible link to the earlier days of the Royal Australian Navy.

Notes

Prologue

1 Dowling, B. *A Bushie's War 1940–1944*, self published, 22.
2 Oral History of Rear Admiral G.R. Griffiths, Australians at War Film, Archive #1146, 10 April 2002.

1: A Country Boy

1 *The Sydney Herald, 17 March 1834, 3*

2 Plomley, H.J.B., *An Immigrant of 1824*, Tasmanian Historical Research Association, Hobart, 1973, 27.

3 Busby, J., *A Treatise on the Culture of the Vine and the Art of Making Wine: compiled from the works of Chaptal, and other French writers; and from the notes of the compiler, during a residence in some wine provinces of France*, R. Howe, Government Printers, Sydney, 1825.

4 Anon., *An Interpretation of the Log of William Dalrymple Kelman on board Triton on the Voyage Leith to Hobart Town 7th September 1823 – 19th January 1824*, 6.

5 Busby, J., *A Manual of Plain Directions for planting and Cultivating Vineyards, and for Making Wine in New South Wales,* R. Mansfield, Government Printers, Sydney, 1830.

6 https://www.waitangi.org.nz/discover-waitangi/treaty-house/

7 Ramsden, E., *James Busby: The prophet of Australian viticulture and British Resident at New Zealand, 1833–40*, self-published, Sydney 1941.

8 Ramsden, E., *James Busby: The Prophet of Australian Viticulture*, Royal Australian Historical Society Journal & Proceedings, Volume XXVI, Part IV, Sydney 1940. 366–67.

9 *The Sydney Morning Herald*, 7 May 1842, 2 and 3. The consul was also reported as Monsieur Taramond on page 2.

10 *Maitland Mercury and Hunter River General Advertiser*, 13 March 1884, 5.

11 *Ibid.*, 15 March 1884, 1.

12 *The Sydney Morning Herald*, 29 November 1881, 4.

13 Griffiths, G.R., *Family Griffiths 1788–1976*, Self-published, Sydney, 2003, 115.

14 *The Newcastle Morning Herald*, 28 August 1914, 5.

15 Gunn, J. & Gollan, R.M., *The Report on the Wine Industry of Australia*, Government Printer, 1931, 10.

16 Oral History of Rear Admiral G.R. Griffiths, Australians at War Film, Archive #1146, 10 April 2002.

17 Griffiths, G.R., *Family Griffiths 1788–1976*, *op. cit*, 119.

18 *The Sydney Morning Herald*, 23 December 1936, 6.

19 *Maitland Daily Mercury*, 15 January 1937, 6.

20 *Ibid.*

2: Life at the Naval College

1   *Royal Australian Naval College Magazine*, Government Printers, Melbourne, 1938, 21.

2   *The Argus*, 9 November 1936, 10.

3   Hamer, D., *Memories of My Life*, South Wind, Singapore, 2001, 62.

4   *Ibid.*, 85.

5   McGuire, P. & McGuire, F.M., *The Price of Admiralty*, Oxford University Press, Melbourne, 1944, 23.

6   *Ibid.*, 22.

7   *Ibid.*, 23.

8   *Ibid.*, 23.

9   Interview with Rear Admiral Andrew Robertson by the author, 27 September 2019.

10 Interview with Rear Admiral Rothesay Swan by the author, 21 January 2020.

11 Rear Admiral G.R. Griffiths, discussions with the author, 7 August 2020.

12 Oral History of Rear Admiral Guy Griffiths, 2009.

13 *Royal Australian Naval College Magazine*, Ramsay Ware Publishing, Melbourne, 1939, 240.

14 Oral History of Rear Admiral Guy Griffiths, 2002.

15 Interview with Rear Admiral Andrew Robertson by the author, 27 September 2019.

16 *Royal Australian Naval College Magazine*, Government Printers, Melbourne, 1941, 5.

3: Midshipman at Sea – HMS *Repulse*

1   Hayes, J., *Face the Music: A Sailor's Story*, Pentland Press, Edinburgh, 1991, 125.

2   Court martial of Commander G.S. Stewart RAN, 2 June 1941, 7821123 (NAA).

3   Rear Admiral G.R. Griffiths address to Sydney Rotary Club, 21 October 1980.

4   Oral History of Rear Admiral G.R. Griffiths, Australians at War Film, Archive #1146, 10 April 2002 & as modified in an interview with author 3 August 2019.

5   Dowling, B., *A Bushie's War 1940–1944*, self-published, 23.

6   Oral History of Rear Admiral G.R. Griffiths, Australians at War Film, *op. cit.*

7   *Ibid.*

8   Oral History of R.W. Fraser, Imperial War Museum, Archive Number 8267, 16 August 1984.

9   Rear Admiral G.R. Griffiths interview with the author 3 December 2018.

10 Oral History of Rear Admiral G.R Griffiths, Australians at War Film, *op. cit.*

11 Midshipman G.R. Griffiths, S.206 Report by Captain W.G. Tennant 10 January 1942. (NAA).

12 Dowling, B. *A Bushie's War 1940–1944*, self-published, 24.

13 Hayes, J, *Face the Music: A Sailor's Story*, Pentland Press, Edinburgh, 1991, 130.

14 Oral History of Rear Admiral G.R. Griffiths, Australians at War Film, *op. cit.*

15 Oral History of R.W. Fraser, Imperial War Museum, Archive Number 8267, 16 August 1984.

16 Oral History of Rear Admiral G.R. Griffiths, Australians at War Film, *op. cit.*

17 Matthews, E.J. Recollections at https://www.forcez-survivors.org.uk

18 Interview with Rear Admiral G.R. Griffiths with the author, 27 May 2019.

19 Pool, R., *Course for Disaster: From Scapa Flow to the River Kwai*, Leo Cooper, London, 1987, 49.

20 Interview with Rear Admiral G.R. Griffiths with the author, 27 May 2019.

21 Roskill, S.W., *Churchill and the Admirals,* Pen & Sword Military Classics, Barnley, 2004, 199.

22 Jones, D., *Australia's Argonauts*, Echo Books, Geelong, 2016, 404.

23 Admiral T.C. Hart USN, Diary entry for 6 December 1941, Admiral T.C. Hart Papers (USNHHC).

24 Report on Action by Captain W.G. Tennant, 1; TEN 22/1, Papers of Admiral W.G. Tennant (NMM).

25 Captain L.H. Bell RN, letter to the First Sea Lord, HMS *Express*, 10 December 1941, (NA UK).

26 *Ibid.*

27 Griffiths, G.R. (speech), *The Loss of Repulse and Prince of Wales*, undated (Griffiths Papers).

28 Captain L.H. Bell RN, letter to the First Sea Lord, HMS *Express*, 10 December 1941, (NA UK).

29 Pool, R., *Course for Disaster: From Scapa Flow to the River Kwai*, Leo Cooper, London, 1987, 59.

30 Hayes, J., *Face the Music: A Sailor's Story, op. cit.*, 140.

31 Report on Action by Captain W.G. Tennant, 1; TEN 22/1, Papers of Admiral W.G. Tennant (NMM).

32 Griffiths, G.R. (speech), *The Loss of Repulse and Prince of Wales*, undated (Griffiths Papers).

33 A Tribute to Jim Crumlin & HMS *Repulse*, undated (Griffiths Papers).

34 Report on Action by Captain W.G. Tennant, 1; TEN 22/1, Papers of Admiral W.G. Tennant (NMM) and Hayes, J., *Face the Music: A Sailor's Story*, Pentland Press, Edinburgh, 1991, 141.

35 Vice Admiral Sir John Hayes, letter to Rear Admiral G.R. Griffiths, 19 October 1992 and Vice Admiral Hayes' Patron's Message to the HMS *Prince of Wales* & HMS *Repulse* Survivors' Association Reunion, 1992 (Griffiths Papers).

36 Dowling, B., *A Bushie's War 1940–1944*, self-published, 32.

37 Maurice Pink's interview was contain in an article by Tony Rennell. It was

published by the UK *Daily Mail* see https://www.dailymail.co.uk/news/
article-2072359/Britains-Pearl-Harbour-The-Japanese-ambush-left-Navys-
finest-ships-the-sea-800-men-dead.html

38 Oral History of Able Seaman R Wood, Number 8251, 1984, (IWM).

39 Oral History of Able Seaman R Wood, Number 8251, 1984, (IWM).

40 Oral History of Rear Admiral G.R. Griffiths, Australians at War Film, *op. cit.*

41 Notes contained in TEN 22/1, Papers of Admiral W.G.Tennant (NMM).

42 Hayes, J, *Face the Music: A Sailor's Story, op. cit.*, 145.

43 Cain, T.J. *HMS Electra*, Futura Publications, London, 1976, 175.

44 Cain, T.J. *HMS Electra*, Futura Publications, London, 1976, 175.

45 Oral History of Petty Officer C.S. Rogers, Number 11326, 1990, (IWM).

46 Address by Rear Admiral G.R. Griffiths to Military History Society of NSW, 7 March 2020.

47 Hamer, D, *Memories of My Life*, South Wind, Singapore, 2001, 130.

48 Rear Admiral G.R. Griffiths interview with the author 3 December 2018.

49 Hamer, D, *Memories of My Life*, South Wind, Singapore, 2001, 133.

50 Oral History of Rear Admiral G.R. Griffiths, Australians at War Film, *op. cit.*

4: The Lucky Ship – HMAS *Shropshire*

1   Salopia, F., *Horatius Mk. II.*

2   Rear Admiral G.R. Griffiths interview with the author, 8 December 2018.

3   Cablegram from Secretary of State for Dominion Affairs cablegram to Prime Minister of Commonwealth of Australia, 29 August 1942, A5954, 424581 (NAA).

4   Telegram from Private Secretary to the King to the Governor General of Australia, 12 September 1942, A5954, 424581 (NAA).

5   Letter from M. Logue to V. Logue, 7 January 1943 (Logue Family Papers).

6   Hayes, J., *Face the Music: A Sailor's Story*, Pentland Press, Edinburgh, 1991, 119.

7   Sub-Lieutenant G.R. Griffiths S.206 Report 12 March 1943 (NAA).

8   *The Melbourne Age*, 8 October 1943.

9   *The Sydney Morning Herald*, 5 October 1943, 4.

10 D.H. Mattiske, email to the author, 21 December 2019.

11 Nicholls, S., *HMAS Shropshire*, The Naval Historical Society of Australia, Sydney, 1989, xvii.

12 *The West Australian,* 8 September 1943, 3.

13 Griffiths, G.R., *Outline of Naval Career*, unpublished (Griffiths Papers).

14 Nicholls, S., *HMAS Shropshire*, The Naval Historical Society of Australia, Sydney, 1989, 62.

15 Rear Admiral G.R. Griffiths note to author, August 2019.

16 Oral History of Rear Admiral G.R. Griffiths, Australians at War Film, *op. cit.*

17 *Ibid.*

18 *Ibid.*

19 *War Cabinet Minutes,* Numbers 2989–3331, 6 September 1943-4 February 1944, Volume 14, A5954, 689725 (NAA).

20 Lieutenant G.R. Griffiths, S.206 Report, 5 May 1944 (NAA).

21 Rear Admiral G.R. Griffiths, interview with the author, 3 December 2018.

22 Letter from J. Osborne to Rear Admiral G.R. Griffiths, 8 January 1980 (Griffiths Papers).

23 Captain C.A.G. Nichols DSC, RN Confidential Performance Report summary sheet. S.206 dated November 1942, ADM 196 Series (NAUK).

24 Russell, R., *Memories of HMAS Shropshire,* H.M.A.S. *Canberra-Shropshire* Association (N.S.W.), 1992, 7.

25 Rear Admiral G.R. Griffiths, interview with the author, 3 December 2018.

26 *Ibid.*

27 Rear Admiral G.R. Griffiths, *Life on the Line* podcast, 18 September 2017.

28 Interrogation of Admiral Toyota Soemu, OPNAV-P-030I00, 317.

29 Rear Admiral G.R. Griffiths, interview with the author, 3 December 2018.

30 Rear Admiral G.R. Griffiths, *Life on the Line* podcast, 18 September 2017.

31 Gill, G.H., *Royal Australian Navy 1942–1945,* Collins, Melbourne, 1968, 509.

32 Oral History of Rear Admiral G.R. Griffiths, Australians at War Film, *op. cit.*

33 Swan, R.C., *The Battle of Surigao Strait,* 15 December 2019 (Australian Naval Institute).

34 Nicholls, S., *HMAS Shropshire,* The Naval Historical Society of Australia, Sydney, 1989, 128.

35 *Australian Naval History* podcast, *The Battle of Leyte Gulf,* Season 4, Episode 17, 25 November 2019.

36 *HMAS Shropshire Action Report 1–18 January 1945,* 24 January 1945 (NAA).

37 Letter from Vice Admiral Sir Richard Peek to A.W. Grazebrook, 22 January 1988, & Commander E.S. Nurse AS 206 dated 15 October 1945 (Jones Grazebrook Papers).

38 Rear Admiral G.R. Griffiths, interview with the author, 8 October 2019.

39 Rear Admiral G.R. Griffiths, Address to the 2001 King Hall Naval History Conference.

40 Anon., *The Cruiser and the Kamikazes: The Story of Japanese Suicide Attacks on HMAS Australia at Lingayen Gulf, Luzon 4th-9th January 1945,* J.M. Armstrong Papers.

41 Letter from Commander W.S. Bracegirdle to A.W. Grazebrook, 14 February 1989 (Jones Grazebrook Papers).

42 Oral History of Rear Admiral G.R. Griffiths, Australians at War Film, *op. cit.*

43 Rear Admiral G.R. Griffiths interview with the author, 3 December 2018.

44 Oral History of Rear Admiral G.R. Griffiths, Australians at War Film, *op. cit.*

45 Commander US 7th Fleet letter to C-in-C US Fleet, 13 April 1945, MP1185/8, 440593 (NAA).

46 HMAS *Shropshire* Action Report Lingayen Gulf, 18 January 1945, 4, MP 1185/8, 440593 (NAA).

47 HMAS *Shropshire* Recommendation for Honours and Awards, Lieutenant G.R.

Griffiths, 1 February 1945 (NAA).

48 See website http://www.itsanhonour.gov.au/honours/awards/imperial.cfm .

49 Rear Admiral G.R. Griffiths, oral history, Naval Heritage Centre, 2009.

50 Rear Admiral G.R. Griffiths, interview with the author 1 September 2019.

51 Report Commanding Officer HMAS *Manoora* to Commander Task Unit 78.2.2, 1 July 1945, Operation OBOE Two Operations, Report of Wave Leader, Wave 7, contained in HMAS *Manoora* Report of Proceedings (AWM).

52 Collins, J.A., *As Luck Would Have It: Reminiscences of an Australian Sailor*, Sydney, Angus and Robertson, 1965, 155.

53 Silkett, W.A. *Downfall: The Invasion That Never Was*, US Army War College Quarterly – *Parameters*, 5 September 2012, 114–15.

54 Rear Admiral G.R. Griffiths, *Life on the Line* podcast, 18 September 2017.

55 Anon., *Porthole: Souvenir of HMAS Shropshire*, John Sands Printers, Sydney, 1946, iii.

56 Oral History of Rear Admiral G.R. Griffiths, Australians at War Film, *op. cit.*

57 Anon., *Porthole: Souvenir of HMAS Shropshire*, John Sands Printers, Sydney, 1946, iii.

58 Rear Admiral G.R. Griffiths, *Life on the Line* podcast, 18 September 2017.

59 Lieutenant G.R. Griffiths, S.206 Report, 28 September 1945 (NAA).

5: The Korean War

1 *Reminiscences of My Naval Career*, Address by Rear Admiral G.R. Griffiths to Military History Society of NSW, 7 March 2020, see https://www.youtube.com/watch?v=SOgzHkxYZOc

2 Oral History of Rear Admiral G.R. Griffiths, *Australians at War* Film, *op. cit.*

3 Jones, C., *Wings and the Navy 1947–1953*, Kangaroo Press, Kenthurst, 1997, 63.

4 *Ibid.*

5 Letter from Mr Francis Crowley to Rear Admiral G.R. Griffiths, 14 November 1991 (Griffiths Papers).

6 Lieutenant G.R. Griffiths S.206 Report, 4 February 1950, 11490365 (NAA).

7 Lieutenant Commander B. Farthing, RAN Retired email to the author, 13 November 2019.

8 Rear Admiral G.R. Griffiths interview with the author, 3 December 2018.

9 Smith, V.A.T, *A Few Memories of Sir Victor Smith*, Australian Naval Institute Press, Canberra, 1992, 43.

10 *Ibid.*

11 Gordon, A.H. *HMAS Sydney in Koreas: The Firefly Observer*, contained in *Reflections on the RAN*, edited by Frame, T.R, Goldrick, J.V.P. & Jones, P.D., Kangaroo Press, Kenthurst, 1991, 292.

12 HMAS *Sydney* Report of Proceedings, 3–14 November 1951, dated 15 November 1951 (NAA).

13 Report by Captain D.H. Harries, 4 March 1952, Navy Office file 5233/1/17, Annex A (NAA).

14 Oral History of J.E. Parsons, S02779 2002 (AWM).

15 Lieutenant G.R. Griffiths S.206 Report, 12 March 1952, 11490365 (NAA).

16 Lieutenant Commander G.R. Griffiths S.206 Report, 21 November 1952, 11490365 (NAA).

17 Commonwealth Navy Order No. 50, dated 3 February 1953.

18 *Ibid.*

19 One of the news reports is contained in the *South China Morning Post*, 19 November 1952, 16.

20 Rear Admiral G.R. Griffiths interview with Vice Admiral D. Shackleton, 2019.

21 Rear Admiral G.R. Griffiths, *To Who It May Concern*, 14 June 1995, 1 (Griffiths Papers).

22 Reeve, J. & Stevens, D.M., eds, *The Face of Naval Battle*, Allen & Unwin, Crows Nest, 2003, 158.

23 HMAS *Anzac* Report of Proceedings (ROP), December 1952, paragraph 39, RCDIG 1072956 (AWM).

24 HMAS *Anzac* ROP, February 1953, dated 2 March 1953; & HMAS *Tobruk* ROPs 1952, RCDIG 1072956 (AWM).

25 Report by Captain D.H. Harries, 4 March 1952, Navy Office file 5233/1/17, Annex A (NAA).

26 HMAS *Anzac* ROP, March 1953, dated 5 April 1953, RCDIG 1072956 (AWM).

27 CTU 95.2.2. ROP, 12 May–26 May 1953, dated 28 May 1953, 2, RCDIG 1072956 (AWM).

28 HMAS *Anzac* ROP, June 1953, dated 1 July 1953, 9, RCDIG 1072956 (AWM).

29 *The Times* (London), *Duke's Inspection of Aircraft Carrier*, 25 February 1956, 4.

30 Rear Admiral G.R. Griffiths' penscripts on draft chapter, January 2020.

31 *The West Australian*, 24 April 1956.

32 Grey, G., *Up Top: The Royal Australian Navy & Southeast Asian Conflicts 1955–1972*, Allen & Unwin, St Leonards, 1998, 24.

33 Contained in the FESR General Directive quoted in *The Review of Service Entitlement Anomalies in Respect of South East Asian Service 1955–75*; Submission by Rear Admiral Guy Griffiths RAN (Retired), 8 September 1999 (Griffiths Papers).

34 Rear Admiral N. Ralph email to the author 17 July 2020.

35 Lieutenant Commander G.R. Griffiths S.206 Report, 28 October 1956, 11490365 (NAA).

36 Commander G.R. Griffiths S.206 Reports, 6 January 1958 & 11 September 1958, 11490365 (NAA).

37 *Navy News,* Volume 2, Numbers 1 & 2, 9; & 23 January 1959, 2 & 2.

38 *Ibid.*, Volume 1, Number 5, 19 September 1958, 1.

39 *Ibid.*

40 http://938.org.au/.

6: First Command: HMAS *Parramatta*

1   Conrad, J., *Command at Sea: The Prestige, Privilege and Burden of Command.*

2   Jeremy, J.C., email to author, 9 July 2020.

3   Commander G.R. Griffiths, AS 206, 1 November 1961 (AWM).

4   Third Naval Member Minute to CNS, 28 September 1961, contained with HMAS *Parramatta* Report of Proceedings, July 1961, AWM 78-290/2 (AWM).

5   Pen script to HMAS *Parramatta* Report of Proceedings, July 1961, AWM 78-290/2 (AWM).

6   *Navy News*, 29 September 1961, 8.

7   *Ibid.*

8   Oral History of Rear Admiral G.R. Griffiths, *Australians at War* film.

9   Penscript to HMAS *Parramatta* Report of Proceedings, June 1962, AWM 78-290/2 (AWM).

10 *South China Morning Post*, 7 June 1962, p.6 & *South China Morning Post*, 8 June 1962, 8.

11 Commodore W.S.G. Bateman, comments on draft chapter, 1 May 2002.

12 Author's interview with Rear Admiral G.R. Griffiths 21 January 2020.

13 Commander G.R. Griffiths, AS 206, 4 January 1963 (AWM).

14 Naval Minute, *Consequences of the loss of Voyager and Damage to Melbourne*, 15 February 1964, 2, 8194321 (NAA).

15 Naval Board Minutes, 26 February 1964, 8194321 (NAA).

16 Interview by the author with Commander John Smith, 26 November 2019.

17 Commander G.R. Griffiths, AS 206, 26 October 1963 (AWM).

18 Captain G.R. Griffiths, AS 206, 18 December 1964 (AWM).

19 Author's interview with Rear Admiral G.R. Griffiths, 21 January 2020.

20 *Ibid.*

21 *The Bay City Times,* 5 April 1965, as well as in *The Advertiser, The Age, The Australian, Canberra Times, The Courier Mail, The Examiner, The Hobart Mercury, The Telegraph and t*he Melbourne *Sun.*

7: Wartime Sea Command HMAS *Hobart*

1   Robles, A.F. letter to Rear Admiral J.V.P. Goldrick, 16 July 2019.

2   *Navy News*, Joining HMAS *Hobart*?, 1 October 1965, 3.

3   Rear Admiral D.J. Campbell, interview with author, 16 April 2020.

4   *Ibid.*

5   Vice Admiral D.J. Shackleton, penscript comments on draft chapter, 26 April 2020.

6   Email to the author by Ian Holmes, 13 November 2019.

7   *Ibid.*

8   *Ibid.*

9   Grove, E edited, *The Battle and the Breeze: The Naval Reminiscences of Admiral of the Fleet Sir Edward Ashmore*, Royal Naval Museums Publications, Stroud, 1997, 62.

10 *DDG in Vietnam and Lessons for the Royal Australian Navy*, Australian Centre for the Study of Armed Conflict & Society, Occasional Paper Series No. 7, Naval Studies Group, 2017, 11.

11 *HMAS Hobart Report of Proceedings*, July 1966, 1 (AWM).

12 Frame, T.R., Goldrick J.V.P. & Jones, P.D. *Reflections on the Royal Australian Navy*, Kangaroo Press, Kenthurst, 1991, 330.

13 *Navy News*, Hobart Commissions on Dec.18, 10 December 1965, 7.

14 *HMAS Perth Report of Proceedings*, November 1965, 2 (AWM).

15 Address by Rear Admiral G.R. Griffiths to Military History Society of NSW, 7 March 2020, *op. cit.*

16 *HMAS Hobart Report of Proceedings*, January 1966, 2 (AWM).

17 *HMAS Hobart Report of Proceedings*, March 1966, 1 (AWM).

18 Email to the author by I.F. Holmes, 13 November 2019.

19 Rear Admiral G.R. Griffiths interview with Vice Admiral D.J. Shackleton, 13 January 2012.

20 Frame, T.R., Goldrick, J.V.P. & Jones, P.D., *Reflections on the Royal Australian Navy*, *op. cit.*, 331.

21 *HMAS Hobart Report of Proceedings*, May 1966, 5 (AWM).

22 Oral History of Rear Admiral G.R. Griffiths, Australians at War Film.

23 *HMAS Melbourne Report of Proceedings*, August 1966, 5 (AWM).

24 *The Mercury*, Hobart, 2 September 1966, 1.

25 *Ibid.*, 2 & 3 September 1966.

26 *Ibid.*, Hobart, 3 September 1966. 7.

27 *Ibid.*, Hobart, 1 September 1966. 10.

28 Frame, T.R., Goldrick J.V.P. & Jones, P.D. *Reflections on the Royal Australian Navy*, *op. cit.*, 331.

29 *Ibid.*

30 *The Canberra Times*, 23 December 1966, 1 & 13.

31 *HMAS Hobart Report of Proceedings*, March 1967, 1 (AWM).

32 *The Sydney Morning Herald*, 8 March 1967, 1.

33 Frame, T.R., Goldrick, J.V.P. & Jones, P.D., *Reflections on the Royal Australian Navy*, *op. cit.*, 333.

34 Vice Admiral R.A.K. Walls interview with the author, 27 February 2020.

35 Reeve, J. & Stevens, D.M. edited, *The Face of Naval Battle*, Allen & Unwin, Crows Nest, 2003, 159.

36 Oral History of Rear Admiral G.R. Griffiths, *Australians at War* film; & *HMAS Hobart Report of Proceedings*, March 1967, 5 (AWM).

37 Frame, T.R., Goldrick, J.V.P. & Jones, P.D., *Reflections on the Royal Australian Navy*, *op. cit.*, 332.

38 *The Sydney Morning Herald*, 2 April 1967, 15.

39 http://usscollett.com/images/photos/bradick_a/a_bradick%20photos.htm#history

40 Dash, H., *HMAS Hobart in Vietnam*, https://www.navalofficer.com.au/hobart1/ .

41 Rear Admiral G.R. Griffiths interview with the author 6 June 2020.

42 *HMAS Hobart Report of Proceedings*, April 1967, 19 (AWM).

43 *Ibid.*, 21 (AWM).

44 *Ibid.* (AWM).

45 *Canberra Times*, 12 May 1967, 8.

46 *Ibid.*

47 http://www.dd-692.com/beau.htm .

48 *Monthly Historical Summary of Commander, United States Seventh Fleet* for May 1967 (USN).

49 *HMAS Hobart Report of Proceedings*, May 1967, 10 (AWM).

50 The pilot was Lieutenant (JG) M. Alsop; see Hobson, C., *Vietnam Air Losses, USAF, USN, USMC, Fixed-Wing Aircraft Losses in Southeast Asia 1961–1973*, North Branch, Minnesota: Specialty Press, 2001, 103.

51 Hobson, C. *Vietnam Air Losses, USAF, USN, USMC, Fixed-Wing Aircraft Losses in Southeast Asia 1961–1973*. North Branch, Minnesota: Specialty Press, 2001, 103. & https: //navy.togetherweserved.Com .

52 *HMAS Hobart Report of Proceedings*, May 1967, 14 (AWM).

53 *Ibid.*, June 1967, 3. (AWM).

54 Captain G.R. Griffiths Form AS 206 dated 14 June 1967, 11490365 (NAA).

55 See https://valor.militarytimes.com/hero/55423#33426 .

56 *Gitmo Gazette*, Guatanamo Bay, Cuba, 18 August 1967, 1–2.

57 *Daily Telegraph*, 30 June 1967, 15.

58 *Ibid.*

59 *HMAS Hobart Report of Proceedings*, June 1967, 7 (AWM).

60 Letter From Mr Charles F. Baird, Assistant Secretary of the Navy to Captain G.R. Griffiths, 30 June 1967 (AWM).

61 Captain G.R. Griffiths Form AS 206 dated 27 October 1967, 11490365 (NAA).

62 *HMAS Hobart Report of Proceedings*, June 1967, 8 (AWM).

63 Robles, A.F., letter to Rear Admiral J.V.P. Goldrick, 16 July 2019.

64 Rae, J.B., email to author 9 November 2019.

65 Commander Carrier Division Two signal to HMAS *Hobart* 310803Z July 1967 (AWM).

66 *HMAS Hobart Report of Proceedings*, August 1967, 10 (AWM).

67 Commander Seventh Fleet signal to HMAS *Hobart* 100816Z August 1967 (AWM).

68 Reeve, J. & Stevens, D.M., eds, *The Face of Naval Battle*, Allen & Unwin, Crows Nest, 2003, 159.

69 Oral History of Rear Admiral G.R. Griffiths, *Australians at War* film, *op. cit.*

70 Captain G.R. Griffiths Form AS 206 dated 14 September 1967, 11490365. (NAA).

71 *Ibid.*

72 *HMAS Hobart Report of Proceedings*, September 1967, 12 (AWM).

73 Rear Admiral M.B. Forrest, interview with author 16 April 2020.

74 Rear Admiral P.H. Doyle letter to Rear Admiral G.R. Griffiths, 11 January 1980 (Griffiths Papers).

75 Rae, J.B., email to author 9 November 2019.

8: Flag Officer

1   *The Straits Times*, 7 September 1967, Singapore, 13.

2   Interview by Rear Admiral J.V.P. Goldrick with Rear Admiral Tan Sri Dato Sri K Thanabalasingham, 15 April 2019.

3   *Ibid.*

4   Commodore G.R. Griffiths AS 206, dated 1 August 1969 (NAA).

5   Ms E. Griffiths email to the author17 May 2020.

6   Interview by Rear Admiral J.V.P. Goldrick with Rear Admiral Tan Sri Dato Sri K Thanabalasingham, 15 April 2019.

7   Commodore G.R. Griffiths AS 206, dated 1 August 1969 (NAA).

8   Guy Griffiths interview with the author 3 December 2018.

9   Captain G.R. Griffiths, S.206, 10 December 1970 (AWM).

10 Rear Admiral G.R. Griffiths interview with Vice Admiral D.J. Shackleton, 13 January 2012.

11 Defence capabilities Paper, 1973, 19, NHD.

12 Tange, A., *Australian Defence: Report on the Reorganization of the Defence Group of Departments,* November 1973, Australian Government Publishing Service, Canberra, 1974.

13 Email from J.S. McGeachie to the author, 8 November 2019.

14 Rear Admiral G.R. Griffiths address to Sydney Rotary Club, 21 October 1980.

15 *Canberra Times*, 23 February 1974, 1.

16 *Navy News,* 21 June 1974, 1.

17 Interview with the Commodore J. McCaffrie by the author, 17 June 2020

18 Oral History of Rear Admiral G.R. Griffiths, *Australians at War* film.

19 *Navy News,* 17 January 1975, 3.

20 Oral History of Rear Admiral G.R. Griffiths, *Australians at War* film.

21 *Canberra Times*, 30 December 1974, 7.

22 *Navy News,* 17 January 1975, 4.

23 Rear Admiral G.R. Griffiths, interview with the author, 6 June 2020.

24 Oral History of Rear Admiral G.R. Griffiths, *Australians at War* film.

25 *HMAS Hobart Report of Proceedings,* January 1974, 2, RCDIG 1073551 (AWM).

26 Governor General's letter to Queen Elizabeth II, 4 January 1975, NAA AA1984/609 Part 1 (NAA).

27 Recollections of Commander W. Ritchie provided to the author, 14 November 2019.

28 *Navy News,* 17 January 1975, 20.

29 *Ibid.*

30 *HMAS Melbourne Report of Proceedings*, January 1974, 6, RCDIG 1073551 (AWM).

31 Guy Griffiths interview with the author 3 December 2018.

32 Commodore G.R. Griffiths, Form PH 168, dated 1 July 1975 (AWM).

33 HMAS *Otway, Report of Proceedings*, March 1975, 2, RCDIG 1074068 (AWM).

34 *Navy New*s, 11 April 1975, 8

35 Commodore R.M. Baird email to the author, 3 August 2020.

36 *Naval Personnel Newsletter*, 6 May 1977, 1.

37 Rear Admiral N. Ralph email to the author 17 July 2020.

38 Guy Griffiths interview with the author 3 December 2018.

39 Rear Admiral G.R. Griffiths Form PH 168, 27 December 1978 (Griffiths Papers).

40 Commodore R.M. Baird email to the author, 3 August 2020.

41 Letter from Rear Admiral G.R. Griffiths to Mr Francis Crowley to, 18 April 1994 (Griffiths Papers).

42 *Navy News*, 26 January 1979, 4.

43 Citation at https://honours.pmc.gov.au/honours/awards/878690 .

44 Vice Admiral G.J. Willis letter to Rear Admiral G.R. Griffiths, 17 January 1980 (Griffiths Papers).

45 Commander I.D.G. MacDougall letter to Rear Admiral G.R. Griffiths, 22 December 1979 (Griffiths Papers).

46 Lieutenant Commander H.L. Daw letter to Rear Admiral G.R. Griffiths, 12 August 1979 (Griffiths Papers).

9: Home From the Sea

1 Griffiths, G.R., Address at the Re-Dedication Service HMAS *Sydney* Memorial, 15 November 1996.

2 Griffiths, *G.R. Griffiths Family Tree* monograph, undated, 1 (Griffiths Papers).

3 *The Australian,* 30 November 1979, 2.

4 Griffiths, G.R., Address at the Resettlement Seminar, circa 1983 (Griffiths Papers).

5 *The Australian*, 26 November 2001, 13.

6 Rear Admiral N. Ralph email to the author 17 July 2020.

7 Australian Institute of Health and Welfare 2010. Cardiovascular disease mortality: trends at different ages. Cardiovascular series no. 31. Cat. no.47. Canberra: AIHW, 1.

8 Take Heart Newsletter. Summer 1995, 1.

9 Purss, C., email to author, 30 July 2020.

10 See https://www.heartresearch.com.au/ .

11 Vice Admiral Sir Hayes message to Force Z Survivors Association 9 December 1997.

12 Griffiths, G.R., interview with the author 20 September 2020.

13 Email from Mr R. Wollmer to the author, 6 November 2019.

14 Mattiske, D., Recollections to the author, 21 December 2019.

15 Griffiths, G.R., Submission on the Defence Review 2000, undated (Griffiths Papers).

16 Oral History of Rear Admiral G.R. Griffiths, Australians at War Film.

17 Griffiths, E., email to the author 19 October 2020.

18 Tuchman, B.W., *A Distant Mirror: The Calamitous 14th Century*, Penguin Books, 1979, xvi.

19 Rear Admiral G.R. Griffiths Trafalgar Day dinner HMAS *Watson*, 21 October 1984.

Bibliography

Abbreviations

AWM	Australian War Memorial, Canberra
IWM	Imperial War Museum, London
NAA	National Archives of Australia (Canberra, Sydney and Melbourne)
NLA	National Library of Australia, Canberra
NMM	Caird Library – National Maritime Museum, Greenwich
RN NHB	Royal Navy Naval Historical Branch, Portsmouth
UKNA	The United Kingdom National Archives, Kew
SPC-A	Seapower Centre Australia
UNSW	University of New South Wales

Books

Adams, J.H., *Ships in Battledress*, The Currawong Publishing Company, Sydney, 1944.

Allen, L., *Singapore 1941–1942*, London, Davis-Poynter, 1977.

Alliston, J.M., *Destroyer Man*, Greenhouse Publications, Richmond, 1985.

Anon., *Australian Army Amphibious Operations in the South-West Pacific 1942–45*, Army Doctrine Centre, Canberra, 1995.

Anon., *Porthole: Souvenir of HMAS Shropshire*, John Sands Printers, Sydney, 1946.

Australian Naval Aviation Museum, *Flying Stations: A Story of Australian Naval Aviation*, Allen & Unwin, St Leonards, 1998.

Bennett, G., *The Loss of the Prince of Wales and Repulse*, Ian Allen Ltd, London, 1973.

Bond, B. & Tachikawa, K., edited, *British and Japanese Military Leadership in the Far Eastern War 1941–1945*, Frank Cass, London, 2004.

Boslaugh, D.L., *First-Hand: No Damned Computer is Going to Tell Me What to Do: The Story of the Naval Tactical Data System*, Available on-line at https://ethw.org

Cain, T.J., *HMS Electra*, Futura Publications, London, 1976.

Churchill, W.S., *The Second World War, Volume III: The Grand Alliance*, Penguin, London, 2005.

Collins, J.A., *As Luck Would Have It: Reminiscences of an Australian Sailor*, Angus and Robertson, Sydney, 1965.

Cooper, A., *HMAS Shropshire: A Vivid Account of the Recapture of the Philippines in WWII*, Monograph 197, The Naval Historical Society of Australia, Sydney, 2002.

Date, J.C., *The Battle of Leyte Gulf 22–26 October 1944*, The Naval Historical Society of Australia, Sydney, 1985.

Dowling, B., *A Bushie's War 1940–1944*, self-published.

Eldridge, F.B. *A History of the Royal Australian Naval College: From its inception in 1913 to the end of World War II in 1945*, Georgian House, Melbourne, 1949.

Fairfax, D., *Navy in Vietnam: A record of the Royal Australian Navy in the Vietnam War 1965–1972*, Australian Government Printing Service, Canberra, 1980.

Fazio, V.B., *RAN Aircraft Carriers 1929–1982*, Naval Historical Society, Sydney, 2000.

Field, J.A., *History of United States Naval Operations Korea*, US Government Printing Office, Washington, 1962.

Frame, T.R. edited, *The Australian Navy in Vietnam: Lessons and Legacies from 1965*, Barton Books, Canberra, 2015.

Frame, T.R., Goldrick J.V.P. & Jones, P.D. *Reflections on the Royal Australian Navy*, Kangaroo Press, Kenthurst, 1991.

Gatacre, G.G.O., *Report of Proceedings*, Nautical Press, Manly, 1982.

Gill, G.H., *Royal Australian Navy 1939–1942*, Collins, Melbourne, 1985.

Gill, G.H., *Royal Australian Navy 1942–1945*, Collins, Melbourne, 1968.

Grey, G., *Up Top: the Royal Australian Navy & Southeast Asian Conflicts 1955–1972*, Allen & Unwin, St Leonards, 1998.

Griffiths, G.R., *Family Griffiths 1788–1976*, self-published, Sydney, 2003.

Grove, E. edited, *The Battle and the Breeze: The Naval Reminiscences of Admiral of the Fleet Sir Edward Ashmore*, Royal Naval Museums Publications, Stroud, 1997.

Hamer, D., *Memories of My Life*, South Wind, Singapore, 2002.

Hayes, J., *Face the Music: A Sailor's Story*, Pentland Press, Edinburgh, 1991.

Hobson, Chris. *Vietnam Air Losses, USAF, USN, USMC, Fixed-Wing*

Aircraft Losses in Southeast Asia 1961–1973. Specialty Press, North Branch, 2001.

Hooper, E.B., Allard, D.C., Fitzgerald, O.P. & Marolda, E.J., *The United States Navy and the Vietnam Conflict, Volume 1,* Naval Historical Center, Washington, 1986.

Hyslop, R., *Aye Aye, Minister: Australian Naval Administration 1939–59,* Australian Government Printing Service, Canberra, 1990.

Jones, C., *Wings and the Navy 1947–1953,* Kangaroo Press, Kenthurst, 1997.

Jones, P.D., *Australia's Argonauts: The remarkable story of the first class to enter the Royal Australian Naval College,* Echo Books, Geelong, 2016.

Jones, T.M. & Idriess, I.L., *The Silent Service: Action Stories of the Anzac Navy,* Angus and Robertson, Sydney, 1944.

Lehmann, G., *A Voyage of Lions and Other Poems,* Angus & Robertson, Sydney, 1968.

Long, G., *Australia in the War of 1939–45 Series One: Volume 7: The Final Campaigns,* Australian War Memorial, Canberra, 1963.

Macintyre, D., *The Battle for the Pacific,* Angus and Robertson, Sydney, 1966.

McGuire, P. & McGuire, F.M., *The Price of Admiralty,* Oxford University Press, Melbourne, 1944.

McIntyre, J. & Germov, J., *Hunter Wine: A History,* New South Publishing, Sydney, 2018.

Money, W. *Captain Bill Money's RAN Memoirs,* self-published.

Nicholls, S., *HMAS Shropshire,* The Naval Historical Society of Australia, Sydney, 1989.

Northcott, M.P., *Ensign 8: Renown and Repulse,* Plaistow Press Ltd, London, 1978.

O'Neill, R., *Australia in the Korean War 1950–53, Volume II Combat Operations,* Australian War Memorial, Canberra, 1985.

Payne, M.A., *HMAS Australia 1928–1955,* Naval Historical Society of Australia, Sydney, 2000.

Pfennigwerth, I., *Bravo Zulu: Honours & Awards to Australian Naval People Volume 1 1900–1974,* Echo Books, West Geelong, 2016.

Pool, R., *Course for Disaster: From Scapa Flow to the River Kwai,* Leo Cooper, London, 1987.

Ramsden, E., *James Busby: The prophet of Australian viticulture and British Resident at New Zealand, 1833–40,* self-published, Sydney 1941.

Reeve, J. & Stevens, D.M. edited, *The Face of Naval Battle,* Allen & Unwin, Crows Nest, 2003.

Roskill, S.W., *The Navy at War 1939–1945*, Wordsworth Editions Limited, Ware, 1998.

Shiplee, A., *Tugboat Tells All*, Parker Pattinson Publishing, Narellan, 2002.

Smith, P.C., *British Battle Cruisers*, Almark Publications, New Malden, 1972.

Smith, V.A.T., *A Few Memories of Sir Victor Smith*, Australian Naval Institute Press, Canberra, 1992.

Stevens, D.M., *The Australian Centenary History of Defence Volume III: The Royal Australian Navy*, Oxford University Press, Melbourne, 2001.

Stevens, D.M. edited, *The Royal Australian Navy in World War II*, Allen and Unwin, Crows Nest, 2005.

Swan, R.C., *Rear Admiral Rothesay Cathcart Swan AO, CBE, RAN (Rtd): Some Recollections*, self-published, 2006.

Walhert, G., edited *Australian Army Amphibious Operations in the South-West Pacific:1942–45*, Southwood Press, Sydney, 1994.

Warner, D. & P., *Kamikaze: The Sacred Warriors 1944–45*, Oxford University Press, Melbourne, 1983.

Woodward, C.V., *The Battle for Leyte Gulf*, Landsborough Publications, London, 1958.

Journal Articles & Papers

Anon., *The Cruiser and the Kamikazes: The Story of Japanese Suicide Attacks on HMAS Australia at Lingayen Gulf, Luzon 4th–9th January 1945*, Armstrong Papers, (NLA).

Anon., *An Interpretation of the Log of William Dalrymple Kelman on board Triton on the Voyage Leith to Hobart Town 7th September 1823 – 19th January 1824*, (G.R. Griffiths Papers).

Brown, C., *Stand by for Torpedo, Collier's Weekly*, 17 January 1942, pp. 12–13.

Dash, H., *HMAS Hobart in Vietnam*, https://www.navalofficer.com.au/hobart1/

DDG in Vietnam and Lessons for the Royal Australian Navy, Australian Centre for the Study of Armed Conflict and Society Occasional Paper Series No. 7, Naval Studies Group, 2017.

Griffiths, G.R., *Brief Notes on the Origin and Connections – Kelman, Holmes & Griffiths*, (G.R. Griffiths Papers).

Griffiths, G.R., *Review of Service Entitlement Anomalies in Respect of South East Asian Service 1955–75*, Submission to the Department of Veterans

Affairs, 8 September 1999, (Griffiths Papers).

Griffiths, G.R., Address to Military History Society of NSW, 7 March 2020.

Loss of H.M. Ships Prince of Wales and Repulse, Supplement to *The London Gazette*, 20 February 1948, Number 38214, pp.1237–1244.

Parker, R., *DDG in Vietnam and Lessons for the Royal Australian Navy*, Australian Centre for the Study of Armed Conflict and Society Occasional Paper Series No. 7, University of NSW, Canberra, 2017.

Plomley, H.J.B., *An Immigrant of 1824*, Tasmanian Historical Research Association, Hobart, 1973.

Official Documents

BR 1736(28) Battle Summary No.34. Naval Strategy in the Pacific – February 1943 – August 1945, Admiralty, London, 1946.

Captain L.H. Bell RN, Letter to the First Sea Lord, HMS *Express*, 10 December 1941, (UKNA).

Cablegram from Secretary of State for Dominion Affairs cablegram to Prime Minister of Commonwealth of Australia, 29 August 1942, contained in *Loss of HMAS Canberra and allocation of HMS Shropshire*, 17 August 1942 – 23 December 1946, A5954, 424581, (NAA).

Commanding Officer HMAS *Australia* to Commodore Commanding His Majesty's Australian Squadron, *Action Report – Operation Mike 1*, 22 January 1945, (SPC-A).

Commanding Officer HMAS *Shropshire* to Commander Task Group 77.2, *HMAS Shropshire Action Report 1–18 January 1945*, 24 January 1945, (SPC-A).

Commander Task Group 74.1 to Commander 7th Fleet, *Report of Proceedings: January–February 1945*, 1945, (SPC-A).

Royal Australian Naval College Magazine, (SPC-A).

RAN *Navy Lists, 1937–1980* (available on-line at www.navy.gov.au).

Report of Proceedings for RAN Ships, AWM78, (AWM).

Report on the Loss of HM Ships *Prince of Wales* and *Repulse*, ADM 199/1149. (UKNA).

Service Records of RAN Officers and Sailors, A3978 & A6769 Series, (NAA).

Service Records of RN Officers, ADM 196 Series, (TNA UK).

Signal from First Naval Member to Commodore Commanding Australian Squadron 150910Z FEB 45, (SPC-A).

Speed Letters from Commodore Commanding HMA Squadron to Australian Commonwealth Naval Board, January 1945 – June 1945, (SPC-A).

Suicide Weapons and Tactics: Know Your Enemy, CinCPac Bulletin 126–45, 28 May 1945.

Tange, A., *Australian Defence: Report on the Reorganisation of the Defence Group of Departments*, November 1973, Australian Government Publishing Service, Canberra, 1974.

War Cabinet Minutes, Numbers 2989–3331, 6 September 1943 – 4 February 1944, Volume 14, A5954, 689725, (NAA).

War Diary (Naval), Admiralty 1939–1945. (RN NHB).

Diaries, Oral Histories & Personal Papers

Australian Naval History Podcast series, University of NSW (Canberra).

Author's interviews and correspondence with Commodore S. Bateman, Senior Chaplain G. Clayton, Vice Admiral I.D.G. MacDougall, Commodore J. McCaffrie, Mr J.B. Rae, Rear Admiral N. Ralph, Vice Admiral R.A.K. Walls & Commander S. Youll.

Interview of Rear Admiral Tan Sri Dato Sri K. Thanabalasingham by Rear Admiral J.V.P. Goldrick, 15 April 2019.

Oral History of Stoker A.W. Bartholomew, Number 8180, 1984, (IWM).

Oral History of Lieutenant Commander V.F. Clark, Number 8905, 1985, (IWM).

Oral History of Marine F.A. Claxton, Number 20134, 2000, (IWM).

Oral History of Vice Admiral J.A. Collins, Mel Pratt Collection, 1975, (NLA).

Oral History of Vice Admiral J.A. Collins, S046522, 1988, (AWM).

Oral History of Seaman R.W.M. Fraser, Imperial War Museum, Number 8267, 1984, (IWM).

Oral History of Rear Admiral G.R. Griffiths, Australians at War Film, 1146, 2002, (UNSW).

Oral History of Rear Admiral G.R. Griffiths, 2009, (Naval Heritage Centre).

Oral History of Petty Officer E. Monaghan, Number 166944, 1996, (IWM).

Oral History of J.E. Parsons, S02779 2002, (AWM).

Oral History of Vice Admiral R.I. Peek, 1977, (NLA).

Oral History of Captain R.A.W. Pool, Number 9248, 1986, (IWM).

Oral History of Petty Officer C.S. Rogers, Number 11326, 1990, (IWM).

Oral History of Able Seaman W.F. Selby, Number 8194, 1986, (IWM).

Oral History of Leading Seaman R.B. Walker, S00708, 28 June 1989, (AWM).

Oral History of Able Seaman R Wood, Number 8251, 1984, (IWM).

Oral History of Lieutenant W.F. Wreford, S00526 (F2786/21), 23 February 1989, (AWM).

Papers of Captain J.M. Armstrong, (NLA).

Papers of Rear Admiral H.B. Farncomb, (SPC-A).

Papers of Admiral T.C. Hart, USN, Operational Archives, (US Navy Yard, Washington).

Papers of Admiral T.C. Kinkaid, USN, Operational Archives, (US Navy Yard, Washington).

Papers of Admiral W.G. Tennant, (NMM).

Papers of Arthur Hubert Turner, 96/22/1, (IWM).

Index

Minneapolis, USS 80, 90
Mispillion, USS 121, 197
Missouri, USS 96
Mogami, IJN 75, 83, 146
Molony, Maurice 50, 53
Money, Bill 158
Mooney, Jack 252
Moore, George 96
Moran, William 20
Morotai Island 71
Morrison, Tom 151, 154
Morrow, James 95
Mounts Bay, HMS 125
Murchison, HMAS 107, 137
Murray, Brian 151
Musashi, IJN 75, 84
My Duyet Thong highway bridge 194
My Trung 183

Nagasaki 95, 146
Napier, HMAS 50, 63
Nashville, USS 65, 69, 160, 162
Naval Air Station, Cubi Point 172
Naval Air Station, Nowra 105
Naval Air Station, Royal, Yeovilton 130
Naval College, *see* Royal Australian
    Naval College
Navy Help Darwin, Operation 224
Navy Office 61, 84, 115, 117, 135–8,
    140, 143, 147, 151–4, 171, 202, 206,
    214–6, 233
Nelson, Gregory 247
Nelson, Horatio 106
Nepal, HMAS 63
Nestor, HMAS 23, 32
New Jersey, USS 112, 116
New Mexico, USS 86
New Zealand 4, 5, 107, 112, 118, 125,
    132, 134, 147, 221, 223, 231, 243

NGS (naval gunfire support) 172, 173,
    175–7, 179, 180, 182, 187, 191, 194,
    197, 198, 199
Nguyen Kỳ 170
Nichols, Godfrey 72, 73, 75, 76, 78, 81,
    84, 88, 91, 92, 95, 98, 108, 142, 257
Nimitz, Chester 64, 65, 96, 219
Nishimura Shōji 75, 79, 80, 82, 83
Nobutake, Kondō 38
Noemfoor 71
Norfolk, HMS 29, 100, 162, 163
Norfolk, Virginia 34
Norman, HMAS 63
Nottingham, HMS 25
Novikov Priboy 219
NTDS (tactical data system) 173, 180,
    182, 215
Nunn, Richard 158

O'Sullivan, Tim 223, 224–6
Oberon (town) 7
Oberon class (submarine) 152
Oboe, Borneo landings 93
Ocean Link, Exercise 135
Ocean, HMS 125
Octagon Conference 65
Okinawa, USS 185
Oldham, George 89, 141
Oliver Hazard Perry class (frigate) 215
Olongapo 172, 181
Olympic Games, Melbourne 133
Olympic, Operation 94, 95
Ommaney Bay, USS 85
Orient, SS 7
Orion (liner) 127
Osborne, James 72, 92, 155, 240
Otway, HMAS 231
Ozawa Jisaburō 75, 83

About the Author

Peter Jones joined the Royal Australian Naval College in 1974 as a 16-year-old cadet midshipman. He retired from the RAN as Vice Admiral in 2014 after 40 years' service. During that time he commanded the frigate HMAS *Melbourne* and later led the multinational Maritime Interception Force during the Iraq War for which he was awarded the Distinguished Service Cross. Since leaving the Navy, Peter has been an Adjunct Professor with the Naval Studies Group at the University of New South Wales (Canberra) and is President of the Australian Naval Institute. His previous book was *Australia's Argonauts*.